WILD HORSE
DIARIES

WILD HORSE DIARIES

Lizzie Spender

JOHN MURRAY

To the memory of my father,
Stephen Spender

© Lizzie Spender 2005

First published in Great Britain in 2005 by John Murray (Publishers)
A division of Hodder Headline

A CIP catalogue record for this title is available from the British Library

ISBN 0 7195 6421 2

Map and photo sections by Kinart
Typeset by Bookhouse, Sydney
Printed and bound by Clays Ltd, St Ives plc

Hodder Headline policy is to use papers that are natural, renewable and recyclable products and made from wood grown in sustainable forests. The logging and manufacturing processes are expected to conform to the environmental regulations of the country of origin.

John Murray (Publishers)
338 Euston Road
London NW1 3BH

Contents

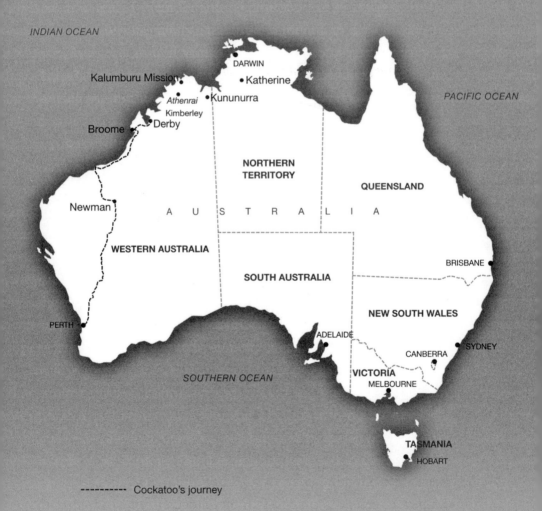

INDIAN OCEAN

PACIFIC OCEAN

DARWIN

Kalumburu Mission

Katherine

Athenrai

Kununurra

Kimberley

Broome

Derby

NORTHERN
TERRITORY

QUEENSLAND

Newman

A U S T R A L I A

WESTERN AUSTRALIA

SOUTH AUSTRALIA

BRISBANE

NEW SOUTH WALES

PERTH

ADELAIDE

SYDNEY

CANBERRA

SOUTHERN OCEAN

VICTORIA

MELBOURNE

TASMANIA

HOBART

---------- Cockatoo's journey

0   400 kilometres

0   100 miles

PART I

THE CALL TO ADVENTURE

A journey of a thousand miles starts with a single step.

Lao-tse, 4th century BC

ONE

My Horse

The poet reached into the recesses of his worn grey tweed jacket and pulled out a battered chequebook. Out of a bulging top pocket he retrieved a black fountain pen. Wheezing slightly, he sat down at the polished dining-room table and started to write. 'What Lizzie needs . . . is a pony,' he said in his assumed American drawl. 'Here's fifty pounds.' He tore the cheque away from the stub and with a benevolent smile, handed it to my father. 'Now, Stephen dear, don't go spending it all on books . . . Remember, it's for Lizzie.' He spoke in the teasing, school-mistress tone of voice he often affected with my father. I was sitting opposite, watching, fascinated by the deep vertical creases and chubby brown moles on his face. The poet seemed to me as ancient as a crocodile, but he was probably no more than fifty.

He was my father's best friend and mentor. They had met at Oxford University and had remained good friends since those heady days, in spite of the fact he was slightly older, and a far more successful poet than my father. The name on the cover of his books was W.H. Auden, but we knew him as Wystan. For two months of every year he would come to London and live with us, taking over my father's study and sleeping on the narrow bed which in the daytime acquired tailored dark green linen covers and metamorphosed into a sofa. For those two months he dictated the terms under which we lived. Wystan would pad around the house in prehistoric carpet slippers, demanding my mother provide lunch on the dot of one, and that we change our ice-trays and corkscrews to some new design he had found in the United States. He always went to bed with a bottle of red wine in one hand and a bottle of vodka in the other. He was well known for his parsimony, but not, it appeared, on this occasion. Fifty pounds was a huge amount of money, and it was being given to my father to buy me a pony by this famous poet who for all his strange ways had seen straight into the soul of a young child.

I was eight years old.

For what seemed like most of my short life, since the age of six anyway, I'd wanted my own pony more than I have ever wanted anything before or since. It was a longing that consumed my waking hours and inspired my night-time dreams. It accounted for my faraway look that was so often commented upon and for my lack of concentration at school. Since I couldn't have my own pony, my life was inhabited by imaginary horses. I created a parallel existence that more often than not eclipsed the real world, based on horses I'd read about, or seen or simply invented, while my real life only sometimes furnished the genuine article. For me, it was never simply a matter of having a mount to ride, or to take to gymkhanas; I was a solitary child and I also craved a four-footed creature as friend, companion, as surrogate family. I understood ponies, and they understood me. Fifty pounds was enough to buy a pony in those days, but only just, as the price of horses in England was kept unnaturally high by the thriving market for their meat just across the channel in France.

That pony was the first of three horses that I would be given in my life. Sadly, Wystan's pony never materialised, nor did the second, but by the time I was offered the third, nearly half a century later, I decided that something had to change, and it would have to be my attitude. I would have to try harder to make things happen.

The third horse I'd been given, I'd seen from a helicopter flying just above the trees in the vast and largely uninhabited Kimberley area in north-west Australia. It was a tall, classy chestnut and it seemed to be blazing with some kind of rare spirit that made it stand out from all the other horses galloping below. It was one of the wild horses, the brumbies, which inhabit the remote outback regions across Australia.

Since I was that small child longing for a pony I'd had a fantasy that I would be shown a herd of horses, and that someone would say to me: 'Take your pick, whichever one you like, it's yours.' The idea came from a film I had seen in distant childhood, its title long forgotten. Sir Lancelot, the knight from King Arthur's round table, is given his choice from a herd of horses after his own horse has been killed under him in battle. He chooses a milky white steed with an arched neck and flowing mane. The horse is duly saddled with Sir Lancelot's silver-encrusted saddle, and the famed knight mounts, only to find himself carried off towards the horizon on a bucking, crazed monster. Eventually he calms the horse enough to dismount and investigate the cause of its misbehaviour. Under the thick leather girth he finds a large burr, put there with evil intent by the man who saddled the horse. Sir Lancelot removes the burr, remounts and canters off into the sunset, and from that moment on, the horse is a dream come true. Whenever I see a herd of horses I play this game. I choose my favourite. I call it my Sir Lancelot moment.

So there we were, up in the skies in a helicopter with no doors, on a property in Australia's north-west, on our way to make a cup of tea – 'to boil the billy' – and then watch the sunset on the bank of an isolated creek. The owner of the property, Celia, was sitting in the back with me. Sitting demurely in front of us was Dame Elisabeth Murdoch, ninety-four and mother of the media mogul Rupert, wearing a delicately patterned pink and turquoise cotton frock. Next to her, Dusty, the pilot, controlled our helicopter.

We were flying over a property off the Gibb River Road, called Athenrai. Celia and her husband Michael had bought the station about five years earlier. Michael claims not to love the outback particularly, but is famously quoted as saying he loves his wife, and *she* loves the outback. Celia has thrown herself heart and soul into protecting the rock art, promoting interest in the evocative and historically important cave paintings, and helping local Aboriginal children, offering them scholarships to schools in Victoria and then at weekends, looking after them in her rambling city house.

The task of running the station had been entrusted to my good friend Susan Bradley, and it was Susan who invited me to stay for a few days at Athenrai, suggesting I take the opportunity to hitch a lift on the private plane that Michael had chartered to bring Dame Elisabeth the eight hours flight from Melbourne. She was to be the joint subject of an article being written for *The Australian* promoting the history of the art and its research.

We were in the middle of nowhere and to me, a visitor from England, albeit someone who had taken every opportunity over many years to visit and explore this extraordinary country, the distances were staggering. We were about 650 kilometres from the nearest shop to the west and 450 kilometres to the east. It was hard even to imagine the distance, the equivalent of London to Edinburgh to the west and London to Paris or Penzance to the east without a single shop in between, just a couple of small road houses, and 150 kilometres from the closest neighbouring homestead. We were in an area the size of Ireland with no fences between us and the Indian Ocean.

The Kimberley is one of the most sparsely populated places on earth. Its raw and ancient beauty is accentuated by the extremes of its two seasons, the Wet and the Dry. When the tropical monsoon storms arrive in December, the land is drenched with torrential rain and electrical storms rage. The vista turns almost overnight into one of lush grasses, eucalypts covered in sparkling freshly washed leaves, and rivers and creeks overflowing with vast torrents of water making the roads impassable for up to five months at a time. Found in this wilderness area are beautiful rock art galleries – paintings and drawings done on isolated rock escarpments by people from earlier civilisations and hidden for centuries from outsiders' eyes.

Now it was the third week of July, and the middle of a comparatively mild dry season, the creeks still spread over the roads, encouraging the 'freshies' – freshwater crocodiles – to bask in the shallow waters on the surface of the roads. The land around was dusty and dry, the grass bleached a dull corn colour.

It would be a short ride down to the creek in the chopper, about ten or twelve minutes, as opposed to the forty-five minutes it would take the rest of our party, winding the sixteen kilometres among the trees in the four-wheel drive. I was looking out the side, enjoying the balmy air and the view, and trying my best not to be too terrified by the void below. Underneath us the trees appeared sparse, but looking ahead they created a carpet of green stretching out sixty or seventy kilometres to blue plateaus on the horizon. I could see the occasional stony bank of a dried-up creek, and then the odd clearing, with tall grasses and bald patches where the dusty red earth revealed itself. My eye was caught by movement in the trees below. Cattle, no doubt. Athenrai had been a cattle station since it was first settled in the 1950s, although Celia and her husband were phasing out the cattle to concentrate on the preservation and study of Aboriginal rock art.

Like a typical back-seat driver, I looked over at Dusty to check that he was concentrating on his job. Helicopters scare me, but it would be unthinkable to turn down such a great opportunity to see the landscape, to get an idea of the scope of our surroundings. We all wore heavy headphones with small microphones, and if we wanted to communicate, we pushed a button on the floor which operated the headphones on the walkie-talkie principle. I glanced back down towards the cattle, they seemed to be moving rather fast and smoothly, and at that point we flew out over a clearing, and so did the animals below.

I sat bolt upright, leaning dangerously sideways to get a better look. 'Horses,' I shrieked into my microphone. I could see two big bays cantering below us, running from the sound and shadow of the helicopter, and then just behind, a dark chestnut with a dark chestnut foal. I was astonished. No one had mentioned horses in the two days I had been on the station. Rock art, cattle, but not horses. That meant that they weren't station horses; these had to be wild, the famous brumbies of the Australian bush. But I'd always thought of brumbies, perhaps because of the sound of the word, as bumble-bee types – uniformly small, brown, round and uninteresting, while below me, without any question, I could see real class and breeding. Dusty bobbed the helicopter around to get a closer look, and Dame Elisabeth and Celia turned their heads in a fairly uninterested way. For them the fascination of the region lay in its Aboriginal art. The horses disappeared into the trees and Dusty straightened out and continued towards the river. A few minutes later we came upon another group and this time Dusty slanted the helicopter down and followed them through the trees.

I was craning my head out the side, breathless, forgetting my fear of heights in my eagerness to get a closer look at the five horses cantering together. They were led by an impressive black horse with a white star in the middle of its forehead. Next to him were two scruffy looking, pinky coloured young horses, a chunkily built bay and then behind, weaving among the trees, a statuesque chestnut with a crooked blaze – a broad band of white starting high on the forehead, sloping over one eye before crossing the other way to peter off over a nostril.

It was love at first sight. There was something about this horse, something in its spirit, and the way it moved, floated, that took my breath away. My old fantasy of choosing a horse from a herd clicked in, I pushed the switch to the intercom, pointed and yelled above the roar of the helicopter engine, 'That one there, the chestnut, that's the one I want.' It was my Sir Lancelot moment.

Dusty swung the helicopter around and dipped it down to take a closer look. 'I'd say he's a colt,' he called, as we hovered back up into the air, and then swooped down again, chasing between the leafy branches after the horses, the skids of the chopper narrowly missing the foliage. We found the horses again as they came out into another clearing, muscles bunching and releasing under their gleaming coats as they stretched out into a gallop. This was a horse in a million – the harmonious confirmation, the power, the fluidity of movement, the proud tail carriage. Then we lost them, catching up a few minutes later with another small group down in a gully; all very nice horses but not star-quality, not like the bright chestnut with the crooked blaze.

A few minutes later we arrived at the destination, landing on a big flat rock just a few metres from the creek itself, joining the others who were already busy putting up the canvas chairs and setting the billy over the fire. I threw a fishing line baited with raw meat into the creek, and within seconds found myself pulling out sooty grunters – the local rather muddy strain of bass – netting them out of the smooth black waters onto the river bank. I took out the hooks and threw back the small ones, keeping a couple of the larger, to throw onto the barbie for Dame Elisabeth.

Celia was sitting nearby on a rock looking thoughtful. 'Lizzie . . .'

'Yes.' I moved a little closer to hear what she had to say.

'I've just asked Susan about those horses we saw. It appears that there are about six hundred of them running wild over Athenrai. I've asked her who they belong to, and she says, well, they're on my land so they belong to me. So that horse you saw, Lizzie,' she said quietly. 'The one you liked. It's yours.'

I wiped the fish slime off my hands onto my new shorts, smiled and then blinked a few times. It seemed that I'd been waiting for this moment since I was six years old, and so it was a little hard to take in. 'Celia . . . Gosh. Thank you. That's incredible.'

'Susan told me how much you love horses . . .'

'Celia. Thank you.' I walked back to the river bank and threw a newly baited line into the river. A horse. Mine. One that I had seen and fallen in love with. I was elated and a little confused.

We drank strong tea brewed in the billy can, and then moved on to gin and tonics and corn chips. I sat on smooth stones still warm from the heat of the day and watched the sun sliding down fast, blazing intense yellows and oranges, behind the trees on the other side of the creek. I was weighing up Celia's words. My own horse. The beautiful chestnut – but was this the kind of horse you owned only in theory, which stayed running around in the wild, a story to tell, *a nice idea*? Was that Celia's intention? Or was this a horse you came back and found and made yours, for better or worse, for the rest of its life? Did anyone ever catch brumbies? If so, how?

It was the turn of the others to fly back to the homestead in the helicopter, so I climbed into the front seat of the Toyota Land-cruiser driven by Susan's old friend Chris North. Squashed in the back were three of the researchers and Nicolas Rothwell, the journalist who had come to write the piece on Dame Elisabeth. Susan had befriended Chris North about fifteen years earlier when he was working on a station near Carlton Hill, just outside Kununurra. Ten years ago, taking just a swag and a hold all, Chris had walked away from the station, intent on dedicating his life to writing, and the exploration of the Kimberley. Chris spends months of the year wandering, camping out alone, or with Aboriginal elders, his battered hat forever pulled down over his lived-in face, investigating every rock, gully and cranny. We set off for home, Chris swinging the heavy vehicle around over tracks hardly visible to the untrained eye, especially not at night.

After a few minutes silence he spoke. 'So Celia gave you the horse you saw from the chopper.'

'Yes.'

'You'll never catch it.'

'Oh.' My spirits began to sink. There was the answer to my question. Of course! It was just an idea. I would never actually own that horse.

'Or, at least, you can . . . You could try,' he added.

'Yes? You think so?' I turned and watched his profile as the car bumped over the dried mud tracks, the felt of his hat now dipping so low over his eagle-like nose that it was a miracle he could even see the road, his smile tight with the information he was about to impart, or not, as he chose.

'Won't be easy.' He was playing me like a sooty grunter on the line, enjoying every moment.

'Well yes, I realise that.' Humility in the face of the task was mandatory.

'Only way you'll be able to do it is from a chopper.' He paused for effect.

'Yes . . .' I answered, tentatively. I had a sense from the expression on his face that things were about to get a lot worse.

'You'll have to shoot the lead mare,' came a voice from one of those sitting in the back. 'And the stallion.'

'Yeah. Shoot to kill,' Chris continued. 'Then you gotta shoot your horse with a tranquilliser gun; that's gonna be hard, gotta be a crack shot, because you have to hit the horse at exactly the right angle for the dart to go in, and the drug to take, and those horses have tough skin, I'm tellin' you. And then supposin' you do all that, then as your horse falls to the ground, wham, down hard, you'll have to land the chopper quickly and get to the horse fast, and inject it with something else, as sweat's gonna pour from that horse. A horse can sweat out the tranquilliser drug in a matter of minutes.' He paused again. I was too shocked to even comment. 'It's not a pretty sight, believe you me,' he added for good measure. 'Seeing the horse all crumpled up on the ground, sweat pouring from it.'

'Is that the only way to do it?' I asked.

'Yep.'

This was the first I'd heard of the concept of the lead mare. I assumed that a lead mare would help a stallion keep control of the herd. The stallion does the prancing, snorting and neck-arching, but all the time, there is a controlling female in the background, the silent power behind the throne. I presumed that these two would defend any attempts to steal a member of their herd, and I reckoned that Chris and the others must know what they were talking about. I certainly knew nothing about catching wild horses.

'If it involves killing a horse, or two, hunting or maiming my horse, then that's it, there's no way I'm going to do it.'

He laughed. 'Out here we kill them all the time, they're regarded as vermin. I've killed about two thousand, back in Queensland, for pie meat. Forty-six cents a pound.'

I didn't know anything about the brumby culling programs. I

sank back into my seat and looked out the windscreen. A kangaroo, startled by the headlights, was hopping slowly away through the saplings into the bush, front paws idiotically small in comparison with its enormous powerful haunches.

That evening we had a party, a barbecue under the poinciana trees. There were at least twelve of us, including the rock art expedition, the journalists, Andy and his wife Ann, the couple who worked all year on the station, and a few of the volunteer researchers who had driven over from the Aboriginal community at Marunbabidi. Dame Elisabeth claimed she had never eaten a fish that she had actually watched being caught, so I set to work, persuading one of the researchers, Dan, who had helped me with the fishing, to clean out the guts and innards. As I wrapped the sooty grunters in foil, I noticed that people were looking at me in a strange way. They'd heard about the gift.

I tossed the fish onto the heavy stone barbecue and helped to turn the steaks and chops as I mulled over the situation.

Even if, by some God-given miracle, I managed to find this horse again, running wild in the limitless bush stretching across millions of acres, then what? I would have to work out a way to catch it without hurting it, without endangering its life. And catching it would be only the first step in a very long and difficult journey. How on earth could you even begin to break in a wild horse, an animal of enormous power, strong enough to maim or kill a person? Why would a wild horse want to submit to human dominance? Would it be cruel to take a horse out of an apparently idyllic existence in the bush? I had hardly ridden, let alone schooled a horse, for more than a quarter of a century. I'd never gentled, or broken in, a horse from scratch, although it had been one of my ambitions, a lifelong desire. All the same, I'd had enough experience of horses to have a healthy respect for the risk factor involved in working with any unbroken horse, let alone one that had never been handled, never even seen a person. I had been presented with an almost impossible task, finding a horse in an area almost the size of England with no fences, just a lot of trees and creeks, which could make it difficult to use the old-fashioned round-up on horseback method, or the more modern method using quad bikes; and even then, supposing we managed to catch and tame it, I'd need to transport it – somewhere. Where? We have a flat in London, although we are hardly ever there, and a *pied à terre* in Sydney; neither has a garden, let alone somewhere to keep a horse. We have a lifestyle that makes staying in one place a rarity.

So they could stop looking at me as if I were some eccentric about to pursue the impossible dream, because the sad truth – I thought – was that I am a very sensible person, prone to weighing up obstacles and sane considerations, and allowing them to take their rightful precedence over mad follies.

The next day I went up into the skies again. Celia had given me another generous present, a helicopter ride to visit an Aboriginal rock art site, only very recently discovered in a remote cave. (Helicopters, although a mandatory way of moving around that part of the world, are expensive, costing about six to eight hundred dollars an hour to keep up in the air.) Chris had been prevailed upon to be my personal guide. Peter Eve, a professional photographer from Darwin, came along to take some more photographs for the piece that was being written for *The Australian* newspaper about Dame Elisabeth's visit and her support for the rock art research.

Dusty was piloting us again. A strong-willed but rather silent man imbued with a quiet wisdom and great knowledge of this part of the world, he proved to be a skilled pilot, hiding his many talents behind a short dense beard. We had no sooner risen into the warm air above the station than Dusty, with hardly a word, swung the helicopter off in the direction we had been yesterday, where we had seen my wild horse. It could be like looking for a needle in a haystack, except that horses are territorial and so we held on to the slim chance that we might find the colt in more or less the same place.

First we came across a herd of about ten: mostly cob-like duns. The pale gold stallion with his black mane and tail was prancing, snorting and shaking his neck up at the helicopter as if it were a rival stallion come to steal his mares. All the rocky land covered with trees looked exactly the same to me, but within about five minutes, Dusty was pointing down at a clearing telling us that this was the place we had seen my horse, and after a few more minutes of combing the surrounding woodland, we found them.

There he was again, the chestnut horse, still blazing his way through the tall dried grasses with his tail and head held high and nose out like a prize-winning racehorse, still the same heart-stopping fine quality. My first instinct had been right; he was a truly exceptional horse. I felt thrilled to my bones. Running along-side him was one of the dirty pinky beige companions of the day before, and the impressive black horse that I could have sworn had a good dose of Thoroughbred blood, only now it seemed the black horse had not a white star, but a white blaze. As Dusty dropped the helicopter down to get as close as we could, I saw that my chestnut had at least one beautiful long white stocking on his hind legs, something I had not noticed the previous day. Was he really a colt? I was conscious of softer contours than I had been aware of the first time; she could be a strong and fast filly, and young, maybe only about eighteen months old.

Chris, sitting beside me in the back seats of the chopper, came onto the intercom. 'About two hundred dollars I'd say – of cat meat.' He was smiling his characteristic smile, a devilishly wilful slant of the mouth that seeks to provoke, but I was too thrilled by the sight of my horse to take offence. I was also conscious that, in the front seat, Peter was snapping away with his large professional camera, recording this moment for posterity. Even if I never saw my horse again, at least I would have a photograph to remember him by. So near yet so far, I thought, as I committed the image to memory, the vision of my beautiful horse galloping over the red earth.

Dusty swept the chopper up back high over the trees, over areas of sparse green swamp, until we came to a large clearing. It was an area about the size of half a football field, slightly raised from the land around it, almost devoid of vegetation, and piled with large sandstone rocks that looked rather like scones stacked on a biscuit tray. Dusty landed on a flat area and we climbed out of the helicopter and set off.

I was surprised by the cave, I would have called it more of a stone archway. I always think of a cave as being somewhat like a hollowed out gourd, more or less any shape but fully covered with one defined opening, the sort of cave I have seen in Europe and especially in Greece and Turkey. Chris explained that these rock art caves can be any natural rock formation that has been used as shelter and where the Indigenous artists were protected from the elements while painting. Some of the caves had also been camp-sites and there researchers had found evidence of stone utensils, cutting implements and even spearheads.

We looked at examples from three different periods of art, all in this same area, but done many thousands of years apart. The oldest and most primitive consisted of just hollows in flat rock, 'cupules', where indentations had been created by someone using a tool and therefore they could be categorised as art. The next, and for me the most beautiful, were the finely drawn mulberry-coloured figures, tall and elegant, with tall decorative head-dresses, tassels and sashes, some of them appearing to be dancing. These are known today as the Bradshaw figures or *Gwion Gwion*, dating back over two ice ages and by far the most sophisticated images. They seemed to be 'tattooed' into the rock in intricate detail, and with their height and fine-boned elegance the figures reminded me of Masai warriors, and of the ancient cave paintings on the Greek island of Thera (Santorini). It was hard to believe that these exquisite figures had existed for over thirty thousand years and had been seen by only a handful of people. They are protected by their isolated location and by the fact that they are very difficult to find in such inaccessible country. These are probably the oldest and least-known natural art galleries on earth.

Next we went to the most recent paintings, which are thought to have been created up to two thousand years ago. These were the Wandjina figures: large haloed heads without mouths, said to be the spirits that God put on the rocks to protect the country and to bring the rains. These striking figures are steeped in Aboriginal mythology, and were painted by the antecedents of today's Aborigines from the Kimberley area, some of whom still tell the stories of their fathers' and grandfathers' Wandjinas. They were painted on rocks that are close to water, and always include images of food sources. They are rendered in the brown, yellow, white, black and red ochres that echo the surrounding country, at least in the dry season. Some are fading and peeling, as the ochres do not stand up to the weather as well as the mulberry stains of the Bradshaw figures.

As we clambered over the pale stones in the intense dry heat, Chris pointed out to me the drawings of yams, or the long-necked sweet water turtle, or the kangaroo, or more layers of Wandjinas, and each with a story to tell. I nodded along enthusiastically, but my mind was straying. After nearly half a century of waiting I could finally say the words 'my horse', but my chestnut brumby was running wild in the bush. While it was wonderful, tantalising, it was also cruel.

That night, late, I sat cross-legged on my iron bed, crouched over my computer, and by candlelight wrote an email to a few of my closest friends.

I have a horse. After forty-five years of longing.

Perhaps 'have' is too strong a word.

It's the third horse I've been given in my life. The difference is, this one actually exists. She is the most beautiful chestnut filly with a white blaze and one long white stocking. She moves like a dream and so I've given her a name. Maia. It means illusion and desire. She is part Thoroughbred, Arab, Australian stock horse and brumby. I think. She's about twenty months old, I reckon, and she was given to me twenty-four hours ago. I'm only guessing she's a she because I've only seen her from above, from a helicopter – twice.

To put it mildly, there are a few practical difficulties, like catching it, training it and, if one gets that far, shipping it somewhere and keeping it. Of course, I am immediately dreaming about doing all of those impossible things.

I've been told that there are about six hundred horses running wild on this property which is about a million acres in size. Not that anybody has counted, and they say that for every horse you see, there are ten hiding. As for the breeding, we know little more than rumours at this stage. We've heard that good horses were turned loose from this property a few years ago when the bank foreclosed on some previous owners, so some of the horses could be old saddle horses running free. And we've heard there is Arab blood from another property further north, a Catholic mission.

Terrible situation really – mad!

I've been given a horse and there is damn little I can do about

*it unless I come here next year and give it a try — however long
it might take, months . . . or years!*

I was looking forward to their replies, their take on my great event.

The next morning, Dame Elisabeth and Celia climbed back up
the steps into the elegant silver propeller plane and flew over to
Melbourne; the other seats were taken by volunteer researchers going
home. I elected to stay on for a few days. The Kimberley is one of
those places it's hard to leave, hard to tear yourself away from.

As the plane flew overhead, we settled down at the table in
front of the main homestead, next to the bougainvillea vines, looked
out over the green lawns of the gardens, and ate coddled eggs for
breakfast, looking forward to a little quiet time. Nicolas Rothwell, the journalist from *The Australian*, was getting ready to write
his article; Peter, his task as photographer done, was preparing to
leave the next morning on the long drive back to Darwin; Susan
was going to catch up with station duties that had been somewhat neglected in the excitement of the last few days.

Susan Bradley had been a good friend since she and I had met
in Darwin about thirteen years ago, when she and her husband
David had been running their own cattle station, Carlton Hill,
just outside Kununurra. They had sold the station a few years later
and spent the following years wandering the world before heading
home to Australia. Susan's love of the Kimberley and the rock art
had led her to Celia and Michael and the purchase of Athenrai,
while David was spending much of the year in England running
his own veterinary practice. Before Carlton Hill, he had been a
flying vet but had now developed a preference for working with
small animals.

'So what'll you call the horse?' Susan asked me.

'That's the third time you've asked me that, Susan.'

'Really?' she laughed.

'Yes. Really.' I knew that Susan was not by nature the faintest bit vague. There was something else going on and I thought I'd half figured it out. 'Susan, you're hoping that if you just keep talking to me about my horse, then eventually I'll go off back to England and my life and forget about the whole thing.'

She laughed again. 'You could come back and find it, I suppose. We could *try*. You'd have to wait until the next dry season, next May.'

'So I understand. You're hoping that by next May I'll definitely have forgotten all about it.'

I felt kind of hurt. None of them seemed to have any idea how precious this territory was to me. What came to mind was a line by the Irish poet, W.B. Yeats: *Tread softly because you tread on my dreams.*

That afternoon Susan suggested she and Peter and I should go out in the Toyota to try to get one last glimpse of the chestnut and take a photograph of it from the ground. She was going to prove to me that she was taking me and my dream seriously.

She instructed Peter and me to stand in the back, holding on to the rail, Peter with his heavy camera slung around his neck. We set off down a rough track, and within minutes the two of us were clinging on for dear life as Susan thundered the vehicle along at a rate of knots, swinging sharply off the road and lurching into the undergrowth without warning to avoid fallen logs or tall saplings that had taken root in the middle of the track, never for a moment losing speed. And every few hundred metres, Peter and I had to duck quickly, screaming with laughter, to avoid low-hanging branches. She made no concession to the survival of her poor passengers. This was quite shocking to me, but also quite wonderful. After twenty minutes of this and squinting into the undergrowth for the sight of a horse, our eyes red and smarting from the dust, I started to consider the character of my very dear friend Susan.

It occurred to me that if Susan had been given a horse and had wanted to have it as her own, in spite of all the obstacles, the difficulty of the challenge, it would be in the yards by the end of the week. That would be logical as Susan makes her home for at least half the year in the outback, while I live between Hampstead in London, and the twenty-seventh floor of a building in The Rocks, Sydney, with a great deal of travelling in between. But then it occurred to me that if Susan lived in London and I lived in the outback, such is her energy and willpower that the horse would still be in the yard by the end of the week. She would somehow manage to make it happen, having no doubt persuaded me to help.

Was I missing something? At the age of fifty-three, I was getting the feeling it was time to reassess my approach. This challenge felt like a gift from fate, from the universe, from God. Was this a chance in a million that if I didn't pursue, or at least make a sporting attempt to achieve, I would always regret? Would I be bobbing around on a Zimmer frame in an old people's home aged one hundred and two, saying to anyone who'd care to listen, 'Remind me again, why did I never have my own horse, what was so important or so impossible?'

I had the strong feeling that the horse had chosen me – this was no chance sighting. What, I asked myself, is the point of being fifty-three if you don't at least try to make the impossible happen and finally have the courage to throw caution to the winds? All the more so if it is a dream that has taken root in your heart and, despite a lifetime of distractions, simply refused to go away.

TWO

The Pony Years

I was five years old when my mother took me for my first riding lesson. The year was 1955, and England was only just emerging from the postwar depression. The rationing of food and clothing had ended three or four years earlier, and clothes were still expensive and in short supply. While pregnant with me, my mother had owned only one maternity frock, a navy wool pinafore, which she had worn with different coloured blouses, and so when the pinafore needed cleaning, she had been forced to spend the day in bed.

We lived in a crooked and rather small white stone house in St John's Wood, which is now one of the more sought after and pricey areas of London, but in those days was considered to be a bohemian backwater, bordering on leafy Hampstead, which was definitely the enclave of long-haired eccentric artists.

My brother and I would play with the neighbours' children on vast, rocky bombsites, overgrown with weeds, relics of attempts by the German Air Force to flatten the nearby St John's Wood army barracks. Our favourite of these 'playgrounds' my brother and his friends nicknamed the 'Maggot Place', and this prime site now houses London's exclusive American school. Matthew, my brother, was five years older than me, and the rest of the gang, consisting of Gilbert and Nicky Jacobsen, their twin brothers, Henry and Quentin, the Susskind boy from across the road and Hooty from around the corner, were all about the same age. I was a girl in a boys' world, the youngest, the hanger-on, the little sis, trying valiantly to keep up with their boy-games. We would swing wildly from a rope tied to a high branch of the Jacobsens' pear tree, letting go at the very highest point of the swing to crash down onto their mother's compost heap. Or we would hurtle down steep pavements on homemade go-karts – wooden boards mounted on roller-skates with rudimentary steering engineered from a cross-board and manipulated by means of parcel string, frequently tumbling onto the street when the kart refused to turn or the string broke. Cars were few and far between in those days, and always seemed to be upright, black, and fortunately usually moving slowly.

The stables where my mother took me for my riding lessons were in a cobbled mews street called De Vere Gardens, off Kensington High Street in central London. The horses lived on the first floor, one storey above ground level, and one of my first memories is of seeing these giant creatures, fully tacked-up in double bridles and smart brown leather saddles, stepping gingerly down a wooden ramp, dropping their heads for stability. The sound of their metal-shod hooves rattling on the cobbles rang out as they stepped into the street.

The riders mounted from stone mounting posts that had survived from the turn of the century, when the mews had been used to stable the horses and carriages of the gentry. I suspect that, having been only five years old, I would have been lifted onto my pony. At first my legs had been too short to go into the irons, and so my little feet in their lace-up brown leather walking shoes had to be tucked into the loop of the stirrup leathers.

From there, we set off across Kensington High Street and into Hyde Park, where we would spend the next hour or so walking and trotting along Rotten Row, the sandy track that winds around the edges and centre of the park. To this day tourists wearing jeans, anoraks and cycling helmets are to be seen clinging on to sad horses as they plod their way wearily around the famous circuit.

Horses had never been part of the Spender heritage so it was generous of my parents to splash out shillings they could ill afford on my riding lessons. My father regarded my love of horses with some amusement – he claimed I must be a throwback to his mother's side of the family, the once wealthy banking side, the Schusters. Wealth that had somehow never quite filtered through to our side. Great-Aunt Gwen Schuster had hunted sidesaddle with the Heythrop until she was eighty-four. She cut a magnificent figure, her silver hair tucked up under the top hat, black veil over her blue eyes, lipstick perfect, and the full navy skirt of her tight hunting suit swathed across the side of her Thoroughbred.

She was also the first person I knew to own a dishwasher, and when we went to visit her, after we'd finished tea, we would all watch with fascination as she carefully washed the plates, cups and saucers before loading them into the machine. I envied all my little second cousins, the Schusters, who had the means to indulge their passion for horses – they all rode like mad and took for granted the possession of their own ponies.

I was never consciously aware of my father writing poetry; it was something that happened behind the closed doors of his study through which Wagner usually blared full blast from our old wooden gramophone. From the room next door, the sitting room, came Liszt, Chopin, Schubert as my mother, Natasha Litvin, who was a concert pianist, practised frantically for an upcoming recital. Matthew and I would experience this musically discordant scene from the polished wooden floor of the corridor separating these two rooms, waiting for a break in the music to knock on the door. When we got tired of waiting we would run down to the kitchen to be fed zabaglione and chatter in Italian with Francesca and Idelma, our cook and nanny, two wonderful ladies whom my parents had met while staying one summer on Lake Garda in the early 1950s.

Everybody else at my Church of England school, Francis Holland, went home to an orderly tea and homework. I came home to two poets, my father and Wystan Auden, or Joseph Brodsky, the Russian poet who later won the Nobel Prize, who had come to live with us after being thrown out of his homeland, sitting around the kitchen table in a haze of cigarette smoke, correcting typewritten pages. Somewhere on the checked, aqua Formica surface under the flying pages I would find a still warm teapot, sugar still in its packet, milk still in the bottle, a packet of ginger-nut biscuits and cups without saucers. There was conversation of which I could sense the intensity but not really take in the words, as I helped myself to a few biscuits and retired upstairs to read *Jill and Her Ponies*, or *Silver Snaffles*.

No one else at school had a father who never did up his shoelaces; who went to the bank to cash a cheque in his pyjama top because he'd forgotten halfway through that he was getting dressed. And although he did go to an office for several years while he was editing the magazine *Encounter*, it was not like anybody else's father's office. It was a scruffy set of tiny rooms near Piccadilly, crammed with dusty manuscripts, and for me provided an Aladdin's cave in the form of a stationery cupboard from which I would be given lead pencils with rubbers on the ends and blank paper dummies of the magazine, which I could fill with drawings and writing.

There were almost no rules at home that I can remember.

Liberal parents believe their children should play an active role in decisions, or at least be trusted to be responsible. Or perhaps liberal parents are usually so busy with their own creative lives and concerns that they just let their children get on with it. Everything changed dramatically twice a year during the few weeks in which Wystan came to stay, because he believed passionately in discipline, and my father believed passionately in Wystan.

'No, you can't stay in your bedroom over lunch, even if you are on a diet and reading Russian poetry,' Dad would say. 'Wystan says you must be down on the dot of one.'

From as young as fifteen we were allowed to stay out until all hours, but not to put an open book face down on a table because it damaged the spine; nor were we allowed to turn down the corner of the page to save a place. We were allowed to read D.H. Lawrence, though possibly not actively encouraged to read *Lady Chatterley's Lover*, but absolutely forbidden to read the children's author Enid Blyton, because her style was considered to be agonisingly prosaic and her child-characters wooden and stereotypical. Every Christmas from about 1956, in an attempt to encourage my brother and me to become writers, my father would give us the most beautiful, page-a-day diaries, made by Smythson's and bound in red Morocco leather. On most days, my entry read 'S.A.U.', which was short for 'school as usual', though occasionally I would add something brief yet apposite like: 'Then just messed around with the boys.'

By the age of seventeen the strain of the free life became too much for me and I ran away to boarding school, calling my father two days later to tell the poor man where to send the cheque for the exorbitant fees.

When I was six we spent the summer in a house we had been lent in a village near Oxford, called Westwell. There were riding stables nearby with gigantic brown horses, and assorted bay ponies, their manes cropped at about two inches long, jutting straight up from their necks. There was also a shaggy little Shetland pony; he must have been all of 10.2 hands, or 42 inches high, and small enough for me to mount by myself. He was called Tommy.

The highlight of the summer was the local pony show and gymkhana, and as there were far more riding-school children than ponies, we had to share. We drew lots, and I won Tommy for the fancy-dress race.

The day dawned. It was one of those endless hot summer days one remembers from childhood. I was up and dressed in my jodh-purs by six-thirty, nervous as hell about my upcoming riding event, and finally at eleven we set off for the show-grounds. There more time had to be wasted as I trailed along behind my mother through the horticulture tent, putting in what felt like several tedious life-times impatiently examining cut-flower arrangements and miniature gardens created in square biscuit tins. Finally it was almost time for the fancy dress race, and we headed for the show ring.

At two-fifteen Joanna, another client of the riding school, emerged from the ring, led by her father, both of them grinning from ear to ear, the blue rosette of second place pinned proudly to Tommy's bridle. Her turn was over and before she had the chance to luxuriate in her triumph she was unceremoniously pulled off the Shetland and I was dropped onto the felt pony saddle in her place. The stirrup leathers were quickly adjusted to my length, and Tommy with his new rider was hastily pushed back into the competition ring.

The purpose of this particular event was to canter up to little individual lines of clothes, dismount, and while clinging on to the reins of your thoroughly overexcited mount, to cram on the neatly folded cardigan, scarf, hat and coat, then try to mount as quickly as possible despite the encumbrance of the added clothing.

Then, holding on to the mane or neck-strap for dear life, gallop ferociously the rest of the way around the ring to streak past the winning-post hopefully in front of the other nine children.

At first, Tommy behaved like an angel. He understood the point of the competition perfectly, cantered fast to the heap of clothes, skidding to a stop as I threw myself off, and stood patiently while I donned the garments. I was ahead of all the other children. I pulled on the long coat that must have belonged to a man of six foot, and turned to mount, but the clothes were hampering my movements. Tommy was standing there looking at me, his little hooves firmly planted on the tails of the coat. 'Get off,' I screamed, pushing at his shaggy front. He had no idea what I meant. He was waiting for me to mount, as he could see the other horses already moving off. 'Tom-mee,' I wailed, tears pouring down my cheeks as I pushed and shoved with all my might. Finally, he stepped aside to get a better view of the departing crowd. I hauled myself onto his back and before I had a chance to get my feet properly in the stirrups, we were off at a fast canter – but still way behind the others. It was at this point that Tommy had an equine brain-wave. Why go all the way around the outside of the ring when, by taking a short cut across the middle, he could reach the front of the herd of galloping ponies? Tommy bolted across the centre of the ring, arriving in front of the other nine ponies, and to cele-brate gave three triumphant bucks. I came flying off on the third, and fell, sprawled across the winning line, disqualified from the competition for our short cut.

For the next few years, we continued to spend our weekends and holidays in the Cotswolds. We had been lent a Queen Anne cottage situated in the grounds of a magnificent Cotswold stone manor house, Bruern Abbey, which had been built on the site of an abbey that had been destroyed a few hundred years ago by fire. The generous man who had lent us the Red Brick Cottage was Michael Astor, the youngest son of the famous American, Nancy Astor, the first woman in England to be elected as a Member of Parliament.

Michael was unlike the archetypal English aristocrat of that era with the stately home and the coterie of servants, living within the traditions of their kind and somewhat set apart from the rest of the world. Michael Astor, possibly because of his American heritage, preferred to live in the thick of whatever was modern, creative and interesting. He was lively, witty and engaging, with the kindest heart of almost anyone I have ever known. The Astors had the sort of lifestyle that would be unimaginable in this day and age for even the wealthiest tycoon, movie star or rock legend. The house was teeming with butlers, footmen, chefs, cooks and maids. I think there was even a pastry chef and a boot boy. In the extensive gardens and greenhouses, eight gardeners pruned, planted and mowed; down in the stable yards, three chauffeurs tended the eight cars, and three old-fashioned grooms looked after the horses and ponies. Michael surrounded himself with an eclectic group of friends and family – artists, writers, historians, politicians, or just people he had met and liked. At weekends the house would be crammed full of happy guests, sitting in the drawing room reading the papers and debating world events, often with a cabinet minister in their midst, or taking off for walks around the muddy woods. The dinners were fabulous, with endless exquisitely delicious dishes prepared by the French chef and his many assistants, the long table bedecked with exotic flower arrangements, the faces of the guests flatteringly lit by the soft light cast by the silver candelabra.

When I was in my teens, Michael would invite me to join the dinners. I found them wildly romantic events, the women flirtatious and attentive in their slinky long dresses, and the men with a kind of sexy confidence gained from their black tie, polished shoes and the theatricality of the surroundings.

Meanwhile I would spend time with Michael's two daughters, though I was always conscious of being the poet's daughter from the cottage and rather terrified of the two confident girls. Jane was a year older than me at eight and was stunningly beautiful – the embodiment of charm – with her mother's cool profile and her father's happy laugh. Georgina was her mischievous, freckled, red-haired younger sister, prone to issuing dares to be naughty, which I hated as I was never, ever naughty if I could possibly avoid it. I believed with all my heart that life was complicated and tenuous enough without the added pressures of getting into trouble.

At night we would leave the grown-ups (the 'groans'), to the drama of their long dinners, and we would have supper in the nursery with nanny. We drank Lucozade (rationed to one cup each), and ate food sent up on trays from the kitchens: baked sole or chicken croquettes followed by the best vanilla ice-cream I've ever tasted, made for us by the pastry chef, flecked with the black of the vanilla bean. Both girls would sleep with their long hair wound up in metal rollers under a hair net, so that it would fall in ringlets. Almost every day the three of us accompanied by a groom would go for a ride through the woods and around the fields on Michael's 10,000 acres of farmland. I would be given whatever pony was going spare, starting with Frisky, a bright bay who pulled like a train and had therefore been abandoned by Jane in favour of a calm, dark bay with a wide blaze called Tiddly-winks. When there was no pony available or no riding arranged, I would bicycle half a mile up a steep hill, turn right into a tiny lane and then freewheel the half mile down to Foxholes.

Foxholes was a rambling farm, separated from Bruern by beautiful dense woods, which in the springtime were carpeted with bluebells and dotted with magnificent purple foxgloves. The farm-house was a large red-brick Victorian building, situated on the highest point of the property behind a typical English apple orchard and in front of another small wood. The whole spread belonged to two elderly sisters nicknamed by Michael the 'Outdoor' and 'Indoor' Miss Baileys.

Indoor Miss Bailey never went outdoors; she stayed in the house baking scones and lying on a sofa listening to the radio, or so I imagined, as I can count on one hand the number of times that I was invited indoors. The few times I saw her she was dressed in a navy blue skirt and cardigan, her white hair neatly curled, and I was struck by the creamy colour of her perfect English complexion, her delicate pale rose cheeks lightly powdered with almost white loose powder.

Outdoor Miss Bailey lived entirely outside, spending her days doing men's work around her farm, always dressed in sturdy brogues, an ochre coloured cotton smock, and thick brown cotton trousers stretched over her corpulent form. She was most at home when tending to the needs of her six beloved gold-coloured Jersey cows. She would sit on a traditional wooden stool, leaning her steel grey hair, cropped into a wedge, against the cow's flank and milk them by hand into a tin bucket. She showed me the 'V' mark-ings on the side of her favourite old cow, born just before the end of the war and considered a good omen for the Allied victory.

At night, she and her black-and-white sheepdog curled up on a big wooden bed out on the balcony of her room. She'd had the fourth wall of her bedroom torn down so that it was entirely open to the elements. She'd sleep wrapped in a pure wool Whitney blanket. 'The mistake most people make,' she'd tell me, 'is having sheets – nasty cold things. Just wrap yourself up in pure wool and you'll be warm as toast.' One particularly hard winter, the farm helper was called up to the house a couple of times to dig the lady and her dog out from under a thick covering of snow.

Later on in my teens, after Indoor Miss Bailey had died, I was invited into the house. I even went to stay one weekend. I noticed then that, during the short amount of time she spent inside, Miss Bailey would complain constantly about the cold, and when she was in the kitchen, she would open the heavy iron door of the slow-oven section of the Aga and place her ample bottom inside.

Outdoor Miss Bailey was a historic figure, one of the first lone women farmers. She and I would potter around the farm together in companionable silence, breaking it only to make a remark about one or other of the animals. She would tell me stories about her early days of farming when Foxholes had been joined to the world by a dirt track, and the only method of transport was horse and cart, or in deepest winter, horse and sleigh. We had one essential thing in common – the love of animals – and it formed a strong bond. For me the real magic of the place was to be found grazing in the top paddock: a motley collection of ponies that looked as if they might have been left behind by the last lot of touring gypsies, but I was allowed to ride them whenever I wanted. There was a thick-set, flea-bitten grey with knobbly knees called Silver, and a little skewbald stallion called Pancake, a small unbroken brown mare, bizarrely named Romeo, and her skewbald foal, the progeny of Pancake.

The fifty pounds for the pony was there, it existed, it had been put in the bank, which I knew was the large, tiled building on the way to the tube station; but the pony did not exist and I was still not convinced that such a miracle could ever happen to me.

First of all, we could do nothing for the next few months after receiving Wystan's gift because we were going to spend the eight months in San Francisco while Dad taught at the university and

I ate thirty-six flavours of ice-cream and rode horses in the American style. What an experience! I left a monochrome life, the black-and-white of postwar Britain, and felt myself bursting into a bright technicolour world of infinite possibilities. I was eight then and I have loved America ever since those first few months of discovery. I hung out with the children of beatniks, often younger than me, but, even so, shockingly painting their toenails with bright red polish. My mother took me to a riding school up in the hills. It was such an adventure to ride on saddles with huge pommels, on horses that not only neck-reined, but could start, stop and turn on a sixpence. I had to give up my San Francisco school as I was so mercilessly teased about my accent. I was chased around the playground by my classmates, thrown to the ground and had my arm twisted until I repeated the word 'turtle' several times, to the general hilarity of my young audience.

Funnily enough I came out of the playground events unscathed; it did not strike me as particularly cruel on the scale of child-to-child meanness. At least it was physical, not mental, torture. In fact I was quite relieved to have a good excuse to be able to leave the American school. It was all too different. Fortunately my mother was academically clever so she taught me at home for the rest of our stay.

When we returned to England, we set about looking for my horse. I wanted a nice looking pony of about 13.2 hands, the right size for me to ride comfortably, responsive, with a good gait, and a sympathetic nature. I had a clear vision of the two of us enjoying life together, setting out for long rambles across the downs, maybe even riding along a beach somewhere, cantering down the hard sand near the water and jumping breakwaters.

On my bedside table was a book that my mother had given me for my sixth birthday, *My Horses and I*, written by a famous show jumper of the times, Dawn Palethorpe. The photographic images from this book are printed across my heart; one that struck me particularly at the time was Dawn as a bouncy twelve-year-old standing next to a lively skewbald pony, both in fancy dress. The caption reads, 'Harlequin and I were exactly the same age, so we had fun growing up together.' That was what I had in mind. A horse that would be my friend as well as my mount, a pony that meant I could ride as much as I wanted, and when I wanted, that I could spend hours in the stable with, just messing around, and go to gymkhanas, Pony Club events, if I could find the formal riding clothes required for these events. I had the tweed hacking jacket, and jodhpurs, but no jodhpur boots, I was still riding in my brown lace-up outdoor shoes. All these imagined scenes I kept in the back of my mind, hardly allowing the full force of the vision to take hold as the disappointment if it never happened would be too overwhelming.

I recall a visit to a horse dealer's farm, where several sad and sorry nags were led out and I even sat on the back of one or two lumpy bays. These were ponies who took no joy in life, and I knew that once this had been lost in a horse it would be nearly impossible to win it back. Their spirits had been broken.

A little later we were invited to spend a day on the Berkshire Downs with Penelope Betjeman, the horse-loving wife of John Betjeman, the popular British poet who later became Poet Laureate. These were famous picnic outings. A group of carriages would set out about ten o'clock on a summer's morning filled with John and Penelope's friends, most of them totally indifferent to horses. The odd serious horse fancier would be given a saddled horse to ride, and for the next few hours we would wander over the downs, the grown-ups enjoying the sunshine and the views, brightly chatting away, roaring with laughter as they shared anecdotes and jokes. Whenever we came to a hill, the guests would be ousted from their comparatively comfortable seats and required to walk, huffing and puffing their way to the top of the grassy slope. After a few of these steep climbs, the guests would become increasingly vociferous in their reluctance to vacate the carriages and interrupt their discussions about art and politics, or lose the flow of a story. At that point, Penelope would call a halt. Tartan rugs would be spread over the chalky earth and wicker baskets unloaded from the carriages, containing delicious chicken sand- wiches and hard-boiled eggs from chickens raised by the Betjemans, cakes, bottles of homemade lemonade and thermos flasks of tea. Anyone hoping for a stronger drink was out of luck as Penelope was strongly against alcohol. This is exactly how I remembered this particular sun-drenched, idyllic day. I was in seventh heaven because Penelope had found a pony for me to try out. His name was Firefly and he was everything you could possibly ask for. He was just over 13 hands; he was a strawberry roan with a white blaze, finely boned, lean and happy, with feet on springs. He would respond to a whisper of a command, and stop with the slightest pressure on the reins.

I was allowed to take him back to Bruern for the weekend so I could try him out. The heaven of wandering out to the stables, to the loosebox borrowed from one of Jane and Georgina's ponies, to find my own horse, to tack up and ride whenever I liked! I cantered him through the woods along wide grassy rides planned by the landscape gardeners to give the best views back to the big house. And then at the end of the weekend, Firefly was sent back to his home.

He cost one hundred and twenty pounds, and we didn't have the seventy pounds to add to the fifty sitting in the white-tiled bank. Seventy pounds was an unimaginable, insurmountably large sum of money, and far more than my father, struggling to earn enough to pay the household bills, could afford. Not only that but there were faint rumblings that Michael's marriage wasn't going well, that he might even divorce his statuesquely beautiful, but icy-cool Scottish wife, and if we lost the cottage I would have nowhere to keep a horse. In addition, I was also on the brink of making the transition from primary to secondary school, so the plan was postponed until I had 'settled down' at my new school, but by that time everything had changed. Michael had divorced, the children had gone to live with their mother, the stables were empty, the grooms gone, and we no longer had the loan of the Red Brick Cottage. The writing was on the wall: I was not going to have my own pony, the fifty-pound honeymoon was over.

There was, however, a consolation prize.

When I was eleven my mother gave me the most wonderful present I have ever received. First we went to the post office where my mother drew out thirty pounds of her savings. Then we drove up to north London in our ancient black Jaguar with its red interior, and there we entered a room full of poodles, all shapes, sizes, colours and ages. We returned home three hours later with a puppy.

When Topsy first entered the house she was just a pompom of glossy black fur from which peeked a wet nose and two mischievous brown eyes. She proceeded to cause havoc, making puddles everywhere, chewing up our shoes, my father's best fountain pen, even my precious travel alarm clock, but only a few months later she blossomed into a vociferous and elegant miniature poodle, fiercely protective of the house, the family and most of all, of me. She was my closest friend and companion, and while my parents were tied up with their careers and their adult concerns, she was always on hand to greet me when I returned from school, wanting to know how I was feeling and full of sympathy when I was down in spirits. She was a consummate actress. In London she would behave like a regular town-loving creature, sleeping on sofas or the end of the bed, watching television, and showing enormous reluctance to go outside when-ever it was raining. During weekends at Bruern she would transform into a would-be terrier, flying along beside me as I cycled up to Foxholes or went riding in the woods, digging up rabbit holes and arriving home covered in mud and burrs.

In the summer of 1962, my parents went back to America. My father had been given another of the short-term jobs lecturing in the States that he depended upon to earn his living. Sometimes, as on this occasion, my mother would accompany him and then I would be sent to stay with a school friend, or my father's secretary, Margot Warmsley, would stay in the house and look after me. My brother had taken to boarding at his school, Westminster, and from the age of sixteen was spending weekends with his girlfriend, Maro Gorky. This time, my parents decided to lend our house to an American acquaintance, Ricki Huston, wife of the Hollywood film director, John Huston, who was coming to London to look for a house and schools for her two children, Tony and Anjelica.

The first time I met Anjelica Huston I was struck by three notions. The first was that she wore her Alice band at the front of her brow, across the hairline. This was deeply shocking and suggested she had to have French affectations because down-to-earth English girls wore their headbands a good two inches back from the hairline. Secondly, she had a black miniature poodle absolutely identical to my beloved Topsy, except hers was in need of a good clip, and I instantly felt the tug of a vocational calling to sort out her dog's hair. Thirdly, she was one of the few chil-dren I'd ever met who lived on the same child-planet as me. We were children of interesting, even brilliant, parents who were so tied up in the drama of their lives or with the exigencies of their work that they were very often absent in body and, even when present, were often preoccupied in mind and spirit. We were going to keep each other company and be friends.

Meanwhile our friend Michael Astor had married a wonderfully romantic and gentle blonde goddess called Pandora, and they had again lent us the cottage. Sadly, though, his children were rarely there as they were for the most part living with their mother in another part of the county, so the stables remained empty. It had been Barbara and the children who had been the keen riders, not Michael; neither he nor Pandora had the slightest interest in horses.

My parents invited Ricki and her two children down to Bruern for the weekend so that Anjelica and I could meet. The two of us stayed up half the night talking and clipping chunks of hair off her poodle's shaggy moustache and dreadlocked feet with dressmaker's scissors. In the morning we cycled up the hill to see Outdoor Miss Bailey, and went riding. Anjelica rode the skewbald Pancake, cantering across the fields and jumping logs, and I was instantly full of admiration. She'd ridden a stallion without a murmur of fear – this girl was all right.

Luckily Anjelica seemed to like me too. Of course I had the advantage of holding the high-ground of age at that all-too-brief window of time when being older is advantageous. I was twelve years old, an impressive thirteen months older than Anjelica.

For the next five years I spent all my school holidays with Anjelica on her father's property in Ireland. St Clerans was a greystone, Georgian house with a sprawling estate complete with stables, walled gardens and a folly, stuck in the middle of green fields and woods, about fifteen miles from Galway, on the West Coast.

Anjelica's mother, Ricki, was one of the great beauties of her time. Her face had appeared on the cover of *Life* magazine when she was only seventeen years old and this life-changing event had propelled her to Hollywood where she had met and soon after married John Huston, already a world-famous writer, film director, actor, adventurer and former champion boxer. He was forty-six. She was half-Italian with the dramatic dark hair and eyes and creamy skin that Anjelica has inherited. Ricki was possessed of a serenity, an elegance and an original style about the way she lived and dressed that gave her beauty a timeless quality.

Both Ricki and John Huston, my 'borrowed' family, were extraordinarily generous to me and always treated me exactly as if I were one of their own children. During term Ricki would take Anjelica, Tony and her extra child, me, to the theatre, the ballet or opera at least once a week. These were the golden days of British theatre, when the theatres were run by actors and real theatre people rather than administrators. We saw Vanessa Redgrave and Tom Courtney in Chekov's *The Seagull,* Peggy Ashcroft in *The Cherry Orchard*, Laurence Olivier in *Long Day's Journey into Night,* and then, in 1963, we saw *Hamlet*. It was the inaugural production of Ken Tynan and Laurence Olivier's newly created National Theatre Company, temporarily housed in the Old Vic Theatre, and Peter O'Toole, the movie star better know for his portrayal of T.E. Lawrence in *Lawrence of Arabia*, played Hamlet.

Later, I lay awake all night in the cot bed on the floor of Anjelica's bedroom. I was thirteen at the time and my existence had been shaken to its foundations. For four hours I had been transported into the world of Shakespeare by a blond god, Peter O'Toole, playing a character I understood only too well: the outsider. I had not been the slightest bit daunted by the language, I had heard every word as if it had been addressed exclusively to me. That night, I had fallen in love for the first time, and indeed had fallen in love three times over – with *Hamlet,* with the theatre and acting, and with Peter O'Toole. And just to make things even more intense, Ricki had taken us backstage to meet O'Toole. I was no longer going to be the world's greatest showjumper, I was going to be an actress. But then so was Anjelica. It was never really talked about, just assumed, especially by her father. In my mind it was quite clear Anjelica was going to be the Greta Garbo of her age. Occasionally she would pose in front of the mirror, turning this way and that, and yes indeed, she closely resembled that famous movie star. So for the next five years my acting ambitions remained a dark secret, and it would be many years later still before I would have the courage of my convictions.

Anjelica was unlike anyone I had ever met; she was wildly imaginative and romantic, totally fearless, possessed of her mother's charm and style, and her father's creativity and sense of humour. During holidays at St Clerans she and I spent our days running wild around the countryside, riding our ponies, cleaning tack, messing around the stables, and improvising hare hunts with our motley pack of house dogs. In the evenings we would sprawl on the thick cream carpet of the sitting room among John's collection of pre-Columbian art, and watch John Huston films on the projector: *Moulin Rouge*, *Treasure of the Sierra Madre*, *The Misfits* and *The African Queen*. If John was there with his coterie of movie people, we would stay up until the small hours, dressed in nineteenth-century French ballgowns, playing poker with John Steinbeck, Peter O'Toole, or various other colourful Hollywood characters. We lived a life as exotic and theatrical as one of John's movies. We would go to bed at one or two in the morning, about the time that the grown ups moved on into night-time sessions in the authentic Japanese bath that John had installed in the lower regions of the house. Most of my school friends never even got to meet their idols, while I got to run around all night with mine, Peter O'Toole. I remember Anjelica and I, dressed as ghosts, riding up and down the front lawn in the moonlight, being chased by Peter in his *Lawrence of Arabia* costume.

Anjelica had her own ponies. First, a feisty brown mare called Vicki who had a talent for knowing just how badly behaved she could be and get away with it. She would be an angel with little children and a cheerful little demon with anyone she felt needed testing. She would do anything for Anjelica and jump stone walls of any height. When I remember Vicki I always think of her with a thoroughly mischievous expression on her bright little face.

Next, Anjelica had a dappled grey Connemara mare. John, a crazed romantic at heart, encouraged Anjelica to ride side-saddle – encouraged to the point of command. The only other rider still hunting side-saddle with the Galway Blazers was Lady Ampthill, who was the same generation as my Great-Aunt Gwen.

Paddy Lynch, the groom, whether under instruction from the Hustons or of his own accord I don't know, would buy a pony for me to ride and hopefully improve, and then, when we went back to school, he would sell the pony for a nice profit. The first holidays, Paddy presented me with a black gelding with a broad white blaze. Anjelica and I immediately named the pony Tom Jones, as we had recently been greatly enamoured of Albert Finney playing the title role in the film. We had spent the entire day in the Pavilion Cinema, Piccadilly Circus, seeing the film through four times. This was one of the first indications, along with my admiration of Charlton Heston in *El Cid*, that there might be something in this 'boys' lark after all. The black pony had 'feathers', long hairs on his lower legs, and had only ever been in a cart before. Paddy trimmed off the feathers with his clippers, put a saddle on the pony's back and gave me a leg-up. To my surprise, the little black pony seemed to have no objections to this arrangement, and for the next three or four weeks, he was almost mine.

One time I turned up to a cross-country competition, all ready in an embarrassingly optimistic way to ride, in case anybody had a spare pony. It emerged that a horse could be entered twice, so some kind person handed me the reins of a dark brown pony and pointed me towards the start. Only as I crossed the starting line did it occur to me that I had not had time to learn the course, but the pony seemed to know his way, so I just sat there, taking each fence as it came – a clear round! He had a strange jump, a sort of wriggling motion rather than a leap. I think I came in second, the pony second to his own first.

Lady Hemphill was one of the Hustons' neighbours in Galway. She was a striking blonde with a stylish look, reminiscent of a femme fatale from one of those black-and-white movies of the forties. I could always imagine her dressed to kill in black, drawing a pistol from a clutch purse with a gloved hand and shooting a man dead with one shot. Her daughter Angela was petite and fluffy, and was the proud owner of an elegant dun pony called Thundercloud, who lived in one of the sumptuous looseboxes at Tulara Castle, the Hemphills' home. It was Lady Hemphill who lent me Patsy Fagan.

She strolled up to me at a Pony Club meeting, where I was standing under a tree in the rain dressed up in my riding outfit but with nothing to ride. 'Oh, Lizzie, there you are. Tell you what, I've got a pony I'm bringing on to sell. Next show, I'll throw him in the back of the box for you. Balinarobe, next week. That way you'll get a ride.'

Patsy Fagan was a dream horse, he was beautiful and totally responsive. He was dun coloured – gold with a black mane and tail – which is a classic colour for a Connemara pony, and he was the first Significant Dun in my life.

I was last to ride into the ring at Balinarobe Horse Show. The class was 'Style and Appearance', pronounced '*sht-oil and app-hear-ance*' – West Coast Ireland's version of showing. I was sitting back in the saddle, keeping the reins of the double bridle long, and my hands back, to show off Patsy's beautiful neck. I could see from the moment we entered the ring that the judges were unable to take their eyes off this pony. Angela, Lady Hemphill's daughter, was in front on Thundercloud, and was heavily tipped to win — she always did as Tulara Castle was the local stately home — but on that day the judges could not resist giving first prize to Patsy Fagan. Almost before I knew it, I was cantering around the ring to the audience's applause, with the red rosette pinned to my horse's bridle. In my entire childhood, this was my most perfect moment of glory.

No sooner were we out of the ring than Angela, who'd come only third, threw herself off her disgraced mount, ran over to me and, grabbing hold of my leg, physically pulled me off my golden pony. For the rest of the holidays she rode Patsy, and I was lucky enough to ride Thundercloud, also a great little pony.

The great gifts of my childhood were the chances I had to run wild in nature, coming into the house at the end of the day exhausted, having run through fields, climbed trees, fallen into rivers and rolled in wet grass, the chance to forge enduring friendships doing these things.

I can't imagine my childhood without these grounding ex-periences. For me they were fundamental to my sense of self, and gave me a solid starting point, before all the complicated adult stuff started layering in on top.

THREE

Significant Others

For the next couple of decades, horses faded into the background as other more urgent life concerns took precedence. At this time I was not very good at holding down steady jobs, or indeed, steady boyfriends, but I was blessed with a wealth of friendships and experience. I knew in the back of my mind that one day I would be a writer and so to me to live life to the full was what mattered most. The idea had been firmly planted in my mind the day my father gave me that first red Smythson's diary. 'So, Lizzie, maybe one day you'll be a writer,' he'd said, 'and then you'll thank me for these little books because they will be your future. All you have to do is keep writing, all the time, do you hear?'

Growing up as I did, there were few enough rules, and so on the very rare occasions my father told me to do something, I listened. I reckoned I'd be ready to start on my first novel by the time I was forty.

Anjelica, in her late teens, had moved to America to pursue a career in modelling and so our paths had separated. Except for one memorable trip to Mexico to visit her father in the early 1980s, it would be a good twenty years before we fully resumed our friendship. Meanwhile, in my own late teens I moved away from my parents' home, but only across London to Chelsea to lodge with a college friend. I now faced the reality of earning my living and paying the rent. I learnt shorthand and typing and started looking.

My first job, when I was aged nineteen, was for a charming and dynamic young man only a few months older than me who published a magazine called *Student* from a chaotic house belonging to his parents near Hyde Park. I sold advertising space for the magazine, for which I was paid two pounds a day. I also made the sandwiches at lunchtime with the help of a telephone engineer, Bert, who although on the payroll of the national telephone company never seemed to make it in to work and instead used to spend his days with us. As we left the shop where we'd bought the ingredients, Bert used to clank, his pockets bulging full of shoplifted items: tins of sardines, tuna fish, condensed milk and anything else that had caught his fancy. Part of my duties were to help run an advisory centre for people in trouble, which my employer ran from the same premises. I would be on the phone trying to convince the Royal Air Force to buy a full-page recruitment advert, while an unwashed and somewhat incoherent hippie would be standing in front of me describing some giant striped caterpillars that were currently crowding his vision. As often as not before starting work I would have to shift several homeless teenagers camped out in sleeping bags under my desk, moving them along to the corridor so I could get to my papers.

At the end of each day I would go to my employer's office at the back of the house to claim my salary – two pound notes – which I was required to forage out of the back pocket of his jeans. He was a great guy and we got on well. Often he would come with me to sell advertising space and such were his charisma and powers of persuasion that he was able to sell anything to anybody.

One day after I had been working there about a month, I went into his office to find my boss sitting with his feet on the desk staring rather moodily at the six black telephones ranged before him.

'You know what my ambition is?' he asked me.

'No. Tell me.'

'To have all these phones ringing at once, each one with a call from a major newspaper, all clamouring to speak to me.'

I sat down opposite him, allowing us both a moment of reverential silence after his confession. I quietly surveyed my ambitious and unorthodox boss, his wild curls of red hair all over his forehead, his square black glasses, tight blue jeans and sloppy sweater. Poor guy, I thought, not a chance; he'd need to buy a proper suit for a start, employ a few sane people, cut his hair and cut down on all his crazy schemes.

How wrong could I be? His name was Richard Branson.

My jobs were for the most part gratifying and interesting, even if they never seemed to last very long. I wrote features for a teenage pop magazine called *Mirabelle* in the early golden days of glam rock, ghosting the David Bowie column, inventing the letters to and from Donny Osmond, and interviewing groups such as Queen when they were barely even heard of, let alone famous. I took photographs of Queen with my tiny Rollei B35 camera; Freddie Mercury and Brian May were so incredibly nice, enthusiastic, charming, sane and intelligent in comparison with most of the rock artists I interviewed. I would drag the teenage editor of the magazine, Paul Cohen, along to their concerts, Paul protesting every inch of the way, and when I walked in they would stop playing whatever it was they were playing and Freddie Mercury would lead them in a few bars of 'Hey Big Spender' in welcome.

But between the interesting jobs, in order to earn money and keep myself afloat, I would take whatever came my way. I suffered a few months of secretarial hell, temping, and then in my mid-twenties, I took courage in both hands and followed my first love, acting.

I auditioned and succeeded in winning a place to the toughest and hardest of drama schools, Drama Centre. Aged twenty-five, I qualified for a mature grant and also to have the fees paid by the local council, so I threw in my latest job as fashion editor for a magazine called *Hi* and enrolled for the three-year course. I was over the moon with excitement, having finally committed myself to something about which I was passionate. I missed riding and horses in this phase of my life, but the hard work and financial constraints left very little space for them.

Every now and then, though, a horse would come into my life and leave its mark. Beauty was one of these.

In 1976, I was travelling around America during the summer holidays from drama school, with only one hundred and twenty dollars in my pocket to last the entire twelve-week trip. I visited my drama-school friends in Vancouver and Salt Lake City, and friends of my parents in New York, Martha's Vineyard, San Francisco and Los Angeles. I also went to Aspen, Colorado, to visit my godmother's daughter, Connie Harvey.

My godmother, Muriel Gardiner, had been a friend of my father in the late 1930s in Vienna. They had shared a hut in the Vienna Woods and my father had written poems to her, calling her 'Elizabeth'. Muriel came from a wealthy Chicago meat-packing family and had married an Englishman, then gone with her young daughter, Connie, to Vienna to study psychoanalysis with Sigmund Freud. Once there, she had used her dual nationality and her cash to help Jewish families escape from the Gestapo.

In the summer of 1976, Connie was building a ranch up in the mountains near Steamboat Springs. As there was no homestead yet built, we were sleeping in tents and rising early to shovel gravel, not my favourite occupation, so whenever possible I would escape to something that really interested me – rounding up cattle on horseback. I would ride a quarter horse, Beauty – pronounced 'Bewdy' by her urban cowboy owner. Bewdy was horribly out of condition and looked rather pathetic with the huge western saddle on her back, but she had the sweetest nature and was very pretty. She was dun, cream with a black mane and tail, and after Patsy Fagan, she was the second Significant Dun in my life. She and I would invariably get lost among the trees high in the mountains, so I would dismount and confer with her, and between us we would come up with a scheme: I would call out, she would watch me, and then she would let out an ear-splitting neigh. We'd take it in turns. We never got a response so eventually I would remount, give Bewdy her head and she would find her way back to the others.

Later in my stay, another horse I was riding, a well-trained ranch horse, saw a snake and ran backwards, shaking violently. I tried to dismount but ended up on the ground with the horse on top of me and a broken pelvis.

I spent the next week in Steamboat Springs Cottage Hospital, and Bewdy's owner would visit me every day. He would come quietly into the room dressed in his cowboy hat and denim shirt with silver rivets and say a quick 'Howdee'. Then he would put a framed photograph on the bedside table. It was a picture of Bewdy, kitted out in a magnificent silver-inlaid saddle. To begin with, I made a few attempts at conversation, asking him about his work or Bewdy's history, but words were not his thing – he would answer with a monosyllable and then drop his eyes to the floor. For the next half an hour we would sit in contented silence, each thinking beautiful thoughts about Bewdy, after which he would stand up, retrieve the photograph and leave. It was like a meditation. On the last day, he left me the photograph of our little horse in its wooden frame.

Mellita was the next horse that left a mark. In 1965, Michael Astor had sent me on a Mediterranean cruise to keep his daughter Jane company. Jane was going through a somewhat difficult time in her life and so chose to spend most of the cruise firmly locked in her cabin. My father had given me a letter of introduction to an old friend of his, another poet, Brian Moyne, one of the patriarchs of the Guinness brewing family, who was on the boat with his wife Elisabeth and seven of their nine children. After those ten days together, we became friends for life. It so happened that Brian's children were all horse lovers and bred Arabs and Anglo-Arabs (horses with both Arab and Thoroughbred blood) on their rambling property in Hampshire, and such is the generosity of this family that I don't think I have once rung their house without immediately being invited to go down there to visit.

One weekend twenty years later, in early autumn, I was riding through a large paddock with Brian Moyne's oldest son, Finn Guinness, and suddenly all around us were young horses, about twenty of them. It was one of my Sir Lancelot moments, and so just for fun I imagined that I had been given the gift of my choice out of the entire herd of rapturously beautiful young creatures: the greys, chestnuts and bays, cantering along and kicking up around us. At that moment, a young bay filly with long eyelashes, came up close and looked straight at me. There was something extremely beguiling about her look, her quality, her fluidity of movement, her extreme grace.

'Finn? What's the name of this young filly?'

'Mellita,' he answered. 'She's an Anglo-Arab.' For the next few years I watched the progress of Mellita. She became the favourite horse of Finn's American wife, Mary, but sadly, years later, was kicked by another horse and was found with a broken leg. She had to be put down.

Mellita had two foals, both male. The first had also been

damaged, cutting himself so badly on a granite rock that he, too, was put down. The second was only a foal when his mother died, and so Mary raised him by hand. She saw the horse had talent and put him into training to be a three-day eventer. His name is Tamarillo.

Tamarillo is 16. 2 hands, and is one-third Arab. In 2004, ridden by William Fox-Pitt, he won the Badminton Horse Trials, the toughest three-day event in the world. In the same year, Tamarillo was the star of the British team at the Athens Olympics. He is thought to be one of the best horses in the world, and has his own fan club. I hope this means that I have a good eye when it comes to a horse.

In 1978 I graduated from drama school. The course had been emotionally and physically tough as we worked our way through a multitude of disciplines, from Ancient Greek theatre to Brechtian, from St Denis improvisation to the emotionally taxing method acting of Uta Hagan. Whenever in my first year I and the other female students found ourselves really tired and miserable, there was one particular third-year student we would go to for a hug and chat that would be guaranteed to cheer us up. He was one of the most brilliant classical actors the school had trained, and was not exactly good looking – but very attractive. His name was Pierce Brosnan.

My year, Group Fourteen, had been seriously depleted by the demanding course. Out of thirty-eight students who had turned up fresh-faced and eager to work on that first day, three years earlier, we were down to fourteen. Almost all the twenty-four students missing from the graduation line had been expelled, mostly for reasons of tardiness, an unwillingness to work a twelve-hour day, five and a half days a week, or had simply been thrown out for reasons not always clear to the rest of the group – apparently more or less on the whim of our two brilliant but eccentric and wilful principals.

One of them, Yat Malgrem, once a great Swedish character dancer, whispered to me as he handed me my diploma and deposited a kiss on my cheek, 'Oh, Elizabeth, I never thought you would make it.'

'Nor did I, Yat.' I had never been one for sticking at a job for more than a few months, but for me the slavery at Drama Centre had been comparatively easy. I was doing something I loved and that interested me deeply.

Unfortunately it was a very unfashionable time to be a tall actress and I was five feet ten inches. Yat had warned me: 'Oh, Elizabeth, you are too tall and blonde and European.' During the 1970s, the administrators had taken over the theatres and they liked to keep their names in lights rather than the cast's; this was a time for actors who would melt together into an ensemble and it seemed I was not an ensemble type. I kept a bottle of brunette hair rinse in the bathroom cupboard, thinking if I turned up for auditions as a brunette rather than a blonde that would help, but somehow I never dared use it. I could do nothing about my height. Meanwhile I auditioned for everything; gone were the ideals of a classical drama school: 'Oh, I would never do a commercial'. I did everything; I would turn up on a wet day for one line and almost no salary. Occasionally I would get a good part such as Laura Lyons in *Hound of the Baskervilles*, or Michael Palin's wife in the cult movie *Brazil*.

By the early 1980s I could no longer survive financially or emotionally on the occasional acting part. A friend recommended me for a job at an independent publishing house; I went to the interview and to my astonishment, got the job. It was wonderfully restoring to be in control and feel effective, and to have just enough money to pay the bills. It seemed that by dint of acting the part I could actually do the job. But after two years working for a hierarchical company I began to feel stifled. Spending every day in a dark basement in Bloomsbury, watching the clock, struggling to and fro on the packed and sweaty tube, I longed for a way of life that had fewer constraints, more room for adventure and creativity, and space for dreaming. So I took courage and handed in my notice.

I was thirty-four, and I *had* to start to write. It was six years ahead of schedule, but I had no choice. I'd have to try to make it work. I went back onto the books of my acting agent hoping for something that would help me get by, and by a stroke of enormous luck I landed a well-paid commercial playing the archetypal mother with young children in the Fairy Liquid advertisement. Including repeats, the fee represented eight months of the publishing house's meagre salary and so I had bought myself some time to write. It was ironic, as the way things were going, I was never going to be a mother, let alone a young mother.

Hedgehog Wedding was my first film script. I called it *Wedding*, because it was a black comedy about the characters and complications in a country house wedding, then added the noun 'Hedgehog' for no better reason than I thought it might grab the attention of people flicking through the television guide. That didn't stop the journalists who were hanging around the set from coming up with all sorts of far-fetched theories about what it meant. The script was turned down by eight agents and rejected by two television companies, before being seized upon by one of the best film producers at the BBC, Innes Lloyd. My teacher and mentor, Jack Rosenthal, was a truly great television writer – and the kindest of men – so I chose to listen to him and ignore the sheaf of rejection letters telling me that nobody would ever want to see a black comedy about a wedding where the people were privileged enough to be able to afford to rent a marquee tent.

The film was made and broadcast within a year. In a bizarre turn of events, it was filmed at Bruern Abbey, where I had lived as a child. Michael Astor had sadly died of a brain tumour comparatively young, a few years earlier. His widow had sold the big house and retired to live in the Red Brick Cottage, where we had lived in earlier years. The house had been bought by an American who was planning to turn it into a prep school and, at the time we were looking for a house to film in, it just happened to be lying empty. For me, the whole experience became like a film in itself as I wandered around the shell of this once great house, the lawns now bristling with wardrobe and make-up trucks, reliving my childhood memories. I was as much an outsider then as I had been as a child, as it seemed that the author is not always welcomed with open arms onto a film set. *Hedgehog Wedding* was a success, and was thought by some to be the inspiration for the highly successful *Four Weddings and a Funeral*.

Life then suddenly became very busy as I met someone who shared my crazy combination of interests: art, theatre, friends, travel and food. He was an Australian, Barry Humphries, the actor and author, and a couple of years later we married in Italy.

In 1989, Barry had first taken me to Australia. All I had known about the continent was that it was very large and very far away, and that my father, who hardly ever watched anything other than the news on television, had been totally addicted to the Australian soap *Neighbours*, and used to break off writing every day at five to watch it. It was a revelation. No television screen could give a sense of the beauty and scope of Australia, the fabulous towns and cities, each with its own very individual character, its deserted white beaches, its wonderful restaurants. Most of all, however, I loved the magic of the great open spaces. While I had been working at the publishing house we had distributed a book of photographs of the outback. I had rung the photographer to confirm that he had used tinted lenses, as it was not possible that anywhere could have earth that vibrant red ochre and a sky such an intense blue.

'No, no lenses,' I was told. I surmised he was lying.

Among my parents' friends had been the Australian painter Sidney Nolan. He and his wife Cynthia had come to stay with us when we were living in Berkeley, California, when I was nine. I had looked at books of his images, stretches of desert sand with the bleached bones of animals, and thought, Is *that* what Australia is like? Where were the kangaroos and cuddly koala bears?

During that first trip to Australia, Barry took me to stay for a week with another Australian artist, Arthur Boyd, at Bundanon in the Shoalhaven region of New South Wales, which he shared with Sid Nolan. In one of the fields close to the house were a couple of horses. No, it was not a field, it was a paddock, I was told, even though it was at least three acres in size. A paddock in England is a small enclosure at the back of the house, almost a holding area, maybe with a few fruit trees and probably with so little grass that a horse would need extra feeding. A paddock in Australia can be any size, up to hundreds of thousands of acres. A small area for keeping animals in Australia, I was told, is called a yard, never a corral, that's an American term.

Somehow I managed to catch the smaller of the horses, a grey pony with a little Arab blood evident from his perky nature and high tail carriage. I groomed him and tacked him up. I had forgotten what fun it was just to be with a horse. The little grey would watch everything I was doing, playing up just enough to keep things interesting, and while Barry was down in the gardens of the house with Arthur Boyd, covering canvases with thick layers of paint which Arthur would sometimes put on with his hands, I would trot around the woods – sorry, not woods but 'bush', on the little pony, quite astonished by my surroundings. With lush tall green trees and exotic birds, this was more like a subtropical rainforest than just 'the country' as Barry called it, and it was only three hours drive from Sydney. Then the pony would stop dead in his tracks for no better reason than that he could not remember why he was trotting. It appeared that it had been years since anyone had even considered riding him. This would be unheard of in England where a horse is such a valuable commodity, the horse might be sold, but it is very rarely that horses are more or less forgotten. Australia truly was a remarkable country if well-bred horses were just left in paddocks.

The second time I had been given a horse was by my husband. It was 1995 and we were in London. I was woken by Barry bearing a cup of tea. 'Happy birthday,' he said, giving me a good-morning kiss. Then I noticed a few exquisitely wrapped parcels scattered on the bed.

'These are just some small presents; for your big present I would like to give you a horse,' he said. 'You can find one for yourself and I'll buy it for you.'

My husband is exceedingly generous, but I'm not sure the horse was ever mentioned again, and being the kind of person I am (or was), I did nothing about it, just waited. And that was my mistake, as another sort of person would have simply gone out and looked for a horse to buy. I lacked courage and the conviction that in the big scheme of things my wants were of much significance, and I worried about the practicalities of where I would keep a horse. Meanwhile, my husband had no idea what a can of worms he'd opened. Nor did I tell him.

The next year on my birthday, Barry took me to stay with some friends who live on a magnificent old farm in Portugal. Carlos and Tita breed bulls and Lusitanian horses. Lusitanos, along with Arabs, are one of my very favourite of horse breeds. They are impossibly romantic, taller than Arabs, with slightly Roman noses, and long curly manes and tails. They have the gentlest and sweetest of natures and are the national horse of Portugal.

I guessed that Barry was at last going to give me that horse he'd promised; he was in league with these friends and they had picked out a dappled-grey stallion like one of the gorgeous creatures I had admired in their stables. On the morning of my birthday I would find a string leading from the breakfast table to the stables. I could hardly contain my excitement, though I kept the secret during the journey from London, pretending not to know all through dinner the night before, tossing and turning sleeplessly all night.

At breakfast, I found a parcel on my plate. It contained a box of handkerchiefs, admittedly the best and most beautiful handkerchiefs ever created, made by Charvet in Paris, but no string, no breathless excursion to the stables. I never told my husband about my misfounded expectation. I was embarrassed by it, by the way I had allowed my fantasy to run away with me, back into that place where I had lived as a child – my imagination. Before we had even left Portugal I had lost the box of handkerchiefs, though I swear it had nothing to do with being disappointed. I had well and truly come to terms with the fact that I would never have my own horse; that for reasons of pure practicality that was not the path my life was going to take.

FOUR

The Year in Between:
July 2003 to July 2004

On 27 July 2003, three days after I was given a horse for the third time, Susan and I left Athenrai to fly back to Broome. We were planning to spend a couple of days enjoying the beach before I had to return to Sydney.

I was, of course, still thinking about the brumby Celia had given me. I was hoping Peter Eve would soon send me the photographs he had taken from the helicopter and then I would have proof. But was this a horse I could go and find and bring home? My horse. The words alone made me smile.

With the return to civilisation came a return to sanity, and the bare truth was that it would almost certainly be impossible to find this wild creature again. Susan had told me that nothing in the way of setting out to find the horse could be done until the next dry season, several months away, by which time the horse would most likely have moved on to a different area. We might succeed in glimpsing it from a helicopter, if we were lucky and prepared to spend hundreds or even thousands of dollars of helicopter time combing the countryside, but the chances of ever seeing it close-up were slim indeed. As for actually catching the horse and breaking it in – that was merely the stuff of dreams. I found it sad and frustrating to think about the horse that would never be mine, and to add salt to the wound I was starting to receive replies to the email I had sent out to friends from the outback in which I had suggested in a rather offhand way that I might be considering pursuing this crazy scheme.

From Amy Tan

I imagine you someday riding your beautiful horse and, as you feed her carrots, telling her what a wild thing she once was, how you spotted her from the heavens and knew she was divine.
Amy

From Susie Little

What an amazing thing to be given a horse. I think you should follow your dream and see where it takes you. If you pursue it one step at a time, you will soon know whether it is going to be possible. If you come up against a major obstacle that can't possibly be overcome then you will know it was not meant to be. It is perfectly possible to break and train a supposedly wild horse, but I don't think it would be sensible to try and do this on your own.

Can't wait to hear what happens. If there is anything I can do, let me know. Keep me posted.

From Mary Guinness

I think it is a blessing there are so many logistical difficulties with actually obtaining your new horse because in the end they all break your heart. Like men. Except that it is with injury or death. Both

happen much sooner than you plan. Finn is forever giving horses
away here and I am sure if you are not able to capture Maia we
would be more than happy to accomodate you on your next trip here.

So back in Sydney, and then in London and on my travels, I
recounted the events of my stay in the outback to friends and
was surprised at their response. I found myself holding centre stage
with this tale of wilderness and wild horses, and those listening
asked me questions, requiring more detail, wanting to hear the
rest of the story, and in the spirit of the telling I would even suggest
that I was thinking seriously of going back and looking for my
gift-horse. Then someone would say, 'But where on earth are you
going to keep a horse?' Usually they'd speak in a sort of wailing
voice, and I would feel vaguely irritated. How could they make
such a great leap to that point in the future? Weren't they listening?
Didn't they realise that the whole thing was an impossible dream?

And so for the next few months I got on with my life and all
the usual things that take up my time: visiting my husband, who
was again on the road touring; seeing friends; organising our office;
paying bills; looking after our house. Every now and then I would
take a chunk of time to be by myself to work on the novel I had
been writing.

Barry and I spent Christmas back in Australia in our Sydney
flat. It was wonderful and hot, and I thought about the Kimberley
where it would be the beginning of the rainy season, and my horse
running wild in the long grasses, maybe by now in foal, if she
was a mare.

Then in January, Susan Bradley emailed me. She'd been out
driving and thought she had seen the horse.

Yes – the horse I have seen is a classic bright chestnut about eighteen
months old with a large uneven white blaze, which goes down to

its muzzle and reaches each eye. Its mane, forelock and tail were a lighter colour. It was with a larger brown horse with black mane and tail with a small star on its forehead. I couldn't get near them – they were in long grass with some cattle but raced off as I got closer, kicking up their heels – they are in excellent condition and very skittish. Definitely have some breeding and not just brumby stock.

How exciting! My horse, Maia, was still there apparently flaunting herself, placing herself at the edges of my experience, maybe even waiting for me to go back and find her.

It is hard to pinpoint exactly when I made the decision. The moment I changed from saying, 'It's an impossible dream,' to the slightly more positive, 'I might even go back in May and look for my horse,' in a provocative, testing-the-water kind of way, to the ultimate resolve, 'I *will* go back and look for my horse.' I think it was more of a gradual shift.

It was March 2004. Peter Eve had emailed me a couple of the photos he'd taken of my horse that second day in the helicopter. She was so beautiful. I stared at Maia's image and tried to imagine what it would be like to be standing near her.

In April, on my way to San Francisco to visit Barry, who was touring his stage show in the States, I went to Florida to see my Cuban friend, Dolores. Dolores Smithies, so beautiful, so vital and full of love for life and her family and friends was now coura-geously fighting cancer. She told me that the only thing she regretted about her life was getting upset about things, and that started me thinking about regret, about getting caught up with the little details and missing the big picture. You mostly regret what you haven't done, or when you haven't tried hard enough, not the things you have done. I was fifty-three and fate had thrown me down a gauntlet, a chance to experience something I had longed for all my life. Not only that but fate had been kind – not to mention dramatic – a wild horse that I could befriend and train. What an extraordinary chance. What an adventure. Of course I must do it. It might be an impossible dream, but for today, I would do all I could to make it happen. If I could act as if I were the sort of person who did crazy brave things, then maybe I could become that sort of person.

I set to work. I rang Susan and asked her if she would help me at least try to realise the dream, and Susan, not being one to turn down life's challenges, said, 'Yes, of course.' Then I asked her whether she thought this was just a crazy plan. 'N–o–o.' She answered in a way that said maybe, but let's try all the same. When Susan Bradley decides she doesn't want something to happen, she either says no directly, or she fixes it so that it can't happen; she never appears negative in any way, never indulges an obstructive lag. 'But we'll have to wait until June,' she told me. 'It's been a big Wet this year and the area is still flooded. Even getting into the station right now would be difficult, let alone mustering horses.'

She contacted Celia and reminded her of the gift she had so generously made in an unguarded moment, and warned her that we would be trying to find the horse. I was still not convinced that Celia had ever intended the gift to mean the flesh and blood animal, more just the romantic notion of owning a wild horse somewhere out there. I didn't dare ask in case that notion was confirmed and my project cancelled before it started. Better, I thought, not even to raise the possibility. I cleared my diary for June. Barry seemed reconciled to me abandoning him to getting on with his work commitments alone. I'm not sure I gave him much choice. For most of our fifteen years together I have been an attentive wife, cooking nice meals and heading the support team. I am one of nature's caretakers. Putting a positive spin on that, I feel good if I make others feel good. Less positive, a friend once said to me, 'Why do you always focus on the success of others? What about you, what do you want?' So now it was about me 'wanting' and doing something for myself, and others needing to fit in with that. I didn't ask, I announced I was going, and Barry was totally supportive every inch of the way.

I made plans then to fly to Australia. From Sydney I would have to get up to Broome, and then work out how to travel the rest of the 850 kilometres to the station. I planned to spend a month there, with no real idea if this was how long it would take, but a month sounded kind of comfortable. What else did I need to think about? Money, of course.

I had only the vaguest idea of what the costs would be. Indeed I had only the vaguest idea of how we would set about catching this horse. Maybe we would have a round-up, or find one of those famous horse whisperers. Surely it would not cost more than about two or three thousand pounds and for that, there was Auntie Christine.

Auntie Christine was my father's younger sister. She had been the archetypal spinster, living by herself with a large tabby cat for company in a small brick house in north London, and working as a librarian at the British Library. For as long as I can remember, Christine had pure white hair, always neatly curled. She was slim and nervous and never more so than when she was with my father and her other surviving brother, Humphrey. In their company, it was obvious that she had suffered from having been a lone girl in the company of three strong brothers and perhaps that is why she never married, just lived her quiet life, secure within her own walls. But I always had the feeling that inside the heart of this highly strung woman was a spirit of adventure waiting for the opportunity and the confidence to escape.

Auntie Christine had always been my sympathiser on the horse front. Once, in my late twenties, I had described to her a horse I had fallen in love with, an Anglo-Arab called Bysshe, bred by Finn Guinness. Bysshe was dark chestnut with a flaxen mane and tail and a very romantic look, like a horse from a painting. I had tried to work out a way to buy him, but it was out of the question. I was earning barely enough to pay my very modest living expenses, let alone buy and board a horse. A few weeks later I went back to Hampshire hoping to catch another glimpse of Bysshe. He'd gone, been sold to an Italian, and already shipped to Tuscany.

The next Christmas, Christine gave me a little book about horses, on the front of which was a painting of a horse by Stubbs, now hanging in the National Gallery of London. Painted in 1762, it portrayed a dark chestnut with a flaxen mane and tail called Whistlejacket.

'But that looks just like this horse I know . . .' I said.

'Yes,' Christine said. 'That's why I gave it to you. I recognised your horse as soon as I saw that book.'

Somehow it helped, that someone had listened to my horse prattling.

Christine had passed away a couple of years previously at the age of ninety-two, and had generously left me seven thousand pounds. What better way to celebrate her memory than to spend it on an adventure that I'm sure Christine, of all people, would have heartily appreciated. I would allow myself three, maybe four thousand pounds to spend on tack, plane tickets and horse whisperers or more conventional horse trainers. I could always be sensible with the rest.

I was extraordinarily fortunate in that I had the finances to follow my dream without, say, risking our security by mortgaging the house. It wasn't a fully fledged dream like selling up and sailing around the world in a thirty-foot ketch, or moving an entire family to Majorca to run an organic restaurant, or something. In comparison it would be a fairly modest project. Nor would it entirely disrupt our living arrangements. I had no children whose needs would have to be taken into consideration. I had not succeeded in having children, and maybe that was all the more reason to allow myself to pursue my love of animals. I felt that there was a need to nurture revealing itself in this renewed desire to own and train a young horse.

Susan would obviously be in charge of arrangements in the outback, and her instruction to me was to try to get out there in early June for the dry season. Meanwhile she would hunt around to see if she could find someone to help us catch and train the horse. What else could I do to prepare? It was obvious that I would not be able to buy equipment and riding tack in the Kimberley, as the nearest supplier was a couple of thousand kilometres away, so I went shopping.

I planned to start with purchasing a few items in England and getting the rest later in Sydney. I rang my good friend Susie Little who loves horses and has her own, and went down to visit her in the country near Winchester. She took me to a famous saddlery called Calcutt and Sons. The staff there laughed themselves silly at my crazy scheme, and even more so when I borrowed their phone to call the Australian High Commissioner in London to find out if I would be allowed to bring used horse tack into the country. All around the walls of the shop were pictures of tired looking local horses for sale. I stared at the pictures and was glad I was going to the outback for my beautiful copper horse. I bought a secondhand soft leather bridle, almost black from years of cleaning, with a silver-studded browband, my first bridle after about forty-seven years of waiting. Then I bought a black webbing head-collar, a lunging rein and elastic side-reins, essentials of horse breaking ... I was a long way off breaking in a horse, but still.

Meanwhile, earlier in the year, the horse's name had changed.

At first I had called her Maia – meaning illusion and desire – which seemed rather appropriate, only I was also using that name for the main character in a novel I was writing and so things were getting a little confusing. During one of my husband's brief visits to our home in London, we had a dinner party to which we invited the Irish novelist Edna O'Brien. In the middle of the meal, Edna started to talk, and for a moment the others at the table fell silent, in spite of the fact that one or two of them were unusually fond of the sound of their own voices, and listened to her, spellbound.

'So do you all know about Sedna?' Edna asked in her soft Irish voice. 'I am so captivated by Sedna.' No one answered, so she carried on speaking. 'Sedna is a planet that they have just discovered somewhere far, far away beyond all the other planets, somewhere a few million light miles beyond Pluto. I believe she is a very beautiful planet, although they say she is very small. Sedna is red, and they think covered with red dust. To think that Sedna has been there all this time and has only just now been found by man. Isn't that just so wonderful?'

It was about the same time that Peter Eve had sent me the two photographs of my chosen horse. This chestnut horse, reddy brown and shining like a conker, against the red of the landscape. My horse was still out there, she was found, but only from the sky, and still distant, still a law unto herself. From then on I called her Sedna.

Something else significant had happened in the last month back at the station. Susan had captured two horses – well, not exactly captured, they had walked up to the cattle yards from the bush. They could hardly be described as wild as they were geldings, castrated males, and so must have been in captivity before. Susan reckoned they had most likely lived on the station in years gone by, belonging to previous owners, and that they had wandered up out of habit, or following some ingrained memories of hay and feed. She had driven them into a yard and slammed the gate shut. So we had our first horses and we had not even had to go out looking. Was this a sign?

She'd emailed me some photographs. The first was a black horse with a white star in the middle of his forehead. He had to be called Black Beauty after the famous children's book that must have been read and adored by every child horse-lover on this planet. Only the new arrival didn't look quite as smart as the illustrations of Black Beauty that had been in my worn copy as a child. So I called him Tatty Black Beauty, and from then on he was known as Tatti. The other captive was a little bay pony, very ancient it seemed from the white hair on his face. He had a large square jaw so I called him Brad after the movie star Brad Pitt. I was thrilled – we had horses to work with, horses that had almost certainly been broken in and ridden at some time in their past, and if Tatti was not too old, maybe we could use him in our round-up.

While I dream of a stunning bright chestnut wild horse, an elegant creature with a white blaze and white socks, athletic enough to be trained for the Olympics, what I get is an odd black pony with a white star. Tatti is the one in the yard, not running wild, he's the one waiting for my arrival. Is this what life is like? Is it all about keeping your dream, but at the same time enjoying your reality because that might just turn out to be all there is?

FIVE

London to Sydney

It was now June . . .

I was back in London, making arrangements, all set to go and find my wild horse.

For some reason I seemed to be plagued with fear, but fear of what? I was doing nothing life-threatening, sitting in my kitchen in Hampstead with a phone in my hand trying to arrange a ticket that would take me from England to Perth in Western Australia, or Darwin in the Northern Territory. The only way I could rightly describe it was a fear of the unknown, and I would try to talk myself out of it, reminding myself to just take it a day at a time.

I continued gathering information and equipment. It had been about forty years since I'd thought long and hard about bridles. I had a vision of the brick tack-room at Foxholes with its cracked windows and dusty floors housing Outdoor Miss Bailey's array of ancient equipment: fragments of bridles, rusty pelham bits, old work-horse collars. And then back at Bruern, the Astors' magnificent collection of everything money could buy: simple snaffles to formal double bridles, and quality saddles, all placed neatly on their individual metal brackets attached to the wall with the horses' names displayed underneath, and every piece so meticulously cleaned and oiled by the under-grooms after every ride.

Nowadays there is such a plethora of choices: specialist saddles for dressage, jumping, endurance racing, even navy blue saddles made of some sort of synthetic material; items ranging in price from exquisitely crafted and stitched saddles that last a lifetime made by Hermès, the high fashion company in Paris, costing thousands of dollars, to the other end of the scale, a set of leather saddle and bridle obtainable online from an American wholesaler for as little as one hundred dollars.

On one of my online forays, I came across something called 'Happy Mouth', and was astonished to find that bridle bits nowadays can be made of plastic, even apple-flavoured plastic. Surely a horse can chew through plastic? Surely a horse would want to chew through plastic if it tasted of apple? Wouldn't it end up severely mangled?

I considered my choices. I did not want a skimpy snaffle with thin, mean strips of cheaply manufactured leather, I longed for something generous and classical, with stitching and padding. Dark leather would look the best on a chestnut horse. Perhaps a rubber bit would be kinder for a horse that has come in from the wild? I resolved to buy one.

I was beginning to wonder if it was normal to be so turned on by tack. But the truth is, just as I'd had to wait all these years for my first horse, I'd also had to wait to own my first saddle and bridle. I remembered times in my life when I had contrived any excuse to take a short cut through the tack department of Lillywhite's or Harrod's and stopped to gaze longingly at soft new saddles, tempted to splurge all my savings on some beautiful hand-stitched bridle with its shiny eggbutt snaffle bit, thinking to myself, surely one day I will have a horse to wear this.

I watched the film *The Horse Whisperer*, which in the magical way of synchronicity just happened to be on the television. I found the movie irritating and far too Hollywood, yet when the girl goes to visit the wounded and traumatised horse, I cried. I could not make head nor tail of what Robert Redford was actually doing to communicate with or to heal the crazed animal, though I could understand why the female lead would be drawn magically towards him.

Diary entry: Wednesday 30 June

Talking through practical difficulties on the phone with Susan, and then thinking over the substance of our conversation, I come to the conclusion for a brief period that this is just a crazy idea and would have to be cancelled, and my inner response is one of immense relief. I could go back to my normal, sensible life with none of this drama, this stress.

The fear is such that sometimes I have a niggling thought in the back of my mind that maybe the fear is right. I have to remember that nowadays, I can't even ride a slightly fresh horse, let alone a wild one. I try to remind myself that I will take this one day at a time, and obstacles are things to be overcome, not weapons with which to torture myself.

Maybe I don't know the difference between obstacles and real impossibility; maybe this *is* real impossibility and so this whole scheme is just a form of madness. Susan says that I am indulging in negative thinking. I should trust that it will all go according to plan. What plan? I'm not aware we have one. And if she's right, just supposing I do catch the horse – shouldn't I really be considering seriously the question of what to do with it? A horse is a living, breathing, sensitive animal with appetites and needs.

I find myself forced to consider at some length the question of madness.

Thursday 1 July

Today I was talking to my good friend Rosamund on the phone and out of the blue she said to me, 'Well, what *are* you going to do with the horse if it all goes to plan and you catch it?' When Rosamund asks, I answer, because she never wastes time with irrelevant questions. The truth is that I was relieved to be allowed to consider the question that Susan considers negative thinking.

All right, so let's address the question. *I don't know.* That's the only possible answer, and it is such a relief to simply admit it.

I speculate on possible scenarios:

1) The horse will have disappeared, along with its planetary namesake, Sedna, which has now made itself scarce in the heavens.

2) The horse will not be catchable. Or, God forbid, will be killed or damaged in the chase.

3) Having been caught, the horse will turn out to be a mean-tempered, nasty thing with buck teeth and a jagged neck, a hanging coffin head and, worst of all, an unpleasant nature, only fit to be turned loose. (In that case, find and attempt to catch another one? A gorgeous dun Arab-like filly that I can breed from?)

4) It will be caught, but untrainable – too old and too wild. Turn it loose again?

5) It will be all right. We will manage to train him or her, but the horse will still be just okay, not particularly inspiring. Then what? Well, I can always find the horse a good home.

6) It will be so fabulous and extraordinary, such a fortunate juxtaposition of chance breeding, which is why it chose me, looking down from the skies, *it chose me . . .* this horse will be poetry in motion, a horse like Tamarillo, fit to train for the Olympics. Then I will fall in love with it, and the problem will become: *how to change the rest of my life so I can live with my horse?*

•

Last week I went with Mary Guinness to an equestrian Olympic training session to watch her horse, Tamarillo, float his dressage paces with the willowy and incredibly attractive William Fox-Pitt on his back. Being surrounded by horsey people I felt like a duck returning to water. I could not have felt more at home, sitting in the living-quarters of the horse truck with William and his wife Alice Fox-Pitt, chatting about horses. I was surprised to find that I was still fairly knowledgeable on the subject, or at least familiar with the terms, and even comparatively confident. Not that I have actually sat on a horse for months, but even the instructing I heard sounded familiar, the same old phrases: 'riding the horse up to the bit', 'hocks under him'. It appears that nothing much has changed in thirty years, except of course, they now have apple-flavoured bits.

Friday 2 July

My fear is being mildly assuaged by the all-powerful god of the practical, the ever helpful and sane technique of breaking down the project (and its problems) into bite-sized portions.

Susan has found a horse whisperer . . . or at least she *says* he's a horse whisperer. What is a horse whisperer? All I know about Susan's horse whisperer is that he is local to the Kimberley, more or less, and that he's called Ron. If he is a local he should know how to go about catching a horse in that part of the world, and as for the breaking, let's deal with that later. No one who isn't kind to horses will be allowed near any horses I catch, but let's catch them first.

Ron will at least help us catch it, and hopefully break it in.

I have never trained a horse from scratch myself, but after so many years of my childhood spent hanging around stables, I have a rough idea of how horses used to be broken in England. They were usually 'handled' while still young – stroked, led about in a headcollar, sometimes hand-fed and fussed over. Between two and four years old, the serious work would start. The horse might be left in the stable wearing a bridle and saddle to become accustomed to everything slowly, which was good in principle, but very time-consuming, taking weeks, sometimes months. They were also 'lunged' for hours, circling their trainer on the end of a long rein wearing a cavesson, a surcingle and elastic reins, or later, a saddle and bridle. Then they might be long-reined, the trainer walking behind the horse as if driving the horse in a cart, and then finally 'backed' when someone brave climbed into the saddle, hopefully somebody young and fit enough to cling on if the horse started bucking. Bucking, after all, is the most logical step a horse can take in response to feeling a large weight somewhere up on its back near the withers; the horse would register this as the sensation of a lion attempting to translate it into lunch, requiring instant and drastic reaction.

Horse whispering sounded so romantic, so miraculous, if it were to be believed that such a thing could possibly exist. It sounded like a viable prospect for working on a wild horse. I decided to find out more about this mysterious technique.

When I first heard the term 'horse whisperer', I formed a mental image of a rugged cowboy, roughly resembling Robert Redford in appearance, if not sex appeal, probably known for his gruff monosyllabic mutterings and inability to form meaningful relationships with women. This cowboy would sidle up to a wild or crazed horse and, suddenly eloquent, whisper sweet nothings into the horse's ear. At this point the horse's ear flickers, its head drops into a docile pose, and it changes from being an uncontrollable monster into a model of calmness and serenity, having had a spell cast on it by the witchdoctor whisperer, or having fallen in love with the gruff cowboy. The horse then devotedly follows the

Robert Redford look-alike around for the rest of the day, perhaps even the rest of his life.

Of course, this image would immediately fall flat to anyone knowing even the most rudimentary facts about untamed horses. To begin with, how does the cowboy get close enough to whisper in the horse's ear? Try getting close even to a domesticated pony without a bucket of horse feed.

Anjelica Huston had sent me an email telling me about Monty Roberts, who is known as the original horse whisperer, suggesting I buy his book, *Shy Boy*. In this slim volume, Roberts tells the story of following and taming a wild mustang over the space of a few days – in front of a BBC crew and a large and well-planned back-up. Now, having read the book, I decide that 'horse listener' would be a more appropriate term, or even 'horse thinker'. (Only months later did I find out that the title of Monty Roberts' original bestseller is *The Man Who Listens to Horses*.)

I began to get the message that it was about understanding the way horses communicate among themselves and learning and utilising the social rules of the herd. Monty Roberts thinks how the horse thinks, and behaves accordingly. Horses are not vicious by nature, he tells us, nor do they prey on other animals; rather they are preyed upon, and so they only use their immense power in flight or fight to protect themselves and their offspring. His technique seems to be to give the same signals to the young horse as the lead mare would to a badly behaved adolescent.

From my reading I understood that the method Monty Roberts used to capture and tame his wild mustang, Shy Boy, was to follow him on horseback, driving him away from the other horses and the safety of the herd for about thirty-six hours, until the horse turned around and asked to be allowed to negotiate a truce with Monty. Following the principle that if flight is not working and the horse has realised that his pursuer is not actually trying to kill him, the horse seems to register that this might be the same type of situation as when the lead mare drives an adolescent horse out of the herd for bad behaviour. Therefore the horse tries the same methods he would use for requesting acceptance back into the herd.

At this crucial point of acceptance and truce, a horse will become extraordinarily receptive and tolerant of demands as part of the 'deal', and will allow a halter on his neck, hands to be run over his body, let his feet be picked up and will even allow a saddle, bridle and rider on him, if you really want to push the golden moment.

Monty Roberts shows how these same principles could be used to even better effect in a smaller area, a round yard, sending the horse on and away, allowing the animal to work out of his system the usual methods of defence or self-preservation – fight or flight – until the horse shows signs that he is willing to try conciliatory means. This is part of a technique that Monty Roberts has worked out and made his own, calling it Join-Up.

There are a few fundamental differences between Monty Roberts' wild horse and our brumbies. It appears that his mustang had been taken from the wild earlier and must have been handled, as he had been corralled, transported and even gelded before being turned out with a herd belonging to a friend of his running free in a fenced area considerably smaller than Athenrai. Our horses have never, to our knowledge, seen a person, an electric light, or heard music. Their existence may have been occasionally disturbed by a helicopter or small plane above them, and maybe the engine of a car in the distance. For about fifty years these horses have bred more or less undisturbed in the wild.

Susie Little told me about another horse whisperer named Pat Parelli, so I ordered a National Geographic video called *America's Lost Mustangs* in which Parelli rounds up and gentles some wild American mustangs in New Mexico as part of a project to inquire into the horses' Spanish conquistador origins. They rounded up the horses with a group of people on horseback, and then used similar principles on the horses one at a time in a round yard. In the video Parelli also works with a loop of woven-leather rope around the horse's neck and attributes this to an Australian, Kel Jeffery.

Another friend Sarah Dridan, who breeds Percheron horses outside Adelaide, sent me a book, *The Jeffery Method of Horse Handling*, by Maurice Wright. It's about the Kel Jeffery method, which Sarah says is the Australian version of horse whispering. It is a comparatively gentle and effective way to break in horses, and was the forerunner to the American horse whispering movement with its world famous gurus like Monty Roberts and Pat Parelli.

As Maurice Wright describes in the book, while studying law at Melbourne University, Kel Jeffery suffered some kind of collapse, and was sent by the doctors to stay with a relation in the country to recuperate. At this point he had absolutely no experience with horses. The men working the property would be away from the homestead for days on end, and as Jeffery's strength began to return, he grew bored. He'd noticed a few horses hanging around the homestead, in particular a rather nice mare. He had been told she was not being ridden because she was unbreakable. One day, he managed to drive her into a yard. He had no idea whatsoever of the techniques used to break in a horse, but decided to experiment. The only equipment he could find was a plaited-leather rope and so that was all he used. By the time the cattle men returned at the end of the day, the convalescent law student was riding the unbreakable mare around a yard with nothing but a rope around her neck. From there, Jeffery was able to work with the horse with a saddle and bridle. Maurice Wright believes that Jeffery must have somehow managed to put the rope around the horse's neck and execute a few successful 'control pulls' in the early stages. The mare was from that day, in Wright's words, 'always quiet' with Jeffery and he learnt to ride on her. Jeffery invented something entirely new and so led a movement away from the traditional rough breaking methods. He called it 'New deal for horses'. This must have happened pre-1914 as the first demonstration on record that Kel Jeffery gave of his technique was in that year.

A control pull, from what I have read and observed, is a practice of pulling the horse around a little by means of a rope around its neck, always taking care that the rope does not interfere with the horse's breathing, and releasing the pressure on the neck as soon as the horse co-operates. It seems to prove to the horse with discomfort rather than fear and pain that the human is the boss. I am no expert and would not recommend anybody try this or any of these techniques for themselves without working with an experienced horse trainer, as none of them is as easy or safe as they might sound in description, or made to look in the hands of the masters.

On the back flyleaf of the book about Jeffery there was a Queensland phone number. I dialled it, hoping to find Maurice Wright in, hoping to ask him if he knew of anyone up the Kimberley way who could help me. There was no answer. Looking at Maurice's picture in the flyleaf, the style of the photograph, his clothes, and the date of the book, it was possible that he was no longer in the land of the living. But maybe his wife was still alive and maybe she could help me?

Was I getting desperate and clutching at unreal straws?

Friday 9 July

I have arrived in Sydney and been reunited with my husband. Life is pleasant, mainly because life in Sydney is always so pleasant. It is slightly cool and rainy, which is not surprising as it is virtually mid-winter, but even in winter, the weather is miles better than an English summer.

Susan rang, jubilant. Yesterday they went out in the helicopter and saw about a hundred horses in different groups and they think they saw mine.

'We saw a liver chestnut . . . Tatti,' she said.

'Susan, you're not concentrating. Tatti is the name of the black horse in the paddock. My horse isn't a liver chestnut; Sedna is bright chestnut, with a crooked white blaze and two white stockings on his or her hind legs.'

She is coming to town for a few days for a wedding and suggests I go out to the station a week later than planned, so I won't have to sit there in isolation for the few days while she is back in Sydney.

'But, Susan, I might be able to start practising on the two ponies already in the yards,' I say.

'Oh, didn't I tell you? There are four now. Another two wandered up so we drove them into the yards too.'

'Four? How wonderful. How big are they?'

'On the small side. Only about fourteen hands, I think. And Celia thinks your wild horse is a colt. She remembers seeing it from the helicopter that day and thinking there was something very special about it, in its eyes.'

That brings me a sensation of joy. Special. A horse in a million. That is what I thought both times I saw it.

It appears that the two new geldings seemed to be almost relieved to be in captivity after many years of the rigours of the wild. I look at their pictures on my computer. They are a dissolute pair of bays, one with a startlingly large star, more like a starburst, the other a heap of bones fit for the knacker's yard, so I have called them Starsky and Hutch. I'm enjoying the long distance horse naming.

Apparently all four horses have calmed down over the last few days, getting used to human contact and enjoying the free hay.

I'm itching to put into practice all the techniques I've been reading about and everything I can remember from childhood about horse handling. I plan to start with Tatti, my own private Black Beauty.

Friday 16 July

Maybe it's time to have a riding lesson.

Sunday 18 July

Did I say that horse riding hasn't altered in the last thirty years? Well, I was wrong. This morning I went for a riding lesson in Sydney's Centennial Park. Techniques have completely and sneakily changed. A bit like skiing, they are now more or less opposite to what they used to be.

In my good old days, you gripped with your knees and thighs, and it was a no-no for all sorts of reasons to do with the horse's welfare and sanity, not to mention the clarity of controls, to grip with your calves unless you were urging the horse on. Now it seems it's the other way around, and for the sake of the horse's sanity and health you wrap your legs around it and grip with your calves, apparently allowing your knees and thighs to occasionally flap in an ungainly fashion. Once even the briefest flash of daylight between the knees and the saddle was considered the depths of inelegance, akin to eating your peas off your knife or sitting in a skirt with your legs wide-apart. I always thought you wrapped your legs around your lovers, not your horses. No wonder one of my over-forty girlfriends who has recently acquired a horse whispered to me that it feels more like taking on a lover than acquiring a four-legged friend.

And then there was something about keeping your leg on the horse – all the time. In my day you pressed with the calf to denote 'faster', then took the pressure of your leg off. The horse was supposed to remember to stay at that pace, it's not like a car, you don't have to keep your foot pressed on the accelerator – only now it appears you do, you're supposed to keep your leg on the horse, or it will slow down.

So all my old good habits have become new bad habits, exactly like skiing, and it seems that my style is way out of date – I'm riding Pony Club Style, circa 1965. And it's my fault for inventing the phrase which became a good handle for my instructor to, well, mock me.

So this all starts at 11 am in Centennial Park, which has about five riding stables and a big covered riding arena.

I arrived late, having got lost in the labyrinth of the first four schools and hampered by the fact that I'd forgotten the name of the school taken from the *Yellow Pages* where I had booked a lesson. Then I was tediously delayed by the matter of advance credit card payments and signing forms saying I wouldn't sue them if I broke my neck, none of which I remembered doing the last time I had a lesson.

Next I was introduced to my chestnut mount, Jack. There is a look particular to a certain type of lightweight chestnut Thoroughbred, a kind of lean, keen, athletic look, like that of a tennis pro. You'd almost expect the horse to be wearing a sun-visor with a built-in green shade like its human counterpart, the latest Adidas and crisp gleaming white shorts and, of course, white socks, which this horse actually happens to have on three of his legs. You never get that look with a grey or bay or black horse, only a chestnut with white points.

So horse Jack, with me placed firmly on the saddle, sets off to the indoor arena. The rain is bucketing down and Jack can afford to be jaunty because he knows perfectly well that in the battle of the wills which is about to ensue in the ring, he will undoubtedly win, as he is bigger, younger, fitter and infinitely more stubborn than me.

Once in the covered arena, Jack and I walk in circles around my instructor, trying not to collide with the other ten or so mounts and riders circling *their* instructors. Jack, in spite of his debonair quality, quickly settles into a virtually somnambulant state, performing actions on automatic.

He likes it best when Robina, my instructor, talks. Single words he interprets as a signal to switch to a slower pace than the one he is currently performing. Anything more than three words he interprets as a command to swing into the centre, stumble to a halt and fall into a comatose state, ears flopping sideways in ultra-relaxed mode while Robina and I chat. After that only the most strenuous of calf pressing with a few added Pony Club circa 1965 kicks and even a flash of the crop will get him even temporarily active again. One can hardly blame him: if I am bored rigid trotting around and around in a circle, how must he be feeling after years and years of the same, suffering the riding school horse's fate of a different rider every hour, no consistency of commands, and often an amateur rider who hangs on with the reins. It is a tribute to a horse's natural desire to please that Jack tries at all, which he does, even giving the occasional leap into the air, all four legs straight, just to test my nerve and the security of my new legs-wrapped-around-the-horse technique.

To Jack's delight, Robina calls me into the centre of the ring and spends a long time telling me all the mistakes I am making, explaining the gripping with your calves stuff. I look at her with pity and say rather icily: 'That is not how we ride in England.' Adding loftily under my breath, 'Not how the British Olympic team was riding when I was watching them practise their dressage two weeks ago.'

So much for name dropping. It is her turn to look at me with pity. '*When* did you say you last had a lesson?'

'Oh, well, a few years back, I suppose.' I search my memory. Anjelica and I had spent four hours a day for two weeks being drilled at Colonel Dudgeon's riding academy in Dublin in about 1966. Since then I'd had the odd lesson, that would make it coming up for forty years. To cover up I made the rather flippant remark that I'd live to regret: 'Well that isn't how we used to ride in the Pony Club in the sixties.'

Come to think of it, when I watched William Fox-Pitt on Tamarillo at the Olympic training session, his legs *did* seem to wrap around the gelding, but then I assumed that at six feet five inches, his legs were so long, and the horse at 16.2 hands, so comparatively modest in size, that he had nowhere else to put his legs.

So I decided to admit when I was wrong, or at least to try out the new methods and attempt to keep a calm smile on my face. Thank God I was managing not to disgrace myself too much on the horse's back, or at least not to fall off even in the transitions in and out of canter, which are always difficult in such a contained space, and I even managed to execute a passable leg-change at a canter in the middle of the ring.

'Good, now that's much better,' Robina tells me towards the end of the lesson. 'I used to ride like that too,' she admits. 'But only when I was a child.' And I feel about twelve all over again. It appears that my wild horse and I will be on a learning curve together.

I'd only spent about twenty-five minutes on the horse, but when I dismounted I could hardly walk, my knees were gyrating inwards at every step in the most embarrassing fashion. I was pretty sure driving would not be a good idea as my feet were also a little numb, so I sat in the car for a while ruminating. I had thought before the lesson, well at least I can ride; more than that, I'm good. Not so, it appears, and it's back to the drawing board.

Apart from the Spanish Riding School style or maybe dressage where it seems possible from the pictures that wrapping legs has always been the style – it appears to me that people have been riding well my way for centuries. I wonder how they rode in the Charge of the Light Brigade, or during the First World War. I can understand the changes of style that have taken place with skiing. With the help of modern physics and engineering and the invention of new plastics, the design of skis has changed drastically in the last ten years, but not so horses, they've been more or less the same for the last fifty million years or so.

I decided to bring in an independent jury, and emailed a few friends. Everybody, it appeared, had a slightly different opinion. I reckoned my friend Susie Little would be a sympathiser on the tack-addiction front, so I added a little shopping report.

Found a wonderful tack shop here called Goodwoods, it's huge and is almost in the middle of Sydney! I'm like an expectant mother out shopping for a longed-for late child. They said they will take back anything I don't use, so I took the plunge and bought two new bridles, without bits – they were only seventy Australian dollars each – and a beautiful second-hand pigskin saddle, shiny like a conker; I also bought a cavesson headcollar and roller, four headcollars including a pony or foal size, three leading ropes, three numnahs, three girths, a whip, some frightfully smart black French jodhpurs, really far too smart for the outback. They didn't have any of the plastic riding skull-hats that double as bicycle helmets so had to go for the old-fashioned velvet hat, which I so much prefer.

Robert, the shop manager, kept cutting the prices.

I don't know whether Barry, sitting on a bench, radiating palpable boredom, did anything to propel the price-cutting bonanza, but there's nothing like a good bargain to cheer the soul.

'How are you going to break it in?' Robert asked me as we sifted through saddle cloths.

'I've no idea. Know any horse whisperers?'

'Yes lots,' he said. 'The best, they're Argentinian, they play polo with Prince Charles and they're the best horse handlers I've ever seen. They know more about horses than anybody in the world and they can tame anything.'

'Oh, we couldn't afford them.'

'They would do it for nothing, just the plane fare, food and drink. They just like the adventure. Of course they like to party after dark . . .'

Suddenly the smart French jodhpurs didn't look like such a daft purchase after all.

Sunday 25 July

Tomorrow we leave for the outback; I can hardly believe that after all the months of waiting, it's about to happen. Susan has come to stay in the apartment. The guest room has been so full of tack – spread out on the bed, on the floor, in a bag on the floor – that it is now known as the tack-room and will probably spend the rest of its life being called the tack-room. It's now packed and ready for the journey. At four-thirty in the morning we leave for the airport and the beginning of our adventure. Tonight we pack and then go out to dinner because Bruce Beresford, the film director, and his wife, Virginia Duigan, the author, have invited us to Balmain to sit on their balcony overlooking the harbour while they ply us with white wine and delicious food. I think we should be going to bed early, but Susan can never resist an invitation.

Whenever you suggest being sensible to Susan Bradley, her answer is almost invariably this: 'Just remember, you're a long time dead.'

PART II

THE KIMBERLEY

Go confidently in the direction of your dreams.
Live the life you have imagined.

Henry David Thoreau 1817–1862

SIX

Athenrai

About fifteen years ago, Barry and I found ourselves up in Darwin in the Northern Territory, where Barry was performing one of his 'Dame Edna' stage shows. The production was short of dancers so I'd been dressed up in a frighteningly short outfit and pushed onto the stage, leading to rumours around town that Barry had broken up with his girlfriend and was going out with a tall blonde showgirl. I was enormously flattered.

Darwin had been a great discovery for me. When we arrived we knew not one single person, but John and Lyn Parche, who ran the Beaufort, the hotel where we were staying, had taken us under their wings and shown us the sights. We'd seen extraordinary pearls at the Paspaley cave. We'd visited the Saturday afternoon market and eaten green pawpaw salad and laksa soup while watching the sunset over the beach. On our night off, a party was held in our honour at the casino by the owners James and Jane Osbourne.

It came as a welcome change from long nights spent working in the theatre to find ourselves sitting outside the casino under the Northern Territory skies, a black velvet canopy crammed with stars, enjoying the light breeze from the Timor Sea. Down below us were crocodiles basking in the moonlight, and up on the lawn, the Osbournes had laid on a scrumptious barbecue and gone to great lengths to persuade their friends to come from far and wide to meet us. We loaded our plates with barramundi fillets, giant prawns and Indonesian salads, and I had just helped myself to a second mango daiquiri when Susan and David Bradley came strolling across the lawn.

They were a golden couple, they had that aura. We learnt that they owned and ran one of the most interesting properties in the Kimberley, Carlton Hill, a million-acre cattle station just a couple of hours drive out of Kununurra. David was tall, fit, and very good looking, and we were told that he was a brilliant vet and an intrepid pilot. Susan, his wife, was blonde, bright and extremely attractive with a warm and radiant smile. We learnt that they were not just owners of Carlton Hill, but that they both worked on the property in the most hands-on way possible. I soon discovered that my new friend Susan was as much at home staying up all night with a calving heifer as she was dressed to kill at a party in a casino. They immediately invited us to visit, but we regretfully had to refuse as we already held bookings for a tour of Kakadu National Park, followed by a few days at Alice Springs, from where we would travel to see the famous Uluru (Ayers Rock), where Barry had his heart set on taking me up in a hot-air balloon. I was less than enthusiastic about accompanying him on this particular phase of the trip, having harboured a lifelong mistrust of hot-air balloons.

'Of course, you're out of your mind,' John Parche told us not so politely the next morning at breakfast.

'Yes,' Lyn added. 'We've been thinking about it, and we think you should cancel your trip to Kakadu and Uluru. Remember that you can book one of those tourist trips any time you like.

But an invitation to Carlton Hill... If you go, I promise you'll never regret it.' So we cancelled our expedition and went to spend a week with the Bradleys.

Carlton Hill was my first real experience of the Australian outback, and my great love for the Kimberley dates back to that visit. This prosperous station is set on the banks of the Ord River and so, in comparison with so much of the outback, is greener and more varied in terrain. On the property are two mesas of great Aboriginal significance, Buggelmerri and Jiggelmerri, flat-topped hills several hundred metres high, with cliff sides of stratified rock. In the morning they appear pink and pale terra-cotta, but in the sunset they turn a brilliant glowing red.

During the day we would ride Susan's horses over the countryside, among the small trees, catching sight of rare black cockatoos, and small flocks of green budgerigars, and the powder pink and blue galahs. Or I would sit on the river bank while Barry painted the landscape, fortunately oblivious to the risks of the giant crocodiles staring at us from the water. In the evening we would sit on the verandah watching the sulphur-crested cockatoos chattering in the two great boab trees in front of the homestead and behind that, Buggelmerri dramatically changing colour, and over that week the Kimberley began to work its magic.

Barry and I think of ourselves as city people. For us, eleven is an early night, but that first night we were in bed by eight-thirty and asleep by nine. The sky, in spite of its dramatic light show of stars, was just so black and the night so intense, there was nothing for it but to collapse into bed. Every morning I would be woken at five by the rising sun, or the sliding noise of a kangaroo moving across the verandah of the guest house, or the growing crescendo of birds urgently announcing the break of day. And over that week at Carlton Hill, I began to have a strong sense of myself as just another of those living, breathing creatures, a tiny speck, but part of the incredibly powerful natural world. The feeling brought with it a sense of great joy and peace, it connected with my love of nature as a child. To this day, wherever I am in the world, I only have to think back to that week to recover the feeling of being earthed into the natural world.

Susan and I became the best of friends, and have remained so for all these years. In some ways we are alike, and in other ways diametrically opposite, but what we share is the value of friendship. Hardly a week goes by when we don't email or call each other to share thoughts, experiences and things that make us laugh. Susan is extremely observant and has that impish quality of someone who is always on the lookout for the amusing, as well as the serious, side of what she sees. She lives life to the full and throws herself into all the local Kimberley issues and is tireless in her efforts for her Aboriginal friends.

Fate moves in mysterious ways. During the week that Barry and I spent at Carlton Hill, one of the hot-air balloons at Alice Springs plunged to the ground, killing the pilot and all twelve tourists. Couples were found joined together in a final embrace.

Monday 26 July

From Sydney to the centre of the North Kimberley region is a very long way. You have only to look at a map of Australia to realise the immense distances involved, so much of it parched and almost uninhabited land, good for little more than raising hardy cattle.

Susan and I were up at 4 am. It was still dark when we arrived at the airport. At Qantas domestic check-in, I manoeuvred my four heavy bags onto the scales, then I involved the check-in staff member in lively conversation hoping she wouldn't notice the red glowing scale numbers soaring stratospherically. The first case contained the saddle wedged in place with bridles and headcollars and saddle cloths; the next, a travel printer still in its box, jodhpur boots, and more horse tack and brushes; the third held cotton and linen clothing, bags with toiletries and horse-training books and videos, and the last was filled entirely with rechargers and instruction books and quantities of camcorder and camera paraphernalia.

The first leg of our journey was the four-hour flight from Sydney to Perth on Australia's south-west coast – known to be the most remote city in the world. We gained three hours crossing time zones and so arrived at 8 am in time to tuck in to breakfast. From there it was another two hours' flying time up the coast to Broome. Susan and I discussed our plans as we flew over the endless red desert veined with the black of dried-up river beds, and the white crusty sores of salt flats.

Susan had tracked down the horse whisperer Ron Kerr and asked him to come and help us. He had been working on a nearby station called Diggers' Rest, mostly grading roads and mustering cattle, but he is apparently known in the Kimberley to be good with horses and experienced in breaking them in. She could not tell me exactly what techniques he might use, only that she thought she had found the right man for the job and that he would also know how to round up the brumbies.

It emerged that we didn't have much in the way of plans beyond getting to the station and waiting for the horse whisperer, so instead we made shopping lists for supplies we would be able to pick up during our two hour stop-over in Broome.

It was my second trip to Broome. This time we saw nothing of the fabulous white beaches and charming town, nor did we catch a glimpse of the famous camel trains taking tourists onto the beach; but I was deeply impressed by the interior of the huge Coles supermarket where we went to stock up on supplies and fresh food. Then Susan took me to an electrical shop in the outskirts of the town, more like a small warehouse, where she bought a new video player for the station and I purchased a hair dryer and a state-of-the-art walkie-talkie, which I thought we would need up in the hills, where I envisaged we would be camping out, and in the daytime out on horseback looking for our wild horses. I remembered only too well getting lost with Bewdy while rounding up cattle in the hills of Colorado, and had no intention of getting lost in the outback – the consequences would be far more serious.

There are three ways of getting from Broome to the station. In the dry season you can drive the 850 kilometres on rough red roads, dented with corrugations created by the heavy trucks that travel along the Gibb River Road at frequent intervals. For this journey it is essential to be behind the wheel of a heavy four-wheel-drive vehicle. Or you can fly to Kununurra (or drive there over 1,000 kilometres of bitumen road), and from there take the mail plane. The local mail plane is a two-engine Islander, seating up to six passengers (depending on the freight load), and invariably piloted by a fresh-faced young man – smartly dressed and demonstratively conscientious – making up his hours to qualify as a pilot for a commercial airline. The plane stops by the station twice a week, takes four hours, and costs one hundred and sixty dollars for a small seat with almost no leg room, and fifteen kilos of baggage allowance, including your camera and handbag. The third method is to charter a small one-engine plane out of Broome, a sort of local air taxi service. The difficulty of getting into the station was one of the reasons for the last few weeks' delay. Fortunately, Susan had a charter plane arranged.

We took off at 3 pm in the single-engine Cessna, flying first over the coastline with its translucent turquoise waters and spectacular red rock islands, some with pristine white sand beaches, others rising majestically straight out of the water. Then we turned inland over the extensive mud flats around King Sound, an area with the largest tides in the world. Coming out of Broome, the earth was sandy loam, all oranges and reds, which changed dramatically as we headed north-east away from the coast, skimming over limestone ranges with rivers running through them. Further on the landscape changed yet again into an almost continuous carpet of sparse green treetops broken up by patches of terracotta earth, revealing patterns of the winding branches and threads of the river beds, some dried up, some glinting with dark water.

Two hours ten minutes later we made our descent over Athenrai. I saw below us the vivid green of kept lawns, a few buildings, the name of the station written in yellow paint on the grey corrugated-iron roof of a shed, and then the rusty red-magenta strip of the station's runway. As we taxied in, two vehicles came speeding out to meet us, driven by Andy and Ann Hallen, the energetic young couple who live and work all year on the property and who are responsible for the copious daily watering that is required during the dry season to keep the station its oasis-like green. Fortunately the supply of bore water is virtually unlimited. Ann was driving the tray-back ready to load up our bags and the supplies we had picked up in Broome and then take us back the two kilometres to the homestead. Andy was keeping pace on a quad bike with their two young sons, Brody and Jack, clinging on to the back.

The homestead consists of four corrugated-iron houses painted dark green, built on a flat piece of land of about twenty acres. Between the houses and the airstrip are silver corrugated-iron sheds of varying sizes housing machinery, chickens and the children's schoolroom – no longer the famous School of the Air, nowadays they study by plugging into the internet, and speaking to their teacher five hundred kilometres away, by telephone.

I asked to go straight from the runway to the yards to see the four old geldings – the four fellows in The Gentleman's Club, as we have nicknamed the group. I could hardly wait, I was so excited about meeting the horses with which I planned to practise my gentling techniques. So, after dropping my bags off at the second of the homestead buildings, we drove down about a kilometre of rough track to the old cattle yards.

In spite of their obvious age and poor condition, the horses were better looking than I had anticipated after the several weeks of staring at their images on my screensaver in a slide show of digital photos that Susan had emailed to me. Of the two bays, Hutch is older and bonier, Starsky bigger and bolder, and Tatti, the Black Beauty look-alike, is altogether more beautiful, his obviously fine head complemented by an almost light Thoroughbred body. He stands almost fifteen hands while Starsky is around 15.2, and Brad is a cheeky – in both senses of the word – very small pony.

The four horses had done little else since arriving in the yards other than eat hay and doze. When I approached them, they charged around in a show of 'If you think you are going to catch us, you have another think coming'. But no more than that. They're just old gents used to getting their own way and making it clear they don't want any interference in their comfortable lifestyle, and least of all to be bossed around by a woman. They did not seem to be frightened, or in any way dismayed by the proximity of people.

We ate steak and salad and collapsed into our respective houses and to bed early, exhausted by the very long day of travel. Between 4.30 am and 5.15 pm that day we had taken one taxi, three planes and shopped madly. We had flown nearly 7,000 kilometres, a distance equivalent of London to Nairobi. I can hardly believe that at long last I'm here. It has felt like such a long journey even getting to this point, and we have hardly started on the quest itself.

Tuesday 27 July

After breakfast with Susan, I walked back across the lawn to my quarters and pottered around for a while, as I acquainted myself with my new home. The bush starts just a few metres from the back verandah. It seemed strange to think that somewhere out there beyond all the trees are horses . . . somewhere hidden in a gully or grazing under a tree was my horse Sedna, leading her life innocent of the preparations that were being made to track her down. But meanwhile, the first task was to settle in and await the arrival of the horse catcher.

I started to unpack, hanging up my clothes and spreading camera equipment out over all available surfaces. I'm staying in the most gorgeous guesthouse, which I have all to myself, made entirely of corrugated iron. Some clever design has been used as the metal never seems to heat up. The walls outside are painted a dark forest green, and complemented with green and white striped awnings. Inside, the walls are all painted white, the floors throughout are of polished dark hardwood, and the air is cooled by means of old-fashioned ceiling fans. In the middle of the sitting area is a square wooden table with simple cane chairs and just a few beige cushions. To one side is a varnished wooden bookcase, a few of the shelves stocked with local interest books, a few with jars of coloured sands, and several conveniently empty shelves onto which I quickly unload more of my photographic equipment. Across the room is another small table with a telephone, connected to an outside phone line. The house has a pleasing colonial atmosphere, on a modest scale of course.

There are three bedrooms, in decreasing size, with classical iron-framed beds that stand high off the ground – handy for checking underneath for stray snakes and wildlife. They are made up with navy sheets and matching navy Indian-cotton bedspreads, not so good for checking at bedtime (by torch and candlelight) on how many bugs or creepy crawlies have climbed between the sheets.

Susan lives in the main house. It is almost identical except that she has a television set, a satellite cable connection and some wonderful chairs – quite simply designed – made of canvas and varnished wood, with long wooden slats that swing out from the sides on which you can rest your weary legs at the end of the day while watching television, drink in hand. They're called squatters' chairs, so named because the squatter (cattle man or boss of the pastoral lease property) could sit in it with his legs up while his wife waited on him, although in these politically correct times it is now reported that in fact they were for his wife, so that she could put her legs up and still protect her modesty with her long skirts. Susan also has a battery bank which is recharged in the daytime when the generator is on, so if she wants, she can stay up all night watching the tennis. Quite often she spends a week or more alone at the station, and so she relishes these extra comforts.

This is the house where we eat most of our meals and so her pantry is fully stocked. Supplies are brought in by truck – dried and tinned products such as pasta, rice, tinned tomatoes, tuna, coffee, tea, powdered milk, long-life cream, wine, soft drinks and mixers – anything that will keep for several months. All other foods and fresh goods – meat, chicken, vegetables and fruit – have to be ordered from a shop called Tucker Box in Kununurra and brought in on the mail plane. Freight costs are high, so these items are severely limited and Susan has to plan meals carefully.

There is electricity from a generator for most of the day, though it is turned off at about 9.30 pm, after which I find myself fumbling around with torches, candles and oil lamps. On some of the bedside tables, alongside the normal reading lamp are strange lamps with double bars that recharge while the generator is going and only seem to respond to the 'on' switch when the generator is off at night. They illuminate with a ghostly white glow, barely strong enough to read by. From the moment when I hear Susan start the engine of the quad bike to go and switch off the generator in the evening, I know that I have about seventy-five seconds grace. I spring into action, racing around the rooms, switching off lights and finding torches that still have functional batteries and, if possible, quickly brush my teeth as the bathroom is so much easier to negotiate by electric light.

I slept last night in the largest of the bedrooms, which has a queen-sized bed. Two of the walls consist of wide horizontal glass louvres that are kept open this time of the year so there is only fly wire (mosquito netting) between me and nature. I went to sleep with the peaceful rustle of the leaves in the breeze and the endless chirp of cicadas as my lullaby. In the early hours when the dew started to fall it became a little chilly on my head, so I improvised a nightcap using a stretchy black cotton bag and so, when the sun started to rise and rays of light hit my face, I was able to pull the bag down over my eyes and carry on sleeping. I am spoilt with a more than decent bathroom with an excellent shower, and piping hot water always available thanks to the solar panels on the roof. I have a simple but spacious kitchen area and pantry, and even a top-loading washing machine, and then at the back of the house, a huge hardwood deck made out of Western Australian jarrah that looks out onto the trees and tall yellow grasses of the bush. On one side of the verandah, a passionfruit vine is climbing luxuriantly up a trellis of thick horizontal wires to the height of the wooden balustrade, and all around are exotic trees: mango, pawpaw, frangipani, African mahogany, orange, lemon, lime and grapefruit.

For my horse equipment, I have been assigned the corner of a large, corrugated-iron shed; the name Harrod's is proudly emblazoned in crooked and shaky handwriting on a small board near the doorway. Around the walls, wide wooden shelves are stacked with giant containers of God knows what, probably rat poison and fertiliser, then in the centre of the room, more capacious shelves store everything from rolled swags to extra food supplies: a couple of enormous pumpkins, cardboard boxes of long-life milk and tins of tomatoes and spaghetti. Andy had installed long thin planks of wood fixed at waist height, on which he placed six of the most decrepit and rotting stock saddles I have ever seen. I immediately banished them to the furthest end of the wooden planks, and put my newly acquired second-hand pigskin saddle, along with Susan's black dressage saddle and her son's American saddle, in pride of place. On the shelves were bits and pieces of old bridles, just scraps and rusted portions of bits, nothing even faintly usable.

Andy appeared, bearing hammer and nails. He is a cheerful type, the sort of person who gives the impression of whistling while he works, except that he never whistles. He is slim but strong, with the wiry frame of the naturally energetic, and thick rich brown hair falls in loose curls over his eyes. He is trying to give up his light smoking habit, so has an unlit cigarette between his lips. He is first generation Australian as his mother is Dutch and his father German. His wife Ann is a statuesque blonde with shoulder-length hair falling down in crinkled curls. She is as energetic as her husband and can be seen mowing the lawns on the ride-on mower, or flying around on a bicycle or quad bike.

Andy strolled to the end of the shed and put in hooks across the top of the steel shelves, and I hung up my new bridles and headcollars, then cleared a space on the shelves for my tins of tack-cleaning products and horse brushes. At the end I stood back and admired my work. My first ever tack-room.

I went down to the yards, but the horses refused to have

anything at all to do with me, charging around the yard again with their ears back to denote extreme disapproval of this stranger and the disturbance to their quiet and comfortable life. It must be years since anyone has approached any of these horses with a halter, let alone anything as outrageous as a saddle and bridle.

I realise that in spite of all my reading and formative year spent focused on horses, I have no idea how to set about re-training these elderly geldings. So how will I be able to work with wild horses?

Wednesday 28 July

The next morning I was up at six, which is shockingly early for me. The rhythm of the outback is so different, it is hard to stay awake after nine-thirty or ten at night, and even harder to stay asleep beyond five-thirty or six in the morning, which is when your senses tell you that all the natural world around you is awake and resonating with the joy of being alive.

I made a comforting mug of tea and took it out to the verandah. It's a true blessing that these four station horses have turned up. Catching them, reintroducing them to saddle and bridle and eventually riding them will provide a welcome challenge and the chance to recover my riding skills, which have been so woefully neglected. This will keep me occupied while we prepare for the next stage of the adventure, the arrival of Ron, the horse catcher, with his expertise and equipment. The fact that I have no idea what to do next with these grumpy old geldings is not yet a sign of failure. I remind myself of a phrase that is almost single-handedly responsible for keeping me sane: progress not perfection. I will experiment. This will be the first stage of my adventure.

I headed off down to the yards equipped with a selection of my new booty: multi-coloured webbing halters, leading reins, brushes and the crucial ingredient, a silver bucket containing a couple of scoops of high-performance horse feed.

Little Brody, Ann and Andy's son who is six, has volunteered to be my helper, so I went past their house on the quad bike and picked him up. While I waited out by the vegetable patch twenty yards from the house, I watched Brody getting ready on the porch. I saw him take off the thongs he had been wearing to run about the lawn, and don his small elastic-sided leather RM Williams boots to protect his feet, shaking them out first.

I laughed to myself. I recognised the action. The intention was to tip out any stray scorpions or spiders taking a nap in the toe of the boots. I had been taught to shake out my shoes like that when I'd been six years old by my late godfather, Laurens van der Post, who had been a writer, an explorer, a seventh son and a thirteenth child. He had always promised to take me to Africa with him on a trip, to live with the Kalahari bushmen. He had demonstrated the boot-shaking a long way from the Kalahari desert, in his London flat, overlooking Chelsea. At the time he had been wearing a chalk-striped brown suit, with perfectly matching socks and suede shoes (one of which he had taken off to facilitate the demonstration), immaculate white silk shirt, brown knotted silk tie and a monocle in his left eye.

Brody then went inside and brought back with him a large blue insulated bottle of cold water for us both to drink, something I would not have remembered, but those who live out here know is absolutely essential. Brody climbed onto the back of the bike and we sped off down to the yards.

Once there, we unloaded the equipment onto the ground near the heavy wooden poles of the cattle yards, then the two of us leant against the rails watching the horses in the middle of the yard, dozing, paying us just a little attention in case there was any hay in the offing.

'Lizzie, we goin' to ride them horses?' Brody asked.

'Well, not exactly. We're going to catch them first. And then . . . well . . . as far as we know, Brody, these horses haven't been ridden for a very long time, probably since before you were born.'

Brody stared back at me, his eyes rounded in amazement. As I climbed over the rails the horses set off to the furthest corner with their customary display of bad mannered avoidance, ears pinned back, Tatti even adding a few tetchy shakes of his head.

'So how we goin' to catch them horses, Lizzie?' Brody's little voice piped up from behind the rails.

I was beginning to wonder if having an audience for my early fumblings in horse management was really such a good idea, especially such a young and trusting spectator. I racked my brains on the subject of all the research I had been doing, the horse whisperer's techniques I had been studying, but all the information was amalgamating into a jumble in my head. I'd never seen any of it demonstrated apart from a few minutes on video – Pat Parelli working with some wild mustangs in the States, which had seemed to involve a lot of cowboy techniques like lassoing the horses first. And so I reverted to the familiar tried and tested ways of my youth.

'Brody, just hand me over that bucket of horse feed, will you?' He pushed the silver bucket through a gap in the fence poles.

The change in the horses' demeanour was astounding. Years in the wild had done nothing to cloud their memory when it came to a bucket of feed. Within a heartbeat, all four were facing me, their ears pointed alertly forward as they stretched their necks and made a few steps in my direction, eager to investigate this new and thrilling food source. Having broken the ice, I moved on to my version of techniques common to all three gurus – Parelli, Roberts and Kel Jeffery – the basic advance and retreat.

The notion is when trying out something new with a horse,

go just far enough not to trigger flight or fight, read their signals of disapproval and discomfort, almost before they happen, and then instantly retreat, never force them, then immediately repeat the action, this time going an iota further and continuing until the horse has 'accepted' what you have in mind without experiencing fear, or creating a habit of a narky reaction. Before Tatti knows it, he is putting his head into a bucket and a headcollar at the same time, and within ten minutes, I had all four horses in smart new webbing headcollars of assorted colours. Once they were in their headcollars, they immediately switched to docile behaviour. It seems to me that horses are very philosophical about their circumstances.

At ten, after a breakfast of fresh boiled eggs and toasted wholewheat bread, made daily by Susan in her bread machine, we headed out in the Toyota tray-back on a dry run for a rock art expedition she is planning with some guests who are due to arrive from Sydney later today.

We struggled through the undergrowth following the track Susan had made the year before. I could see nothing, but Susan seemed to be able to detect the track through what appeared to me to be just dense scrub. She was swinging the car around in circles to avoid bigger trees, while the kangaroo bar on the front of the four-wheel drive ploughed down the long grasses. On the way back we diverted off the path again through the trees towards a spot where two young brumbies had been seen several times, an area not far from the road. Just a handful of these wild horses, it appeared, had made their territory near enough to the road to grow accustomed to the sight and sounds of cars. First we saw cows, and then more cows, then two donkeys loping along behind one of the Brahman bulls.

Then we caught sight of horses in the distance, two fine liver chestnuts – a sort of dark, rich chestnut-brown, one about two years old and the other barely a yearling. They didn't seem overly concerned about the approach of our white vehicle, in fact they ignored us completely until we were surprisingly close. Susan stopped the car and I struggled out, the video and camera slung around my neck, eager to try out more of the methods of advance and retreat.

I walked slowly towards the horses as they carried on grazing, and at the moment at which they raised their heads to investigate this approaching animal, I stopped in my tracks and looked away, sometimes even crouching or sitting on the ground facing the other way. As soon as I judged they had relaxed and grown used to the idea of my presence, I would move forward again. By now they were watching me with interest, ears pricked, but by the same token, poised, ready to take flight at the slightest provocation. Having aroused their curiosity, and now only about twenty-five yards away from them, I walked a few steps forward and then turned around and walked away. They followed me. This was exactly what I had hoped for. We carried on this game for a good forty minutes. Every now and then they would stick their heads and their tails in the air and trot a few paces away into the bush, the sight of their floating gait quite thrilling, only to move back closer towards me later. At one point while avoiding me they approached to only about ten yards from the Toyota, with Susan sitting quietly inside, filming. Eventually they decided they had seen all they wanted to see of the two-legged strangers and they cantered off into the bush. Susan, as she filmed these antics on her video camera, began by calling it Lizzie's Monty Roberts' method but quickly moved on to calling it Lizzie's Monty Python method.

In the afternoon Brody and I went back to the yards to try putting bridles on Starsky and Tatti. To my surprise, they put up no resistance whatsoever, accepting the bit like the old-timers they are but as if it was only yesterday they were last tacked up. They immediately transformed into pussycats, just dozing quietly by the fence, all but purring. I was amazed by how far we had come and how quickly with these old geldings. Encouraged by this success, I dressed Tatti up in the lunging equipment, cavesson, surcingle, and elastic reins, and tried to get him moving around me. Lunging seems to be such an integral part of horse-breaking in England, having the horse circle you on the end of a long rein in order to get used to wearing the tack, to strengthen the muscles and improve balance, and in an ideal world, learn to respond to voice commands. Tatti looked great in all the tack-shop finery, but after only a few paces of trotting around me, he would head right into the centre of the circle, melting brown eyes pleading with me to make sense of my strange requests.

I fetched the lunging whip, using it as I had been instructed to keep him trotting in a circle around me, flicking it gently in the direction of his hindquarters. Immediately he spun around, eyes riveted on the long black thong, ears tautly pressed forward, entire expression of face and body resonating with the words: 'That, my friend, is a writhing black snake, and if you think I'm going to take my eyes off it for even one second, you're crazy, and you obviously know nothing at all about survival in the bush.' We'd reached an impasse. I had no idea what to do next. It was the blind leading the blind.

I went back to my house, made a cup of tea, and rang Robert, my new friend from Goodwoods Saddlery, the tack shop in Sydney, ostensibly to order a small bridle for the pony. I confided in him my problems with the lunging, and he said it's just avoidance. He said that Tatti wants the security of the centre of the ring with me rather than the work. I have to be firmer with the whip, he said. He also advised strongly against backing Tatti myself when I told him that would have been the plan for the next day if the lunging had succeeded. He explained that a horse has a tolerance level and once you pass that you can be in big trouble, reminding me that horses work on the system of fight or flight, either of which can be very sudden and violent and can end up in a broken limb for horse or human. So he counselled carrying on with the work and waiting for Ron's arrival.

'But Tatti is such a darling, he rests his head sleepily on my shoulder, ears relaxed, his eyes dreamy – so affectionate.'

'Don't be fooled!' Robert answered.

In the evening, after Susan's friends from Sydney had rolled up in their rented Land Cruiser, we headed off down to a peaceful spot on the river bank for a sunset drink. First we swam in the inky-black cool waters of the creek. I kept well behind Susan, because I know something very important that doesn't seem to bother her much, but bothers me: there are crocodiles in these waters.

There are two kinds of crocodiles in the Kimberley. There are the saltwater crocodiles that grow to enormous lengths, eighteen to twenty-four feet – these are the ones that snap their enormous jaws shut on the juicy bodies of humans, cattle and horses, pulling them down under the water, drowning them, then storing them under a ledge in the river to putrefy and to be eaten at leisure over the next few days. These crocodiles, as might be suggested by their nickname, salties, live in the stretches of rivers where the water is still saline, closest to the sea.

The other kind are called Johnson River crocodiles, although they are also known as freshies because they only live in fresh, salt-free waters, the inland rivers and creeks, even billabongs, like the small lake at the back of the homestead. Freshies supposedly don't grow very long and, although by no means vegetarian, they don't eat people, don't even bite – much. I had no intention of testing the theory the hard way by stepping on one or kicking it while swimming. Almost everything bites when provoked, even people.

Afterwards we put up the camping chairs on the flat grey rocks and poured glasses of white wine and gin and tonics. Only then did I think about it. This was the place where I had been almost exactly a year before, standing on this very rock, my red shorts covered with fish slime, when Celia had given me the horse.

I walked down to the river bank by myself and sat down on one of the smooth stones. I looked at the glassy water with the reflection of the rising moon shimmering across its surface. Exactly a year ago. Since then, Susan had put into effect miracles of planning, and I had overcome obstacles of inertia and put aside my care-taking and over-cautious character traits to set about doing something entirely for myself.

The wild horse represents the soul. An American friend told me this and it had stuck in my mind.

About eight years ago, about the same time as I was finally coming to terms with the fact that I would never give birth to our own child, an Austrian friend, Isabelle Rattibor, invited us to go with her and a group of friends on a trip to Poland. From Krakow we had taken a side-trip to the Church of the Black Madonna at Czestochowa, and it was there that I had what felt like a moment of understanding, an epiphany, maybe even a vision.

We had just negotiated our way past hundreds of little stalls selling mementos of the Black Madonna; from key rings, to small plaster effigies, to embroidered placemats with lace borders. The Catholics in our party were moving forward towards the altar, and I was standing by myself somewhere at the side of the nave looking around. There was a mass being said in Italian and the priest's voice was resonating through the cathedral. It was in honour of several bus-loads of Italian nuns who were there on a pilgrimage. Because I had spent so much of my early childhood hanging out in the kitchen with Francesca and Idelma, Italian had been my first language, and the words, as they echoed around, were familiar to me. I looked across the nave and saw beneath a window the sunlight slanting down onto her face, a girl of about six or seven, with pale brown hair reaching below her shoulders. Only what I felt I saw was a soul merely housed in a child's body. Maybe I was just struck by that kind of spirited and wild look that sometimes comes with early childhood. The thought came into my mind with total clarity and precision: why had I not been given a soul to look after? I had a strong sense at that moment that it was within the gift of a higher power, but that I was also being told that it was not because I wouldn't be a good mother. My next sense was that the real question was, what would I be given to take its place? The answer was that I needed to be patient and just wait and see.

Maybe my wild horse will be the soul sent to me for my safe-keeping. Maybe the experience of searching for, finding and keeping my wild horse would be my gift.

SEVEN

Camels and Clouds

Thursday 29 July

This is my third morning. Already I am settling in.

Last night after lights out I found an enormous spider in my bedroom, sitting on the dark-green ventilator slats on the lower part of the wall, just below the glass, and uncomfortably near the iron bedstead. I took the candle and immediately went back to the sitting room and rang Susan for advice.

'Now you're an outback girl, you'll have to deal with it yourself. You'll have to find the insect spray and kill it.'

I never kill spiders. I do the 'glass over the top and card underneath' trick and then let them loose outside, but this one was a bit too big to fool around with. It was substantially built, the size of a small crab, or rather a sort of Art Deco crab, upholstered in dark cream fur. I have no idea what the lethal funnel-web spider looks like and if there is the faintest chance that this spider could kill me before I put into practice my good Samaritan act – even though I have a vague idea that big is good and does not mean dangerous when it comes to spiders – I think I'll have to take Susan's advice. After all, the big black hairy tarantula climbing all over James Bond in that famous scene from *Dr No* was without doubt capable of a lethal bite. I distinctly recall Sean Connery looking very nervous and sweaty as the spider made its way purposefully through his forest of chest hairs. This spider is just as big, only blond.

I found the torch with the strongest battery and sprayed the spider with the insect-murdering potion. It bolted around the room as if I had given it a shot of adrenalin, with me in pursuit trying to keep track of it with the faint torch beam. I felt thoroughly guilty, but there was no going back now. The heel of my boot finished the poor creature off. Next, with the help of a broom, I chased out a little lizard or gecko that had been hanging out on the ceiling, and I remembered the story Susan told me about the American visitor who came running out of her bedroom claiming there was a baby crocodile on her ceiling. Then I lovingly enacted the glass and card trick with two cute black beetles with attractive black and white symmetrically striped backs.

To my surprise, the cavalry arrived to rescue me in the shape of Andy on the quad bike. I thought I was to be left on my own, on principle, for an outback creature initiation. The spider, to my chagrin, turns out to be a harmless member of the huntsman spider clan. I felt even more guilty, and sad. The charming beetles, Susan tells me the next day, are bush cockroaches. From then on I resolve to treat them without pity and spray them to death. So they're just cockroaches in cute outfits. It's interesting how affected we are by appealing appearances.

'And I hear you're afraid of snakes,' Andy said, laughing as he swept the body of the harmless spider into the dustpan. 'Seeing a snake out here is so unusual, I would consider it a privilege. I would just sit still and watch it.'

The next morning at eleven Brody arrives at the door breathless with the import of the message he is bringing me. He tells me I've been invited over to their house for pikelets and coffee, to meet Andy's parents, Anika and Hubert. Anika is Dutch and Hubert comes originally from Düsseldorf. They are visiting for a couple of days, having driven over from Kununurra, 450 kilometres away. Hubert has a small grey moustache, which twirls up at the ends, and I long to ask him how he keeps it twirled; is there some kind of moustache wax available in the outback, maybe some kind of native 'bush turtle' wax, or something found under the bark of a tree? Hubert speaks almost perfect English with only a slight German accent, he rolls all his r's and says '*und*' instead of 'and'.

Ann has made a heap of pikelets, little squashy pancakes made with self-raising flour. We sit at the table outside and eat them with whipped cream, jam and drink cups of tea and Nescafe.

Since 1976 Hubert has been catching camels in the desert. Camels were first brought to Australia in the middle of the nineteenth century, some brought by the Afghans at the time of the goldrush. There are now about 300,000 running wild, by Hubert's estimation. At one time the mail was delivered by camel, not plane, and in the north some of the first settlers used camels to reach the outback, the terrain being too rough for horses and wagons. In the early days, Hubert would catch his camels by lassoing them from his Toyota, but later learnt how to trap them in spearhead traps on the water holes. A spearhead trap works on the principle of a valve, apparently. A one-way gate lets the camel into an enclosure, but not back out. In one particular week he caught three hundred and fifty. He would train them before selling them to people who need them for tourist rides or for work on the stations.

'They are just beginning to catch on how good camels are for this part of the world,' Hubert told me. 'Camels are smart, they never forget anything you teach them. Once I went to Alice Springs where there was a camel I had trained that I had not seen for two years. I called three times, und on the third call, he comes running to me. They never forget anything. They are the best to have in the cattle country because they can eat anything, eat the most poor food rubbish und transform it into protein, und they don't need to drink so often, und they have soft feet so they do not damage the land, unlike horses or donkeys. Und their meat is good to eat,' he added, somewhat unnecessarily I thought. 'They taste good und there is absolutely no cholesterol.

'Camels are family creatures. When I put a new camel in with a group of old ones, then it takes about two years for them to accept the new camel. If a camel gets separated from the herd in the desert, then he will lie down und will himself to die. Und so I never sell a camel on his own, always I try to sell two or three together.'

'Do you breed them yourself?' I asked, 'rather than having to go to all the trouble of catching them?'

'Yes, I breed them, but the babies I breed always I sell.'

'Oh. Why?'

'Because they are impossible. They are spoilt. Camels are so smart, the young ones, they learn your tricks und then they learn how to handle you instead of the other way around. If I want a camel, I go to catch a wild one.'

His words set me thinking. It could be that in England we make that mistake with horses. Perhaps many of those horses and ponies that have behavioural problems have simply been spoilt when young, hand-fed and treated like puppies, and have learnt to use their strength and their threats to get their own way. They have been too smart for us, learnt how to handle us instead of the other way around, learnt how to twist us around their little hooves.

I set off down to see the geldings in a cheerful mood, anticipating a warm welcome from them following the success of yesterday's training session. To my dismay they were seriously unamused that I had arrived without the silver bucket of horse feed and so resumed charging around the yard with their ears back. I managed to fool them by putting a little hay in the bottom of the bucket instead. I felt they should get used to responding to something other than food.

Tatti then assumed a put upon expression from the moment the tack went on and he found himself in the middle of the ring with me trying to lunge him. Of course it's possible that he has been trained to stand still when not mounted – because Tatti's expression of disbelief at my antics, standing there and urging him on with the occasional flap of the whip, is actually comical.

Friday 30 July

Several times a day, starting at 6 am, Susan goes to a little white hut at the end of the airstrip and reads the weather observations for the Bureau of Meteorology in Canberra. She measures the air pressure and temperature, wind and humidity. Susan and Ann are to be heard later in the day discussing clouds.

'Well, Susan, I'd reckon it was 4/8ths CU1 moving east.'

'No, I'd say 2/8ths, strato cumulus number 4 and a cirrostratus 8. The lower was moving east.'

'So you reckon there was a middle cloud?'

'Yeah. Moving south-east.'

I always liked to think that when you see the temperatures flash up on the map of Australia during a television weather report, it meant someone has had to pound down to the weather station on the quad bike at Athenrai at the crack of dawn to take a reading. Now that I know how it is done, I like to imagine that some-times someone has overslept after a few too many beers the night before, and has made up the measurements, standing on the verandah in their nightshirts at dawn and guessing. Not at Athenrai, of course, but on one of the less well run stations. Pilots, I've discovered, read clouds too, they are able to decipher the texture. 'I reckon we'll go around this one, it might have hard edges.' Clouds have hard edges?

Brody has been my almost constant companion since I arrived. He sits behind me on the quad bike, hanging on with a little arm around my waist, reminding me which knobs to push. Twist the main knob to 'on'. Then start the engine. Then kick into gear one, and off we go – at a jerky, noisy, snail's pace. 'Now you kick into gear two,' Brody yells into my ear above the sound of the engine as we bounce along the red sand track down to the stock yards.

'I'm only learning,' I yell back. 'Give me time.' In exchange, I try to teach him horse lore, but Brody is so small and the horses so big, apart from Brad and what Brad lacks in size he makes up for in sheer contrariness. I see Brody trying to pull Brad across the yard, grunting with the effort. Brad's hooves are firmly planted and he ain't going nowhere unless it's to pack his fat cheeks.

'Keep at the side and the front of the horse,' I say. 'Be aware of the horse all the time. Never get too close to the hind legs. If you tie a horse up, from then on he's your responsibility, so use a knot you can untie in a hurry (your father's good at those).'

'What's that?' I say, pointing at a fetlock.

His eyes grow big. 'Foot?'

'No, that bit there is a fetlock. And that?' I say, pointing at the muzzle.

'Nose?' with Brody's accent the word sweeps up.

'No, muzzle. And now, Brody, run your hand down his neck until the lowest bit. The lump, those are his withers.' I get him to measure how high Brad is against him. 'Then you can go home and work out how high Brad is in hands.' I try to explain hands:

a measurement based on the width of a hand but then what that means in the real world is four inches. My words fall onto confused ears, Brody looks at me as if I am from outer space. He shows signs of trying to slope off when the heat gets great, but I ask him to help me clear up. Ann is so good with her kids, she makes them do what is required, so I felt she would appreciate me asking Brody to help with the boring bits as well as the fun.

Early afternoon finds me lying on my bed absolutely exhausted by yet another session with the horses. Somehow it's always a long and tiring experience, by the time I've been to collect the tack.

Eventually I was kitted up and astride the quad bike once more, ready to go, but then there was another delay. There was a strange vehicle parked outside Susan's house, so of course I had to go and investigate.

Two policemen, whom we had spoken to on the road yesterday, had stopped by for tea, cake and a chat. Who can resist a man in uniform? Especially one with a gun . . . We sat in the garden next to the bougainvillea. They took off their guns and put them onto the table, then tucked into Susan's home-baked fruit cake and my real coffee while chatting six to the dozen about the Catholic mission at Kalumburu, up the road, four hours drive west then north.

I was only half tuned in to their conversation, as it seemed to be about local politics and not my business. I waited until a lull in the conversation and then asked them a really important and pivotal question. If on their rounds up near Kalumburu they'd seen any wild horses.

'Oh yeah, we seen plenty,' Chris said.

'What colours?' I asked.

'Charcoal,' he said.

'Then there's other smoky-coloured ones,' Darren added. I had to ask him to repeat it. I have never heard a horse colour described thus. I was trying to imagine herds of smoky- and charcoal-coloured horses.

Later in the afternoon, after Susan had finished her office work, we went out looking for wild horses. Finding nothing, we set off down a different track on the way back towards the property, along the edge of a more deeply wooded area, and now we're bogged – sitting in the tray-back – about ten kilometres from the homestead, waiting for Andy to rescue us with the tractor. We got out of the car to stuff branches under the wheels and I was immediately attacked by giant mosquitoes drilling through my thick cotton shirt to get to my blood, which I am convinced is of the extra-sweet variety as mozzies love me so much, they come from miles around to find me.

So now Andy, an unlit ciggie hanging from his lips, is bouncing the car by crashing his foot on and off the accelerator, and I'm realising there's all sorts of techniques you need to know if you are going to survive in the bush. We are so well protected and comfortable in our houses with all mod-cons that it is easy to forget that this is still a wilderness. We had a couple of nervous moments when we couldn't reach Andy on the satellite phone. The sun was setting and it was going to be too late to walk the track back to the road, running the gauntlet of mud, poisonous snakes and hidden tree roots without a proper torch, so the prospect was an uncomfortable night huddled in the cabin of the tray-back.

With an almighty whumph, we are pulled out of the mud by Andy.

I had a very restless night, itching, tossing and turning. Is it possible I have fleas? Yes, very possible, even inside my ears. I hear the disquieting flap of filigree wings, a slight feathery sensation on my chest. It turns out to be some kind of moth heading rapidly south into the crevices of my pyjama-clad body. There are so many of these insects in the room – inside my ears too it would appear. If only I had remembered to bring cotton-wool buds. It's now 450 kilometres of red dirt road to the nearest shop to buy some.

I was woken in the early hours with a damp sensation on my head from the morning dew. I got up just before dawn and made a cup of tea, and sat on the verandah thinking and listening to nature waking up.

I've been here four days. I'm getting acclimatised and learning useful lessons. Like not to work with the geldings between twelve noon and 3 pm – *always* the time I seem to find myself down at the yards when Brody, the horses and I, are knocked out by the heat.

Fear, however, still sometimes lurks uninvited. Now that I am more than fifty years old it's time to drop the attitude of fear because it really is just an attitude. A habit. An indulgence. It is time to get on with it; do things I have waited my whole life to do.

Spenders are late-starters. My father always said that. This was one of his wisdoms. He took up playwriting in his seventies with a passion that gave him great joy. Another of his wisdoms was that the worst thing you can do is stifle the emotional growth of the person you live with.

Tomorrow we are setting out on an expedition to the nearby Catholic mission at Kalumburu. Susan is kindly taking me there to show me around and so I can see the horses in the surrounding countryside. These horses, from what I have heard, have interesting breeding thanks to two Arab stallions that were given to the mission and then, as far as I can gather, were turned loose. We're going to stay overnight in the little motel there.

And still no sign of Ron the horse whisperer. By the time he arrives, if he arrives, I will be one week into my four-week trip.

EIGHT

Kalumburu

Saturday 31 July

We left Athenrai at 10.30 am on the 180-kilometre trip to Kalumburu.

We rattled along in the tray-back, not the smoothest of rides across the dusty corrugations of the red road, but the most practical because at times we would swing off the road to do a little exploration, looking for wild horses, steaming through the lightly wooded areas and through the scrub, detouring around the bigger trees. While we were still on Athenrai land, only about twenty minutes from the homestead, we found our first horses and stopped to investigate.

There is something indescribably thrilling about finding these wild horses in the bush. Here are these grown horses, looking as well formed and as interesting as horses bred in captivity in England, often better, as I have yet to see a horse that I would not be proud to take home with me, yet somehow, so mysterious. They have been born and grown, and learnt about the world, all without the intervention of man. They escaped from domestic circumstances possibly as long as fifty years ago, and then have carried on breeding successfully in the wild, as if that was always their way. Horses in domestic circumstances need so much looking after, but these horses have nothing. Watching them, I get a distinct sense of family, of a structure, of arrangements made between them for mutual self-protection. And now, here they are, standing still amongst the trees, not running away in fear, watching me curiously, the human animal. They look me over almost as if they can vaguely remember somewhere in their genes or their collective memory that we could be friends, before finally flicking their tails in the air and cantering away. I long to get to know all of these unique characters.

About twenty years ago I went to a nature reserve in the heart of the Camargue region in the south of France to visit a herd of around ninety of the famous white horses that were being kept wild and untouched in a special fenced off area to be observed and studied. The couple managing the project, Patrick and Alison Duncan, told me that they were on the strictest instructions not to interfere in any way with the natural process. For example, if they found a stallion that had been badly injured after a fight with another stallion, they were on no account to bring in veterinary help. The extraordinary thing was, they told me, they would see stallions with long cuts, of maybe a few inches, with gouged flesh hanging down and bleeding, and within a couple of weeks the wound would have healed entirely, leaving hardly more than a scar. Their instructions not to interfere were made doubly hard by the fact that these 'wild' horses were entirely tame, having found the edges of the reserve and discovered how being nice to tourists could lead to readily available snacks. I found it quite hard to stand by while a cute mare and foal nuzzled up to me, but I had no choice because Alison was standing next to me saying: 'Don't even think of touching those horses, they're supposed to be wild...'

We returned to the road, rattling back along the corrugations for another couple of hours. Our next stop was to visit Dusty, the helicopter pilot, and his wife Nina on a nearby station. I was eager to find out if they knew anything about the history of the old geldings.

'Dusty might be in,' Susan said as we drove up to the homestead. 'Or he might be out working.'

'Couldn't we have called them and made a time?' I asked, mildly irritated that we might have come all this way and then missed out on seeing Dusty and Nina. But it seems that things don't work that way out here.

Dusty was out working, but Nina was there with her daughter, Jenny, so we stopped to drink coffee and talk. Jenny seemed to know all about the four old geldings. From our description she thought she recognised Tatti as a gelding that had lived at Athenrai with the previous owners. The others were from Mount Elizabeth, a station about 260 kilometres from Athenrai. Mount Elizabeth had been used as a tourist destination and the horses had been used for trail rides. What had happened to them in between, or how they got from there to Athenrai, was anybody's guess. She remembered that one horse had been called 'Slit' because of an old scar, a slit in his nostril. We identified Slit as the horse I named Hutch. And the pony we call Brad is in fact called Tonka Toy, and known for throwing everybody and being impossible to ride. She fetched a photo album and showed us pictures of Starsky, or Bayjack as he was known, looking amazingly youthful without the sprinkling of grey hairs. We saw shots of Tatti bathing in a river – he had been called 'Boot' on account of his white sock, pretty undignified for such a nice looking horse.

Nina showed us photographs of Dusty working with a brumby, a little bay filly that had been mustered by chance into the yards along with some cattle. It emerged that after Dusty had patiently and gently trained her well enough to ride, and grown fond of her, and she had produced a beautiful foal, then one day, she had walked through an open gate back into the bush with her foal and never returned. If this had happened to me I would have taken it personally and found it hurtful to have bonded with a horse to that degree and then to realise that it could and might just walk away never to return.

Fuelled up with restoring coffee and cake, we hit the road again. Gradually the land started to flatten out and reveal plateaus in the distance, with huge dreamy meadows in between; long grasses and fine white-trunked trees with bright green leaves, the closest you could imagine to a horse heaven. We saw a spectacular black horse in the distance, and swung off the road into the tall grasses to get a closer look.

He was a magnificent black stallion, not unlike the galloping, glorious stallion in the English Lloyds Bank television advertisements. I leapt out of the car and ran in his direction. He stood still, watching us. He had to be posing he looked so magnificent, and when he moved off, he had that wonderful floating action.

We stopped in the middle of one of the meadows – I suppose in Australia it is called a paddock – and unpacked our picnic, setting up our table and canvas chairs amongst the rustling leaves. Grazing near us was a happy little family group, a grey stallion, pregnant dappled-grey mare and a gawky brown teenager. I set up the camcorder and tried to film us and our picnic table using my new tripod, but it was hard to stop the thing from keeling over as soon as I walked away – my fault for not having read all the instruction books. Eventually we got the thing more or less balanced. Susan put on her bright pink lipstick, straightened her hat, and said she hoped we looked very *Out of Africa*. So we ate our lunch of tinned tuna and Ryvitas, counted up our Weight Watcher 'points', then packed up and carried on driving in the direction of the township, passing more and more wild horses.

'First we're going to visit Rose,' Susan told me. 'She's an artist, and she's very excited because one of her paintings has just sold at Sotheby's in Sydney for a huge sum of money,' Susan continued.

We arrived at a run-down shack on the outskirts of the community. There was a yard filled with broken-down cars, and a guy with a long stringy beard was tinkering with one of them; a few old tabby cats prowled around. We went into the house. In the first room there were cot beds on either side of the room, Rose was sitting up on one, and Jack, her elderly husband, was in the other. Then I remembered that the people we chatted to in Kununurra also held court from their beds. Over the door there was a crucifix. That was all I got to see because by this point, after the long car journey and the effect of the cats and dogs everywhere, I was feeling so ill that I had to leave and run back to the car. I sat there quivering and thinking that I really should pull myself together and go back in, because what I had just done was so rude, but I couldn't.

We visited more friends of Susan's; everyone in town was sitting on plastic chairs outside their bungalows. All around were yellow dogs, moving in a cheerful pack up and down the high street. And at the end of the road I could see a little boy leading a small donkey, one of the prettiest I'd ever seen.

So it would be the motel after all. In an effort to prepare myself I had asked Susan a couple of times what the motel would be like. Pretty basic was her answer. I could well imagine it. As we drove around the town I noticed a couple of small billboards for the motel, even boasting air-conditioning. We'd be all right. I'd stayed in places like that in the States while still a small child in 1959, when my mother had taken my brother and me on a tour of the west – Las Vegas, Death Valley, Yosemite Park, Los Angeles, which in those days still had sweet-smelling air and blissful orange groves. Around the national parks we'd stayed in very basic motels; desolate, simple box cabins with noisy air-conditioning and near the reception, the ubiquitous soft drink cooler with rows of root beer in glass bottles. So I was well prepared for 'basic'.

Or so I thought. At one end of the community was the church of Our Lady of the Ascension, built of cream corrugated iron with an almost new red roof. The old roof had been full of holes from when the Japanese had bombed Kalumburu in 1942, which meant that the statue of Our Lady would get wet during the church services. It had taken fifty years to find the money to replace the roof and Susan had been instrumental in helping raise the funds. All around the church were lawns and huge luxuriant bushes of shocking pink bougainvillea. I was keen to get to the mission motel, check in and have a cup of tea and a shower before going to mass, but Susan was still carrying on an extended conversation with a nice-looking young woman, wearing a blue and white striped T-shirt and denim skirt. People in the outback have an inexhaustible capacity to chat about local events, land commissions, declarations, and so on. I was beginning to feel like a child. *Are we nearly there yet?* Reliving the irritation of waiting for parents who stand around chatting and never tell you what's going on.

It had been at least five minutes since I last asked Susan so I asked her again. 'Are we going to the motel?'

'Yes, in a minute,' she answered, somewhat impatiently. 'I'm just waiting for Bernadette to fetch the key.' I was feeling more and more like a child, with no power over my circumstances, never quite sure what was going on, what the plan was. I felt disorientated, like I was one remove away from events.

But at this point, taking the hint, the girl in the striped T-shirt walked off, and returned a few minutes later with a key. 'Number two,' she said. 'It's a twin.'

Peter Eve took this stunning photograph from the helicopter the second time we saw my beautiful horse, the chestnut in the foreground.

Another image of my gift horse. PETER EVE

Above: Wystan Auden and me. STEPHEN SPENDER

Right: An early affinity with four-hooved friends.
STEPHEN SPENDER

Death Valley, Nevada, 1959. I manage to find myself a ride – on a white mule.
My brother Matthew looks on. STEPHEN SPENDER

Riding Frisky at Bruern Abbey. STEPHEN SPENDER

Penelope Betjeman's picnic day on the downs. Myself on Firefly, Matthew and our father Stephen. NATASHA LITVIN

Susan Bradley swimming (with the freshies) in the waterhole at the picnic spot on the King Edward River. CHARLES ASHTON

Above: The old geldings who wandered into the yards from the bush, Starsky (*left*) and Hutch. LIZZIE SPENDER

Above right: With Wilhelmina, the large piglet. SUSAN BRADLEY

Right: The first arrivals, Tatti Black Beauty (*behind*) and Brad, the pony. LIZZIE SPENDER

Sitting on the rails of the cattle yard at Athenrai, wearing my smart new French jodhpurs. SUSAN BRADLEY

The Hallen family on one of the station quad bikes. *Left to right*: Brody, Ann, Jack and Andy. SUSAN BRADLEY

The arrival of the mail plane at Athenrai. LIZZIE SPENDER

Brody tries to lead the bad mannered pony, Brad. LIZZIE SPENDER

Richard Bradley canters Tatti. LIZZIE SPENDER

Gathered around the Land Cruiser considering plans for the temporary yards.
Left to right: Maria, Ron, Richard and Susan. LIZZIE SPENDER

I have a vague memory that the policemen who stopped by for fruit cake and coffee had mentioned that there were a few construction workers staying in the motel. 'Shouldn't we book?' I had asked Susan. But she hadn't answered.

So we took our key and climbed back into the Toyota.

I had been looking optimistically at attractive semi-detached bungalows sprinkled around the mission, as small as dolls' houses, assuming these were the motel rooms as the motel belongs to the mission. But as we drove away from the church, the bungalows became less and less bougainvillea clad and my spirits started to sink. Finally we left the compound and headed off through the streets of the town itself for a few blocks. Eventually we swung off the road at a sign announcing 'Mission Motel', and came to a halt.

We were in a yard about fifty feet square; on three sides the area was bordered by rows of what looked like joined-up meat safes, or restaurant-sized ice boxes, with square doors in the middle and a large aluminium handle to secure the contents. These are dongas, transportable units with small barred windows at the back, one per unit, that would have been brought out to the area by mining companies and then sold locally when the mining companies left. There were numbers on the doors. On one side there were a couple of green portacabins, one marked 'shower' and the other 'toilets'. In between were a couple of outdoor sinks. This set-up made the campsite in 'MASH' look like pure luxury. I didn't mind the ablutions blocks, I'm used to those from outdoor Australian life, but I couldn't see myself climbing into a meat safe and closing the door behind me, and didn't Bernadette say I'd be sharing the meat safe with Susan?

At the other end of the row of aluminium boxes was the mess room and an outside table. Sitting at the table was an assortment of unshaven men in singlets, shorts and thongs, swigging beer and playing cards to blaring music from a ghetto blaster, and watching with deep interest the arrival of two blondes, willing it seemed, under the circumstances, to overlook our comparatively mature years. These were men who had not seen their womenfolk for weeks. Cabin number two turned out to be squeezed into a corner, right behind the mini beer garden and carousing company.

As I yanked my bag off the back of the Toyota, slung it over my shoulder and headed towards the grinning company, the feeling of despair merged with rising adrenalin and anger. Yes, I'd slept on beaches in Greece, in a basic tin shack at Coopers Creek in the desert in South Australia, and in a tent high in the Rockies in the freezing cold, and in a stifling, bare cement shoe box under the runway at Athens airport, only a few yards beneath the bellies of departing aircraft. I had even camped on a disused ferry at Piraeus, to the dismay of my Athenian friends. Yes, I was fully qualified to have a sense-of-humour failure, without letting myself down and being a spoilsport.

'Susan,' I started. 'You know you really have to warn people.'

She looked at me amazed. 'What are you talking about?'

'You have to warn people that they are going to have to put up with all this.' I was waving my free arm as discreetly as I could considering we had an audience.

'But everybody loves this excursion, they think it's a real experience . . .' Now her voice was rising.

'It's a total nightmare . . . I mean, just look . . .'

'I've brought ambassadors here, high court judges, Elisabeth Murdoch – they all loved it,' she retorted.

'Susan. I have slept in all sorts of appalling conditions, but *this* . . . It's Saturday and we're right behind them.' Panic was beginning to set in as I envisaged the night ahead. Could I maybe camp in the car? The construction workers were all around. I broke off, to converse as calmly as I could manage about local fishing conditions to a few passing workmen who were just setting off carrying rods. I'm English, I'm a stoic, I was trying hard not to over-react, but it was getting harder. A little voice in my head was squeaking: you don't have to, you may feel like a child, but you're grown-up now, in fact you've been grown-up for rather a long time, you don't have to do anything you don't want to do.

'And,' I hissed at Susan once the fishermen had disappeared out of sight, 'we could have just come here on a day trip. You know, that would have been an idea.'

'And the reason we didn't come for a day trip is I didn't want to do the four-hour drive back in the dark,' she hissed back.

'I quite agree, but couldn't we have come earlier and left earlier?'

'No. I like to come to the Saturday evening mass.'

'Couldn't we at least sleep in a room that isn't practically in the middle of their bar, their beer garden?' My adrenalin was spiralling out of control.

'No, this is the only room they have left.'

I refrained from screeching, 'Well couldn't we have booked?' I steeled myself to preparing my body for the imminent severe confinement of the donga.

'I'll think of something,' Susan said, and flung her bag back into the tray-back. I followed suit. We set off back to the mission for the six o'clock mass.

Father Sanz, the old Spanish missionary who had made the mission his home seventy years previously, dedicated the mass at my request to the memory of my Cuban friend Dolores Smithies. She had lost her battle against cancer and had passed away a few weeks earlier. Susan had brought a candle in a delicate glass jar, which we left burning under a statue of the Virgin Mary.

After mass, it appeared that somehow the entire population of Kalumburu had already heard about the motel incident and so various middle-aged couples, led by a tall bony man wearing a classic safari shirt and shorts, called Rod, had appeared out of the woodwork and offered us spare rooms for the night. I was quite looking forward to accepting one of these invitations as I was still unaccountably attached to the bougainvillea-swathed white tin semis and felt sure that at least one of these invitations had to come from some couple who lived in one, with a white-tiled bathroom and biscuits in a tin with flowers painted on the sides. It turned out that the nicest and neatest of the dollhouses belonged to Sister Visitation and Sister Scholastica, the two nuns, one Spanish and one Basque who had arrived at the mission sixty years ago and had lived there ever since. Sister Scholastica, due to her infirmities, now made her way around the community on a quad bike. But Susan, unbeknownst to me, had made her decision and all invitations were politely but firmly refused without discussion. Only six months later, when we were laughing over our memories of that day, did she confess to me that she had decided not to speak to me for at least an hour as a result of my appallingly bad behaviour.

At six-thirty we hit the road again, jolting along at a speedy 120 kilometres an hour all the way back to the station in the dark, except when we had to slow down to avoid fresh-water crocodiles basking in the shallow waters covering stretches of the road. At home we collapsed in front of the television for a late night episode of 'The Bill', and each consumed a plate of left-over risotto. It felt good to be home.

Susan found an email waiting for her with more information about the geldings from Debbie Holt, who had lived on Athenrai in the early 1990s.

Are the horses you have in branded? We only used horses for the first year we were there and the boys had to run them in and try each one to see if it had been broken in or not as there was no horse book. There were a few interesting rides! There were two black geldings I remember who were very quiet. When my dad came to stay he rode them as he was getting a bit old for tricky horses.

I rode one of them out to some rock art with a friend. It was on Mother's Day 1993 and it was really strange because we were nearly at the site when my horse started groaning and arching his back downwards beneath me. It seemed as though his back was really hurting and he could not stand me being on him. I got off and took the saddle off. I looked and felt over his back but everything seemed to be okay. We started off again, but not long after it all started again. Old Harry, being an old bushy, said he thought the horse was putting it on and to ignore it. Anyway we had not gone much further when my horse decided he had had enough and lay down with loud groans. I took the saddle and bridle off and tried to get him to sit up but he just lay there groaning. I was sick with worry but there was nothing we could do and Harry wanted to go on so we left the horse, saddle, etcetera behind and I walked the last kilometre in to the site. We took photos, had lunch and made our way back after about two hours and I expected to find the horse dead at the very least but he was nowhere in sight. I carried my saddle back to the fence we had gone through (not a pleasant walk). And who should be waiting there and prancing around but my former transport. Harry did not have a hope of catching him as the horse knew every trick of avoidance. I am not sure if he would still be there as this was eleven years ago now. I do not know if someone had trained him to do tricks or if he was really in pain. He could have just been a lot smarter than me!

If he is still there give him a hug and my best wishes.

Regards, Deb

NINE

Horse Catcher

Sunday 1 August

The horse catcher hasn't turned up. Every day he postpones another day. Sometimes I believe that he is never going to come. I will be engaged in the Zen exercise of waiting for someone who is never going to turn up, *Zen and the Art of Waiting for the Horse Catcher.* It would mean developing the art of patience, and the last thing I feel right now is patient.

This morning I hear that Ron has diverted to attend the rodeo in Kununurra.

'So how long will the rodeo take, Susan?' I'm all but drumming my fingers on the breakfast table.

'Ah well, the rodeo, that's only a couple of days.' She pauses. 'Might take a couple more days to, you know, recover. Depends on how much he drinks,' she adds, laughing.

In my imagination, I see the only version of a rodeo that I know, the American rodeo, as I've seen it in movies: bronco busting, lassoing from a horse's back, throwing calves to the ground, and in the midst of all this, our horse catcher: bow-legged, rugged, a spotted handkerchief knotted around his neck, leaning against a rail, beer in hand, watching and then taking his turn, and in no hurry whatsoever to move on to Athenrai.

With the delay comes the revisitation of fear. Fear of what? I keep asking myself in an impatient way. Fear of the sheer scale of the plan, even just fear of the unknown. And a kind of exhaustion. I feel I have expended so much energy playing around in the yard with my four old station horses, without even having had the opportunity to ride them. I've spent so much energy just getting through the day and the heat here, running through the charcoal woods practising my advance and retreat methods, almost pretending to, well, be a horse myself which is just about as pathetic as the huge collection of tack that I have accumulated and am now cleaning, like little clothes for the baby that will never be born, and I have a few of those tiny garments too.

I'm tired. Or am I just feeling weak because suddenly I feel powerless, waiting for something I am not convinced will ever happen: Ron's arrival. Just keep thinking, one day at a time.

Sometimes there are distractions, like when Susan breaks off from the routine of running the station to pursue one of her other careers, that of local celebrant. This evening a couple from Perth have booked a sunset wedding.

They arrived late, having managed to lose the only other guests – the best man and maid of honour – on the road on account of the other couple's four consecutive punctures. The engaged couple had decided to keep it simple and not to invite any family members, just to run away and get married quietly on their own. I thought planning to arrive at about three-thirty for a sunset wedding when the sun sets at 5.45 was cutting it fine under any circumstances, let alone in the middle of the bush. The heavy Land Cruiser bearing the engaged couple trundled down the drive at about four-thirty. They had been camping out for the last few days, so the first requirements were showers, shampoo and a hair dryer. Susan then pointed them in the direction of the river bank – about forty-five minutes drive. By the time the bride-to-be was walking down the aisle or at least heading across the flat stones – all by herself, looking radiant and happy dressed in her short white lace dress and clutching a bouquet of bougainvillea, it turned out to be a rising of the full moon wedding rather than sunset, with just the two of them, minus their friends. The rest of us stood in for all the other roles. The bride later said that she was in the middle of writing a novel to be entitled *After Sunset*, which seemed spookily appropriate.

I had only heard about the forthcoming nuptials that after-noon, and so my mind went into overdrive, thinking the whole scheme quite mad and that because everybody was so late, it should be postponed until the next day; but I kept quiet as Susan and I bounced along the dust track in the bull-catcher to the river bank. I was nursing the wedding cake, baked that afternoon by Ann and iced with a thick layer of condensed milk whip, on my knees, narrowly saving it from a sticky fate on the roof of the car. The wedding actually turned out to be magical. As is so often the way with Susan, somehow, at the last possible moment the impossible falls into place.

She lit little votive candles and put them all over the rocks, and then scattered more pink and white bougainvillea between the candles. I was given the job of photographer, with Susan's digital camera. Andy played best man, Ann was the maid of honour and their two little blond sons made the most enchanting pages. It turned out we didn't need anyone else, The couple seemed thrilled by the whole event, and it was incredibly romantic.

Then we followed the wedding with a moonlit barbecue a little further along the river bank. Andy had built a fire within a surround of stones, and we barbecued meat and baked damper (a type of yeast-free white bread) in a big iron pot, boiled the billy, and chased the strong tea with chilled white wine. We found the euphoria of the newly-weds quite catching.

The next morning there was news when I ambled over to Susan's house for breakfast: the horse catcher is on his way! Do I dare believe it?

Sometimes unexpected spanners are thrown into the works, the latest is Susan saying, 'Ah well, we'll have to move the horses from the yards when the cattle come in.'

'Cattle, what cattle?' I ask horrified.

'The cattle muster,' she says.

It's the first I've heard of those yards being used for cows. I have visions of the lovely tame old geldings being booted out, wandering off into the wild, new smart headcollars and all. Not to mention the wild horses if we ever manage to catch any.

'What cattle muster? I thought you didn't really have cattle on this station?'

'Ah yeah, well, that's the point. We do have some, and we need to get them moved to one of Michael and Celia's properties where they have more cattle. One that's properly geared up for them.'

'So when will it be? How soon?'

Susan doesn't really have an answer for that. 'Kimberley time,' she says. It's the timing for things around here, and it means next week, next month, next year...

'I'll just go and check on the geldings,' I say.

She looks amazed, and somewhat amused. 'They'll be okay.'

But really I just want to see them. Say hello. Make sure they haven't wandered off through an open gate. Cut themselves on wire. Died of old age.

I give them some hay. Tatti, after putting on a little show of being uncatchable, comes up and eats and rests his head on my shoulder, enjoying being stroked and fussed over, and reminding me why I love him. I now feed him in a separate part of the yard so that he doesn't get kicked by the pony or chased away by the bays. That said, we're all getting bored of putting the saddles and bridles on and then taking them off and never going any further. Brody, me, even the horses. No longer do I see the little figure in a white cotton hat running down the long track to the yards hugging the huge blue water bottle. Brody prefers to spend his time wrestling with his younger brother. I hear the cries echoing across the lawn from their house.

After lunch Susan and I set out on another search for wild horses. We found the liver chestnuts but today they were not in the mood to play, rather behaving as if we were tedious interruptions to urgent eating plans. They cantered off, the elder with his tail high, flagging some Arab blood in there somewhere.

On the way, as I jumped in and out of the front seat of the car opening and closing gates, picking up Coca-Cola and beer cans discarded by the truck drivers who career along this road at surprisingly frequent intervals, as many as four a day in the Dry, I was thinking about this 'horse thing'. 'She's mad about horses.' You hear the phrase all the time and it is usually said of a woman rather than a man. Why is it that for people who love horses, the feeling is so strong?

A horse is no household pet, their size alone can imbue an edge of danger, and so there is the challenge of reaching an understanding with an animal that is powerful enough to trample you to death. Dogs are privy to every facet of home life and give unconditional love, while horses are infinitely less available. They don't sit in your lap, lie on your bed, or jump up and down when you suggest a walk; nor are they as independent or capable of disdain as a cat, and they never sharpen their claws on your furniture.

Horses are wonderfully attentive, even when putting on a show of bad behaviour they always remain somehow connected. It's as if they enjoy hanging out with people – sometimes I get the distinct impression that we amuse them. It's a sincere, strong connection of the senses, centred around touch and constant interpretation of each other's body language.

Horses are enormously strong, yet capable of infinite gentleness. My English friend Susie Little said to me, with a laugh: 'Well isn't that exactly what we women look for in a man?' They are immensely sensitive – physically and emotionally – and, in spite of their thick skin, a horse can feel a fly land on its hide and then twitch that particular square inch of flesh. They pick up instantly on moods and states of mind: fear, unhappiness, happiness, impatience, confidence or lack of confidence.

There is a grace, a nobility, about horses of quality that expresses itself most persuasively in the way they move, especially horses such as Arabs that seem to float. Then there is the joy of riding a good horse; to be transfomed from a ploding human, forever earthbound, to a creature that can fly. To ride a horse so well trained, so tuned in to you, that you have only to think about turning, or changing gait, and the horse, as if reading your mind, obeys, perhaps sensing some tiny shift in weight or tensing of a leg muscle prior to the actual command.

Horses have a sense of fun which I will not even attempt to describe, but anyone who has spent time with them will know what I mean. There are horses that seem to be always smiling.

I swear if Ron hasn't arrived by tomorrow, I'm going to risk all and back Tatti before we both expire from boredom.

Tuesday 3 August

I was woken by the sound of a truck, which in my half sleep I thought might just herald the arrival of Ron the horse catcher, so I shot into action and leapt out of bed. Everybody else gets up at about five but I have managed, temporarily, to revert to my usual very civilised hours of sleeping, midnight until eight or so.

I was too late to see the vehicle, and the sound of the truck was not followed by any flurry of excitement, just Brody turning up on the doorstep with the old-fashioned whistle that we had bought to train the horses, and which had arrived on the mail plane.

Susan walked across to announce that she has heard from Ron, and that they have stopped over and camped somewhere on the road and so we'd better have breakfast ready and waiting. By now I am practically beyond believing it will happen but a couple of hours later, in time for morning smoko, a large truck rattles down the drive followed by a dusty red Nissan four-wheel drive. Both head straight to the cattle yards without even pausing. We leapt onto quad bikes and headed after them in time to see that our horses are as surprised as we are by their arrival. They watch fascinated as the newcomers are unloaded from the truck. It turns out to be a motley crew of horseflesh.

The first to be unloaded is a huge, scarily thin bay ex-racehorse with a dozy expression, more like a camel or a conger eel than a horse, hip bones like jutting knives. After that comes an attractive chestnut gelding, then an Appaloosa pony, followed by a pretty palomino mare. The Appaloosa has eye cancer, the chestnut and the big bay are lame, and the palomino is in foal, Ron tells us. Are these the horses that we are supposed to ride for our round-up? The station geldings, Starsky and Hutch, stand alert and tall by the fence, saying hello to the newcomers, while Tatti is playing it laid-back and cool in the middle of the paddock and looking quite classy, in his Black Beauty way.

Having secured the comfort of their horses, Ron and Maria stroll over in our direction, in no hurry, the two of them echoing each other, the same relaxed, loose-limbed walk; they are definitely a pair. They are both dressed in dark blue denim – dusty from the road – and the ubiquitous outback felt hats and RM Williams elastic-sided boots.

Ron is not the bow-legged, rugged cowboy I had envisaged. He is tall and quiet, not shy but almost; he has a wide, attractive face crowned with dark curly hair, a broad smile and, like most people who are exceptionally good with animals, an instant magnetism and power. If I had to portray him on stage, I would begin with a big cat. He has the soft but powerful movements of a panther, the sense that he is always somehow moving, even when he is sitting still, and he has the square angles of a big cat around his face, his frame, his hands. He is always centred, always alert, even if outwardly he gives the appearance of being ultra-relaxed, even dreamy. He communicates with space, and with energy. He stands just close enough and at the right angle to be friendly, to be warm, but until he knows you, he stays out of your space. I would guess that he is no more than forty, and Maria I imagine is around thirty.

Maria is slim and good looking, almost petite. She is like an African gazelle, hiding her narrow face with its freckles and her large hazel eyes under a wide-brimmed hat, but still there is a strength of character there. She is half the pair of them and at the same time so much her own person.

We walk up to the main house for coffee, fruit cake and a conference. I was feeling an enormous sense of relief. I had been concerned for the last few days that if Ron was not going to turn up, we would have to look for someone else, but Susan hates to discuss 'what if' plans, regarding them as negative thinking, and so I had had no choice but to trust her. Secretly, I had been on the prowl looking for a local horse breaker, someone within a couple of thousand kilometres, in case Ron turned out not to have the talent or the abilities for horse training.

Months later, Susan admitted that she found my not-so-secret attempts to find a horse breaker thoroughly irritating as, in her mind, she had it all figured out. She had met Ron when he had been working at another station, and had decided that he was the perfect man for both jobs and we need look no further.

The first thing that emerges is that no one, least of all Ron, quite knows why he has brought the four horses. It seems to be a Kimberley misunderstanding, an idea that has been lost in trans-lation. I had made the suggestion that we would need properly trained, fit horses to ride while rounding up the brumbies, and Ron thought he had been asked to bring them so that I could do some recreational riding, because the next thing that emerges is that we are not going to use horses to round up the brumbies – something I hadn't truly realised up till now.

Over coffee Ron starts to talk, quietly describing his working life mustering cattle, grading roads – the work he does to survive and finance the payments on his car, and then smiling the most when he talks about his work with horses, the five hundred horses he has broken in, the horses he owns. These are scattered all around the country as he has no permanent home. A few board in a paddock belonging to friends and more than a few are turned out on the marshlands near Wyndham. Here is a man who really loves horses. But not so much in what I now begin to see is the English way that so often turns a horse into something between a horse and a puppy dog, an animal that lives within the four small walls of a loosebox, never to stay out in the rain because there is a nice warm stable available, wearing coats, and hand fed sugar lumps or polo mints. Ron loves horses for what they are. He does what the horse whisperers do and thinks the way they do. He loves the land and has a connection to it; he is a true bush man, a man of the bush.

Then I talk. I tell Ron and Maria my dream, my plans for Sedna. They listen in silence, just occasionally smiling, but I get the impression they are intrigued and enthused by the quest. After all, they love horses.

Ron's arrival has caused an immediate surge of action, now we can move forward. Susan gets on the phone to Dusty and fortunately he can come over in the helicopter almost right away; Ron and Maria go down to their quarters, to unpack and settle their dog and her two puppies. They are staying in another corrugated-iron house, the one furthest from the main homestead and on the way to the yards. It is usually the men's quarters, has no kitchen and is called 'The Hilton'.

We reconvene at three. Our plan is to head into the skies in the helicopter to try to locate Sedna, or failing that, to see what other horses are around that we could try to bring in. And what am I feeling apart from great excitement and anticipation? A great dose of fear. Was it ever so?

Is this how it works, I get closer to my dream and then fear turns me back? Fantasy, I'm quickly discovering, is not to be sneezed at. In fantasy, not only does everything go entirely your own way, but you never have to suffer the consequences, deal with the practicalities and impossibilities, do the homework, or feel the fear.

Homework, as I explain to six-year-old Brody when he stumbles over to the house, complaining how boring his school work is, is a necessary part of life. 'Everything in life is a bit fun and a bit homework,' I tell him. That is not the exact quote as I was given it. The quote I was given many years ago is that life is twenty per cent sex, and eighty per cent washing up.

Dusty arrives in the helicopter at about 2.45 pm. 'He'll have the clock on, and be counting the time,' Susan says, so I count it too. How much? Six or seven hundred dollars an hour. At 3 pm we take off, Ron and Susan sitting in the back and me in the front.

There is one thing I can never get used to in the outback, helicopters without doors. I am sitting in the narrowest of seats and on my left, starting three inches from my body, there is nothing except The Void. I am only held into my narrow seat by a single simple buckled seatbelt, exactly like that in a car.

Will it hold? What if my camera knocks against it, and then it springs open of its own accord? I take some comfort in the fact that I have never known a car seatbelt to spring open. I lean forward, the seatbelt gives generously, easily enough for me to slip out of its webbing grasp. I decide that my priority for the next hour or so will be to endeavour not to fall out of the helicopter when it swings, swoops and then hangs sideways in the air. Ahead I can see the windscreen and if I put a hand out I can clutch onto it. I know from previous flights my left hand must creep slowly there from in front of the body or else it gets blown back in a way that reminds me all too graphically of the speed of this machine. I can hook my right elbow behind Dusty's seat, which is fine except that my right hand is supposed to be engaged in filming with my video camera. Talking of which, the camera is likely to be one of the first casualties, falling out of my lap into the trees.

We swirl up into the air. I've noticed that helicopters have a strange, oily way of quivering themselves up into the air which is almost sexual. I was anticipating this interesting sensation but as it turned out I was far too worried about the void to pay any attention.

We swing out across the country, the air beautifully balmy, the landscape stunning; we skim over a sea of green treetops, just a few metres above the leaves, heading towards a wooded plateau on the horizon, the light soft, and beyond the plateau it appears almost blue. Directly below us is baked terracotta earth interspersed with the palest corn-coloured grasses.

Within five minutes we have our first sighting: a group of about five horses, mostly chestnuts and bays, followed soon after by the most wonderful muscular dun stallion escorting two creamy-coloured young mares. As with all the horses we see from the helicopter they are cantering, eager to get away from this giant bird/stallion in the sky but not apparently distressed. Susan even has the feeling that they are playful.

I tried to film but as I could hardly see anything on my video screen, just the faintest of dark shapes which could have been horses . . . or trees. I would just be zooming in when Dusty would swing the helicopter around; once he swooped down and turned at the same time, and I swear I very nearly fell out, then he tipped the other way and I slid across the seat and nearly landed in his lap. It took my stomach a good couple of seconds to catch up with the rest of me.

There followed a long period when we saw no horses. I was beginning to feel disappointed. Maybe there were not as many out here as we'd thought. Susan suggested we head back to the homestead, taking a big loop past the microwave telephone tower, and then suddenly it all started happening.

Ron points at some horses out in the distance. I look away from the instruments which, I have discovered, is the safest place to focus my eyes in an attempt to fool my woefully inadequate inner ears that we are more or less straight and steady. We see a group of three chestnuts and go closer. The front horse has long white socks and a white blaze. It's a miracle.

We've found Sedna! It has to be her. What a gift! There she is, as if she has been there, waiting for us, all this time. How quickly things can change. Only twenty-four hours ago I was ready to give up hope.

Sedna, it appears, is now part of a sweet family. She has a handsome dark chestnut stallion, and a tall foal, with her colouring, but with a flaxen mane and tail, and from the size of Sedna and her bulging sides, she is expecting again. So after twelve months of speculation we now have confirmation that she a filly, not a colt. My only concern is that she could be rather smaller than I remembered. And suddenly there are horses everywhere. We see thirty or forty, most of them magnificent, ranging from one young thing on its own to groups of ten or twelve. We see bright chestnuts, flashy gleaming bays, stunning muscular duns, romantic palominos, quite a few the chestnut colour with flaxen manes and tails, one perfect black horse running with a pure white milky steed. The largest group we spot is heading across a creek. A bay mare with a blaze does a spectacular head-over-heels fall, but climbs back onto her feet and keeps going. Her foal, a tall bay with a strikingly large star, waits for her.

We see a big black horse Ron says he's broken, an old station horse. When it comes to a horse, Ron has an amazing eye; how he can tell this from such a distance we have no idea, but then Dusty goes low and we see the marks on his back – Ron says it is a mark from the saddle in the heat, something to do with friction caused by salt and sweat. Towards the end we see a tall mule, keeping up a fast canter with its companions.

All the way back to the station, Dusty and Ron talk over the system, discussing where Ron can bring the truck, build the camp, find a fence. They are really on top of things, this adventure seems to be taking on a life of its own, finally gathering momentum. We land. We've been in the air for an hour and twenty minutes.

Back at the homestead, we look at maps, scribbling in places where we've seen horses, where to build a yard or a road, and then Dusty heads off home. Then, before I have had a chance to digest the dramatic happenings of the last couple of hours, we head down to the yards for the next urgent task on our list. For Ron to back Tatti and Starsky.

He pulls a saddle off the top of his red Nissan Patrol, a hefty Australian stock saddle now covered with a layer of red dust from the journey.

'So you've had saddles on them an' that?' he asks me.

'Yes.' I hand him Tatti's bridle.

I stand by the fence with Maria and watch. It's wonderful to watch Ron around horses. He has an easy familiarity with them, and a sort of nonchalance that has them immediately interested and not playing games of avoidance. Everything he does seems almost like an afterthought, almost playful – he makes my method around horses seem so deliberate and so overbearing, so Pony Club circa 1965. First of all he walks around the yard, picking up the odd branch, then he firmly shuts the gate into the next yard. Not content with the chain at the bottom, which might leave the gate looking slightly open at the top, he ties the top shut with bright pink twine from the hay bales. Next he strolls past Tatti, reaches out and catches him by the headcollar, leads him up and down, and then brings him back to the fence. Ron looks him over, feels his legs, notices a scar just above his hoof, and comments that this bad cut was probably why he was turned loose and not taken away by the previous owners. He doesn't even tie Tatti up, the horse just stands there, his ears drooping mule-like which signals to me that he's feeling content and safe. Ron puts on the bridle, but Tatti is so bored by this routine that he hardly even bothers to wake up, and his wayward ears are stuffed under the headband, the bit into his mouth and the throat lash done up in a second. Ron picks up a smart purple saddlecloth, puts it on and then swings on the stock saddle and fastens the girth. For a moment Tatti's head goes up in surprise – he's used to a saddle, but this one is particularly big and heavy. Tatti gets no tea and sympathy, however. Ron is already trotting him up and down, leading him by the length of the reins, and then suddenly he is up and in the saddle and Tatti hasn't even had time to decide what he thinks about the saddle, let alone Ron's weight. He takes Tatti up to the line of fence at the side of the yard and trots him up and down, always close to the wooden fence posts, and turning him inwards, always, towards the fence. Tatti decides that with all he has to think about, the most pressing consideration is the annoyance of having a bit in his mouth attached to reins that are forcing him to flex his neck, so he throws his head up continually but by now Ron has him cantering around in a circle. He brings him back to me, swings his right leg over Tatti's neck, slides to the ground and hands me the reins. The whole riding part of the exercise has taken about five minutes. Ron has played Tatti like a fisherman plays a trout, keeping the line tight, but never jerking against the weight of the fish.

'You think I'll be all right?' I ask rather nervously.

'Yep.'

Excited that the day has finally come, I cram on the black velvet riding hat hoping Ron and Maria don't think it's too sissy and mount. Tatti walks on, trots, snatching at the bit and distinctly off balance, but there's no meanness in him. I feel safe but not yet prepared to canter. After all, with the length of his hooves he could easily trip over them with my weight on him, or at least that's my excuse. He's responsive to my legs if a little fluffy, jumpy and confused. Not surprisingly, seven to ten years turned loose in the bush doing no more than nibbling at grass shoots and avoiding stallions – it's a long time.

Next Ron takes over Starsky. I have put a side-bar snaffle on him as I have noticed that he would really rather the ring of the bit be pulled through his mouth and come out the other side than bother to turn, and within minutes Ron is doing the same with him as he has done with Tatti.

'He'll be fine. Providin' you don't mind about stopping an' that,' Ron says with a laugh, referring to Starsky's mouth. So often a problem with horses that have been used in a riding school: they have been ridden by so many different riders, quite a few of whom seem to believe the reins are there for the express purpose of hanging on, that the horse's mouth eventually becomes deadened.

Then Ron canters him around the yard and up and down the longer fence, always turning him inwards. Starsky tries out a few little bucks for size, Susan calls them 'pig roots'. I decide to pass on riding Starsky today, in fact possibly at all.

Suddenly everything has changed. We've seen Sedna, we have a plan, and we have Ron and Maria.

Just before I went to bed I took my oil lamp and went to the loo. As I sat down I noticed that in the corner of the tiny room, some fifteen inches from my foot, there was a small stack of dead leaves. Strange, what was a neat heap of brown leaves doing in the corner of a room that is always kept so well swept? Then I realised that the heap of leaves had round yellow eyes which were staring at me with a baleful expression. I drew my feet back as the truth dawned on me. Perfectly camouflaged against the polished floor boards was the prehistoric speckled brown body of a frog. I tried not to panic but I was up and out of the room in a flash, into the kitchen to fetch a glass for the glass-and-card-trick. Or perhaps a white cup so I wouldn't have to see the eyes until he was well out of my territory. When he was safely on the lawn and just before he languidly hopped away I could appreciate, in true wildlife reporting fashion, that he had the most perfect shapely legs and cute delicate toes, in spite of his gnarled and knotted skin.

TEN

Queen Bee

Since Ron and Maria arrived two days ago, serious preparations for the venture have been under way and my lyrical dream is turning heavy metal.

Ron, Maria and Susan are talking about creating three temporary yards, each one ten or fifteen kilometres from the station in a different direction. We will then do three separate musters and gather different groups of horses from the three areas. Creating a yard means transporting and wiring together metal panels made of heavy iron tubing, each one resembling a weighty five-bar gate, into two adjoining enclosures, each about eight metres in diameter with two gates. Of course, to get the panels to the right areas we will first have to forge a rough road through the bush using a road grader. We also need to construct hessian wings – double wire fencing covered with hessian, 350 metres on one side and 150 metres on the other, to create a naturally coloured, funnel-shaped approach to guide the horses into the yards. By covering the wire with hessian we will also hopefully prevent any of the horses from not seeing the wire and galloping into it. The intention is for the helicopter to drive the horses a fair distance before they reach the yards to get them tired enough to not be too destructive, but not so far that they could be damaged from exhaustion. Then, after we have rounded them into the yards, we will leave them there for a day or two until they have settled, perhaps even do some preliminary work on them before bringing them back in the old truck to the yards at the station.

So much for my fantasies about sleeping in a swag under the stars and in the daytime strolling around on horseback picking up stray wild horses.

Susan, apart from her day-to-day management of the station, is on the phone trying to organise a helicopter and pilot. The station helicopter, a Robinson 44, is too big and heavy to manoeuvre for the exacting work of horse mustering. We would be better served by a two-seater Robinson 22 which can spin and move close to the ground. Dusty, although a brilliant pilot and cattle musterer, does not have particular expertise with horse mustering. Horses are trickier than cattle, they move faster, and are more likely to separate into small groups. Susan's found someone called Ben, from Kununurra, but he is proving hard to pin down.

Ron and Maria were up this morning at five, collecting the ramp they will need for loading horses into the truck. Both the ramp and the heavy road grader have been borrowed from Tulla, the next door station. They towed it halfway yesterday before the trailer got a flat, very much an occupational hazard in this part of the world. As there was no spare tyre, they had to leave the ramp overnight and go back this morning to pick it up.

Next, they will be knuckling down to the hard work of preparing the tracks we will need as Ron starts on the grading of ten or twenty kilometres of scrub. Until a few days ago I had no idea what grading meant, but now I know it describes smoothing and levelling the ground (could be the remains of an old track or could be virgin territory, still covered with scrub, saplings and rocks), into some kind of a road. In our case it needs to be flat, wide and strong enough to take the truck which will carry the material for the yards in and then hopefully the horses out.

Meanwhile, we have new visitors.

Susan is known to be the Queen of the Kimberley, as there is no one with a greater general knowledge of the entire area than she, be it the land and the properties, or the rock art, the Aboriginal communities and individuals, and even what to do if your vehicle breaks down. She is charming, amusing, loves people, creates delicious meals and is an incredibly generous host. And so people are constantly dropping by. Some are friends or recent acquaintances or even friends of friends, but anyone who can, makes a point of visiting her, bringing with them stories of city life and politics, and gifts. Australians never arrive empty-handed. We welcome the fresh foods and chocolates.

Lea is one of Susan's good friends. She is an American who lives in Sydney and has brought with her two teenage nieces, lots of fresh vegetables, grainy bread and Veuve Clicquot champagne. More to the point, she has bailed me out with a couple of items of which I was in dire need: a large container of vitamin pills, and a family-sized pack of cotton buds for my itchy ears. Susan, the great hostess that she is, has packed up the car with a picnic and taken them off for a good old trek into the bush, while I settle down to the first quiet day I've had here since I arrived.

There is a huge amount of activity and everyone is incredibly busy. What am I doing?

Nothing.

I am sitting on my verandah with my feet up, watching a beautiful young wallaby in the middle of the lawn only about five yards away, eyes like a young doe, little front paws displayed delicately in front, like a lady showing off a fine new pair of gloves.

Even after fifteen years of coming to Australia two or three times a year, I am always thrilled by the sight of kangaroos and wallabies in the wild.

I'm not used to being the Queen Bee, the one with the chequebook, I'm used to being a worker bee, in the thick of things with my sleeves rolled up. Are all Queen Bees lonely?

There are logistical reasons for my Queen Bee syndrome. Out of pure consideration, I am being spared the grind of the heavy work. And we are spread out over different houses and all working in different areas so even meeting for meals is difficult, as it means locating the others. Most of our daytime meetings are chance encounters. Our walkie-talkies only have a four kilometre range, and it would be simply ridiculous for everyone to have to keep breaking off from what they are doing to keep me informed, especially as there is always a moment-to-moment improvisational quality in the way that things are done around here; it is in the nature of the flat tyres, the rusted vehicles, the rugged land. My questions are always answered willingly, and if I can manage to find Susan in her house or somewhere about the property, she usually has a pretty good idea of what is going on.

I stick my head out the front door in time to see Maria flying by in one of the station vehicles, oil drums tied to the back and the dog hanging out the window enjoying the air. It looks like fun.

I could make a point of volunteering more strenuously for heavy duties, but I don't. The fact is I'm rather enjoying my solitary time. Isolation is a familiar state for me and it has its compensations, one of them being its very familiarity. When I was a child living in the cottage of Michael Astor's house in Oxfordshire, at times I would find myself suffering from feelings of isolation that hit harder when you are very young. I was the poet's daughter in muddy red corduroys, cast-offs from Michael's daughters. I felt light-years away from their ivory-towered existence. And so I invented for myself a little tour that took me up the gravel road from our cottage to the main house, Bruern Abbey, into the back door, through the corridor of the servants' quarters under the house and then out over the black and white checked marble floor of the hall into the front drive. From there, I would walk around the manicured lawns to the front of the house, then along a cobbled road below the big terraces and back to the cottage. I walked in a purposeful way, as if very busy on some errand, but in fact I was just wandering along, hoping to run into someone to play with – one of the children, or even a sympathetic adult.

I had my ways of escaping isolation, the most effective of which was to lose myself in the company of animals, especially ponies. To this day, I am never the slightest bit lonely when I am with a horse.

While I am sitting here scribbling in my journal, I am having to keep an eye on the geese who are headed straight for the vegetable patch, though of course, not *straight* because then they would get caught out and chased away. They have a master strategy. To begin with, they are taking the scenic route, coming down the red sand road from the animal sheds, past Susan's house, then strolling past mine, then Andy and Ann's, just beyond which the vegetable patch is situated. One of the geese keeps a look out, while the other forges the path and occasionally stops to pick at something on the road. Most of all the look-out captain is keeping an eye on me, sitting on the steps of my house writing. They play grandmother's footsteps. Whenever I look up, they stop waddling, and pretend to be enjoying the afternoon air. I look back at my work. When I look up again they are about ten metres further on, but appear again to be standing stock still sniffing the breeze or admiring the sunset.

The next time I look up I see the geese have disappeared . . .

I leap onto the quad bike and arrive just in time to find them hot-footing it through the tomato vines in the direction of the precious chard. I give them a ticking off and they set off back to the farmyard complaining loudly.

The thing about the geese is you have to catch them in the act, you have to actually find them waist-deep in the rocket, or else they just deny the whole thing and wait looking aggrieved until you've gone back to your work when they have the perfect opportunity to decimate the lettuce and basil before you can decently get back on their case again.

Andy, Ann and the children have gone to Kununurra for a few days, so I have decided to make myself useful and feed the animals. It can't be that hard, just throwing a bit of feed at poultry and a pig.

I let Wilhelmina, the large piglet, out of her cage while I try to figure out the various vats of food and the details of who gets what. I decide to begin by filling the chickens' drinking troughs. The pig comes along for the ride. She indelicately and insistently snuffles the back of my legs, tickling me with the ring in her nose, until, deserting the chickens, I turn the hose on her, thinking that will teach her to keep her distance. Not a bit of it, she simply adores the impromptu shower and stands stock still squealing with delight. So I move on to preparing her bran swill and with the promise of food I am able to lure her back behind bars. The chickens meanwhile are throwing themselves kamikaze fashion against the netting of their cage, making it almost impossible to get in without letting them all out. Finally I succeeded. They weren't the slightest bit interested in the chicken feed, but virtually attacked me in a manner all too reminiscent of Hitchcock's masterpiece *The Birds*, flying full-tilt at me to get me to relinquish the supermarket plastic bag which they knew contained the household scraps. Once that was emptied on the ground, I witnessed a horrifying beak and claw squabble over who got the knuckle bones from the roast lamb, which ended my belief that chickens were mild vegetarian creatures. By the end of the feeding and watering I had chicken feathers up my nose, pig saliva down the back of my legs, and any amount of gritty stuff in my hair. I was ready for my shower. And there I was thinking I was a country type of a person, well able to roll my up my sleeves and get on with it all in a capable sort of a way. It seems that I am as out of practice with farmyards as I am with riding.

As I potter around fulfilling all my self-appointed outback tasks, observing the immense cunning of these animals on their life-long quests to fill their stomachs, I am thinking, We've located Sedna! The first miracle has happened. Our horse catcher has arrived, and everything is on course. Is it truly possible that I am about to get what I want? My horse? Not likely. Through my life just that feeling of intense longing has always been enough to signal the likelihood that I won't be getting it, whatever it is. The more I want it, the less likely I am to get it, a devilish inverse ratio. Where did this chronically pessimistic attitude come from? Is it possible that this feeling dates right back to childhood and the pony I never got? Will I be able to learn through this adventure to quell those self-defeating prophecies?

It is a well-documented fact that one's sense of power, one's belief in self, comes from those early years, and that through our grown-up years we live with the damage from our childhoods. Lack of self-worth seems to be the cliche of our times. My view is that childhood is like everything else in life: good, bad, positive, negative, and so it is the best possible preparation for what comes after. Our lives are informed in every way by our images from childhood. Adulthood is a great adventure of working them through. Savouring the positive, ferreting out the negative. I always try to remind myself that we have choices in our attitudes. I will find my horse. I have the power to at least try.

•

The next morning, Susan's twenty-nine-year-old son Richard stepped off the mail plane, and came strolling down the garden path in shorts and the classic blue RM Williams shirt, a canvas duffle bag thrown over one shoulder. He has his father's movie star looks and his mother's infectious smile, and at this moment he was smiling broadly with the joy of being back home in the Kimberley.

Richard had come straight from a diving job on an oil rig in the South China Sea where he had been working on underwater repairs. A summer holiday job several years ago for the Paspaley pearling company off the coast of Broome led him into the lucrative but gruelling life of the professional deep-sea diver – and from the strong young boy I had first met fifteen years ago at Carlton Hill, Richard had developed into a man with the physical confidence and the aura of someone whose daily work is testing, even dangerous. From what he told us, sometimes it is purely harrowing, such as when they have to pull up crashed planes and the fatalities from the seabed of the South China Sea or the depths of an African lake. He had just been in saturation, where a group of six or eight divers are sent so deep that the process of descending takes several days in a compression chamber. They live in bunks in a room no more than ten feet by ten feet, and stay to work on the ocean bed for several weeks before ascending the same slow way. As Richard is a writer, the time is useful; it gives him the chance to read everything he can and to write about all the characters he meets and the stories he hears all those thousands of metres under the sea.

Susan had told Richard of the horse project, he had loved the sound of it and had hurried home as soon as he could. Within minutes of arrival he had thrown himself into helping Ron with the heavy work.

Later in the morning Susan and I took a picnic lunch out to the workers. Susan asked me to think what to give them to eat. Ingredients are strictly limited out here, so I came up with the plan of egg sandwiches made with the delicious eggs from my new friends and colleagues the chickens, mashed up with mayonnaise, cracked pepper and sea salt on the grainy bread brought by Lea, and sliced tomatoes of which we have too many. Except at the last minute Susan vetoed this in favour of last week's leg of lamb remains – which I felt strongly was only borderline still safe to eat – some sliced bread that was still frozen, Vita Weat biscuits (which in the event she forgot to pack), tomatoes and some camembert, alas not yet quite ripe. I felt hurt, but said nothing, it would be too embarrassing. We are such good friends, but occasionally and not surprisingly, as we are both strong characters, we enter into a sort of clandestine battle of wills, comparing notes and laughing about it months later.

And so at about eleven-thirty, we set out driving the tray-back the twenty kilometres along the new dirt road until we found our team. Ron was concerned that he had taken the grader off in completely the wrong direction, as wire fences were turning up in unexpected places. But they spread maps out on the bonnet of one of the cars and Richard, who is good at this sort of thing, checked it through with them, made a quick call to Dusty on the two-way radio, and it turned out to be all on course.

This was the first time I had seen the road grader. It turns out to be an impressive and enormous yellow piece of machinery with a digger in front. I had no idea that this project would turn out to have such Herculean aspects, including heavy machinery, extra crew members, extra time and the purchase of half a kilometre of hessian. I had naively supposed that we would have been out catching wild horses more or less a day or two after Ron's arrival. From the looks of things, costs would be soaring. The pound was strong against the Australian dollar which worked in my favour, but I didn't envisage seeing much change out of Auntie Christine's money.

We prepared the billy. We built a wood fire in the road, lighting it with the air cooler from the Toyota that Maria had been driving, which in a timely way had just burst into flames and had to be removed from the engine by Ron and Richard in true heroic fashion. Then an ancient black kettle was hung on a wire contraption in the middle of the fire and Bushell's tea leaves thrown into the black kettle after the water had boiled. We drank tea out of chipped enamel mugs.

Richard is enormously enthusiastic and capable, and ribs Susan in an affectionate son–mother way all the time. I had believed she was infallible until the interaction with Richard at which point I realised – according to the teasing she was getting – she might have a little less idea of what she's doing than I thought. For example, it appears she is not quite clear on the technique of how to read the hand-held GPS that she religiously carries around with her.

'Rich, this doesn't seem to be working. Look, I punched in 53L 1214231 UTM8297664.'

'Mum, that's the reading of where we are now, not where we're supposed to be going.'

'Oh yes, darl. I see what you mean.' Susan laughs in a slightly embarrassed way, going a little pink as she does on the very rare occasions she gets something wrong.

Celia once said to me, 'The thing about Susan is that she's always right about everything, and I don't mean she is one of those people who can't accept being wrong. I mean she is always right.' And it's true. With the odd exception that proves the rule.

In the afternoon I offer to feed the chickens and the pig. Susan, in an act of sympathy against the constraints of the caged life, had pinned back all the doors and had let the animals out about an hour earlier.

'Oh don't worry, they'll drift back to their own pens at about five, ready to roost,' she assured me.

Not a bit of it.

A mob of chickens met my arrival with excitement bordering on hysteria, flocking towards me in a mini charge of the flight brigade. It was half-past five and the pig was on their heels, snorting a welcome. She appeared to be entirely covered in black tar.

By the time I got into the feedshed, I found Wilhelmina was in there with me, she'd stopped slobbering down the backs of my legs and had devised a more constructive plan. As I'd opened the door to the cool room to get the chicken feed, she'd hurled herself in behind me. She'd obviously been lying awake planning this all night and before I knew it she was making a quick advance towards the sack of high-performance horse feed. I gave her a shove with my foot in its soft leather trainer, at which point she promptly bit me. Not really a bad bite, more of an insulted, 'Heh, watch your manners!' bite. I chased her back out of the shed, banging the metal scoop against the walls and bins, and once outside, gave her the bran as quickly as possible to keep her from making any more attacks on my body, I had to water it down into swill with the hosepipe over her head, as she refused to wait while I mixed it properly. Two of the pullets had their heads in the old enamel saucepan along with the pig, but all attempts to remove them were met with furious squawks. Any minute now, I thought, a chicken head will disappear into the pig's mouth along with the swill, but quite frankly I was beyond caring. I chased the last few ducks into the further pullets' pen, sprinkled around a few more pots of chicken feed and then headed home pretty sure that there was still the odd duck wandering loose and a few chickens in the tool-shed laying decorous clutches of eggs inside the boxes of giant screws and car parts – the chickens' favourite laying venue of the previous year. We got about ten beautiful eggs that night. I had a sense of great achievement on that aspect.

Susan made pumpkin risotto for dinner and Richard's favourite dessert, a truly wonderful crème caramel that traditionally she always made for her sons whenever they came home from school. Ron and Maria came over from the Hilton, and we ate under the stars by candlelight, and then went indoors and watched the videos we had taken of all the horses we have seen from the helicopter, those we'd seen while out driving and on the trip to Kalumburu. I asked Ron which ones he liked. He likes the small greys with the rather Arab look that we'd seen up at Kalumburu, and the big milky white steed we'd seen running with the black broken horse from the helicopter on the day of the recce.

Saturday 7 August

Round-up day is now scheduled for Tuesday, although it is still dependent on availability of a suitable helicopter and a pilot with horse-mustering skills, and from the two that Susan is chasing, we have not yet had a definite confirmation. It is also dependent on us finishing the extensive preparation work. Ron's time with us is limited, and I was booked to leave in less than three weeks, so the problem of where the horses should go and live could be as little as two or three weeks away.

My plan is to find somewhere to send Sedna until I have time to make proper arrangements to spend time with her and train her, somewhere where they would be well looked after, where I can visit. Susan says I mustn't worry yet about what to do with the horse, where to send it, she believes it will most likely still be far off transporting, too wild and unsettled, and she could be right about that.

'So what should I do with her?'

'Leave her here.'

'Oh, if that's okay with you . . .' But there was another thought tugging at the back of my mind, an uncomfortable notion, a fear. What about the Call of the Wild? A fence broken by a fallen tree in a storm, or a gate left open, and it would be so easy for a horse to get out and impossible to find it again. I think of Dusty's little brumby that he had trained and grown fond of, which had just disappeared one day never to return.

I think of Monty Roberts and Pat Parelli in their glamorous media-conscious worlds, and their films about catching wild horses. Both had the help of extensive back-up: film crews, family, co-workers, horse trainers, vets, saddle horses, large sums of money, well-padded horse trucks, not to mention their own extensive experience. Watching their films, I was surprised to see that neither of the two wild herds in question seemed to include stallions. We have the possibility of bringing in more than one stallion and having vicious fights on our hands. Even one stallion on his own could be dangerous to us. Parelli and Roberts seemed to know exactly where to find their horses. Admittedly both were working in *considerably* smaller areas of 'wilderness', both seemed to be working in comparatively flat and accessible terrain, while we have trees, trees and more trees, dried-up creeks, full creeks, gullies, hills and everywhere, knee-high spiky grasses hiding who knows what in the way of roots and holes not to mention snakes. A lot of horses and dogs out here get killed by the snakes.

At lunchtime we found the workers almost at the end of the road they are grading. Today they have begun grading the planned temporary yard, in a clear flat area just before a hill. Richard has been helping Ron. They are into all sorts of projects, welding together bits and pieces of scrap from the 'resource yard', in other words, a sort of scrap dump. At lunch, the conversation between them becomes man to man.

'Reckon there could be a wheel spanner in the dog box of the Louisville ball truck?' Richard starts for openers.

'Nah, happened to notice that the extension lead on your sprogget snapped,' Ron replies.

'Ah. Right. What about the one and a half inch sprogget leads in the scrump box? We got them?' queries Richard.

'Could be on the grader, I reckon that's got spiders down both sides,' Ron states.

'So what d'you reckon on the Necrofil – bleedin' down into the hatchet hole?'

'Use chicken wire.'

'Ah yeah? You reckon?' Richard retorts in surprise. He helps himself to a biscuit. 'Got any more tea, Mum?'

Late in the afternoon I saddled Tatti with the second-hand pigskin saddle and, watched by Maria and her dog, mounted. After all these years with so little practice, I'd been nervous about riding Tatti on my own so I'd waited until I could persuade Maria to come down to the yards with me. It's the first time in all my life that I have ridden a horse in my own saddle.

My sweet Black Beauty was an angel and walked and trotted around gracefully, all the time fighting with his own highly strung temperament, but never with me, even the head-tossing settled as I was sure it would once Tatti got used to a bridle again.

For the last couple of days there have been a few stalks of the local spiky grass, maybe about three or four inches long, stuck to the mosquito-netting door of my house at about eye-level, blown there by the light breeze that is sometimes strong enough to create a mini whirlwind in the middle of the road. I keep meaning to rip the stalks off and throw them into the shrubbery. Yesterday, as

I was coming in the door, the grass stalks got up and walked across the wire mesh door. I stood there with my mouth open watching them making their way off onto the house front – it was a very *Alice Through the Looking Glass* moment.

It's quite hard working at my computer in the dark, after the generator has been switched off as it is every night at about nine-thirty. I work by the light of the oil lamp and the torch, and what is indescribably irritating is the insect life that takes to scurrying all over me and the computer screen, as it appears we are the brightest objects around. All sizes of things with wings flutter nearby. They specialise in exploring the glowing map of my face, with tiny fluttery feet, and best of all they like flying up inside my nose, as I am a Russian, flared-nostril type of person, added to which, tonight for some reason, maybe the lack of moon, there are some really big things dive-bombing around the room.

And because there is no moon, there are stars . . .

I've just walked back from the other house. I had to stop and spend time staring up above, being reminded of childhood visits to the Planetarium in London, and having believed all through my adult life that stars never looked as good as they did at the Planetarium. This part of the world confounds that thought. Here, in the Southern Hemisphere and in a place so far from city lights, the sky is filled with stars burning with more luminosity than I have ever seen; a firmament condensed with layer after layer of these pinpricks of light, and behind, the Milky Way wafts across the centre like a soft background mist. The experience of the stars alone in the Kimberley is enough reason to come here and, sitting in the dark staring up at that sky, it feels that nothing can go wrong, that I am being looked after, protected, that there is a natural order of things beyond my power, that all I have to do is trust.

ELEVEN

The Killer

Sunday 8 August

I've been here thirteen days, Ron and Maria five.

Sounds like the pig might be for the chop house, snuffled her last snuffle, bitten her last trainer-ed foot. Richard is volunteering to do the deed and even to hang the prospective barbecue in the room next to his down at The Donga (the name of the little house where he is living), with a bucket underneath. I dread the sound of a shot across the yard. They say that pigs scream when they are taken to slaughter, but Wilhelmina screams all the time, so it doesn't seem that her life is very enjoyable. Any moment she spends not physically gobbling food, she seems to regard as physical torture and mental anguish, or am I just trying to assuage the guilt before the dreadful day comes?

Last night Susan and I did the feeds together after dark. There were only three eggs. Wilhelmina charged the door of the feed shed at the same time that Susan was trying to go in herself, resulting in Susan suffering a bad cut on the corrugated iron of the shed door. I have always known that it's hypocritical to be a carnivore and yet say you mind about animals being killed for meat, especially around a farm, but now I am confronted with the hypocrisy in me. I'm loath to give up meat. I once read a very comforting study which asserted that we are not evolved enough to be able to give up animal proteins.

At eleven we went out and made smoko (morning teabreak) for the toilers down at the path they are grading to the second site. After completing the road to the first site, Ron decided that out of the three projected temporary yard sites, the second one he had found was probably the best and so we are now concentrating on this one. Low hills either side of the valley create a natural funnel effect. By the time the horses are brought over the rise at the end of the helicopter muster, they will already be between the hessian walls, but less likely to notice because of the naturally sloping land on either side.

It's getting really hot in spite of the breeze, but Ron doesn't let that faze him, he works on regardless all day, never faltering, never once complaining in spite of the monotony of the work, not to mention the constant flat tyres. I believe that Ron and Maria are both inspired by the idea of the horses at the end of it all as they both adore horses.

There was a lot of talk today about finding a cow and killing it for beef. The cow is rather unfairly and inaccurately called the 'killer' even though it is the one being killed. I don't know why I'm so shocked; these cattle are destined for the Indonesian meat market, and at least this way one animal doesn't have to suffer the long journeys by truck, the waiting in the yards with hardly any shade down by the port in Broome, and then the long crossing across the Timor Sea to Indonesia.

There was a skinny small grasshopper in the shower with me last night. It was perched on the inside of the shower curtain and I was trying to get it out without it getting wet. Here I am trying to save the life of a grasshopper, but willing to accept a pig or a cow being shot. Why? I suppose the beef and pig killing is not in my hands, and I'm trying to make the adjustment to country life.

Monday 9 August

I have been here exactly two weeks. It feels like half a lifetime and the rest of the world, as it gears up for the Athens Olympics, seems distant and irrelevant.

After lunch the men went out to finish grading the road down to the second temporary yard site. On the way back, they're picking up dinner. They take a roll of sharp knives with them.

'Wanna come?' Richard asks me.

'No thanks.'

They'll take whichever cow fate throws in their path. I suppose it's not really that much different from shooting a rabbit, it is just a bigger animal, with big brown eyes, a wet nose, and that melting look of a Brahman cow which resembles that of a young girl wearing a cloche hat.

Richard likes to wind me up. It's part of a paradoxical element in his character, two sides living together in a state of partial truce. One minute he'll be talking to me about his novel with the sensibilities of a sensitive and observant writer, next minute, after a couple of beers, boasting how a couple of days ago, he ate the sweetbreads of a cow that fifteen minutes earlier had still been inside the living animal. When he looks at me and comes out with these lines, I feel that he is testing a part of himself for its resilience. If I wince and look shocked, then he feels saved – being a writer has not turned him into a wimp. I call it the Ernest Hemingway syndrome, the inner conflict of the action man and the artist.

Maria let slip yesterday that Ron wasn't at all happy with the meals we've been feeding him, Nigella Lawson's pumpkin risotto, my spaghetti bolognese which I was so proud of.

'No offence, but if a meal doesn't have beef ribs or steaks, it isn't a meal,' Maria said. 'That's just the way he is, just the way he's lived.'

One thing is for sure, the way Ron is working, steadily from crack of dawn ('sparrow's' as it's known, short for sparrow's fart), he needs feeding and deserves to be fed whatever he likes. Richard has been making his feelings felt too. 'Oh, Mum, not risotto, again. Can't we have some meat?'

At six I went down to the workshops. The deed had been done, the boys had picked up dinner, and pieces of cow were hanging along a clothesline under the fluorescent lighting – it looked no worse than any old-fashioned butcher's shop. In fact I was already doing a head count, and then a 'cuts of beef' count, and wondering if there was going to be enough for a few good meals.

The rhythm has changed again, with postponement of the round-up, while we wait for the helicopter pilot, and the arrival of still more guests on the mail plane, Jeff and Gemma. Jeff is a retired 'silk' and Supreme Court judge. When they arrived we got into a social groove, with lunch on the lawn and then almost immediately afterwards, we headed off down to the river to cook ourselves a sunset barbecue. I had thought that Ron, Maria and Richard were turning up to join us, they'd been invited, but as it grew darker, it became evident that they weren't coming. I started to get nervous, it was all very well sipping our gin and tonics and counting the first stars in the sky, but I felt that I was twiddling my thumbs, fiddling while Rome burnt. On the way down to the river, the conversation had been ninety-nine per cent about Australian politics, a subject about which I am woefully ignorant. I felt I was in the wrong dimension, ignoring my responsibilities, not doing what I have come all the way here to do, which is quite simply immerse myself in horses, catch my horse and write.

We watched a pair of black cockatoos fly past. Usually they stop in the tree on the river bank but tonight they just went on past, even they were shunning us. Then as night fell, which happens very quickly in this part of the world because it's so close to the equator, we stoked the fire under the metal barbecue plate and threw on the beef ribs and steak from the 'killer', and potatoes.

'This is beautiful fillet,' Susan said to me.

It grew cooler and we brought our camping chairs closer to the flames. The others attacked their ribs, Flintstone-style, and I tried to cut my steak. No go. The knife made no impression whatsoever, no matter how hard I sawed. I tried picking it up in my hands and chewing one end. 'Ah, well, it will be chewy,' Susan had admitted as I lifted the meat off the barbecue. I was prepared for chewy but my teeth made as little impression as the knife. I might as well have inserted a hard lump of rubber between my jaws. I put the steak back on the barbecue and picked up a rib. Tearing Flintstone-style on the ribs was a more successful venture.

The truth is that Ron and Maria seem to avoid our company. I think they have been scared off by the first few days of Nigella Lawson's finest recipes, the romantic table settings under the stars with candles and the table strewn with bougainvillea. They prefer to eat every night with Andy and Ann, and from across the lawns we hear screams of raucous laughter. They don't scream with raucous laughter when they are with us. I feel even more out of sync, and I have to admit to being a little hurt. They have been here a week and I hardly know them. I'd so much rather be with them and talking about the outback, horses and horse breaking, hearing stories from their experiences, than Australian politics with Jeff and Gemma.

Later, in the small hours, as I was woken at 3 am by a friend from New York, Gale, who had got the time difference wrong, I was wide awake and thinking in overdrive about the future.

At the valley site, the temporary yard is complete and the access road almost finished. Now we're just waiting for the helicopter pilot to turn up on our radar screen. We are possibly only thirty-six hours off the big round-up and apart from sending a few vague emails to friends asking if anybody has any ideas, I've done nothing about the looming question of the transport, housing and fate of my horse. Susan says it's too soon to plan, but I don't really think it's right to have no plan when there could be the fate of a living animal at stake.

Susan's philosophy is quite different and very interesting, and I am determined to keep an open mind to her way of planning, or rather *not* planning. She believes that planning is dangerous, not to mention futile, as it is based on the imagined version of future events; and how often do the real events follow the course of the imagined road? Not often, so why make plans based on a purely invented future, when in the course of that planning you could come up against imagined problems – and therefore put yourself off completing a task, following a dream. She therefore appears to regard most planning as negative thinking. For her, a fall-back plan is a plan to fail. Of course there is another possibility, that Susan sometimes has more of plan than she lets on, but by keeping it out of the discussion, she retains more power.

My friend Gale has another point of view. She always plans, she figures out what needs doing, decides on a positive path and leaves no stone unturned following it through. She is crystal clear on the subject of priorities and responsibilities and her reasons for following a particular course of action. She is the person I try to talk to when I get confused on these issues.

Another high-achieving Australian friend, Greta, gives me a different viewpoint which throws a possible light on Susan's mysterious workings. Greta never likes to discuss the ins and outs and pros and cons of a plan because in her mind she has already carefully thought through all the possible outcomes and therefore considers discussion a waste of time, even a danger as it could dilute resolve. In fact Greta considers it somewhat insulting that anybody would question her about the smaller details, or the path of decision, as in her mind she has it all figured out and so any questioning shows a lack of trust or respect. Maybe this is how my good friend Susan thinks, as sometimes I get a distinctly cross look or tetchy reply when I ask her (yet again) about horse breakers or the future plans for the horse I will catch.

Which brings me to one of my character foibles that I like to think is no more or less in the past. In my younger days I harboured a tendency to abdicate my power to a stronger personality – not even necessarily stronger – and in a rather lazy way, to stop thinking for myself, only afterwards realising that if I had kept thinking and not opted out, things could have worked out even better in the long run. I have to be alert to that tendency.

Now, when I have a decision to make, I conduct inner and outer research to find out what I think, I explore options and even ask other people's opinions. I regret this if it suggests a lack of confidence, but I don't regret the process itself, as it gives me a freedom, an unpredictability, not being locked into an habitual way of thinking, and for me it is interesting exploring different viewpoints.

Susan says my horse, if we succeed in catching it, can stay here for now, and while I have settled for that in my mind, I know I need to think for myself. Somehow I didn't manage to convince her that there is no disadvantage in having a plan for what happens to the horse, if we get it, and that this would not be a plan to fail.

This isn't about convincing Susan, though. It's about doing what I think is right. I have every intention of carrying on with the clandestine phone calls and emails, investigating possibilities of how to move my horse, and where to keep it. Because who actually would be looking after the horses after Ron, Maria and I go?

As I lie here in bed and the clock ticks beyond 4 am, I can hear Houdini, the cockerel, crowing, and in half an hour Ron will be up and starting his day. He is working hard, going to bed early and getting up at sparrow's, while I have been up late sitting on river banks sipping gin and tonics and being called 'Patsy'.

Richard has come up with the amusing notion that Susan and I are like the characters from the English comedy series 'Absolutely Fabulous', only we're Ab Fab of the outback — and the idea seems to have taken hold. Watching videos of Susan and me in our hats and Paspaley pearls, setting up our billy and fussing around, I have to admit, he's one hundred per cent right. As long as I get to play the sexy Patsy.

Wednesday 11 August

Today we visited the second yard which the boys and Maria have finished. It is at the end of the most magical valley, with a creek and tropical plants, everything is a vivid green.

'If I was a horse, this is where I would be,' Susan said. I was trying to put out of my mind that I would be taking Sedna away from this little slice of horse paradise. I remembered that a horse's life is never that perfect, that safe.

Last night, Jeff and Gemma told me the story of the Snowy River brumbies. The government decided that as wild horses were not an indigenous species, merely feral, they should be culled on the basis that they were interfering with local indigenous flora and fauna and their hooves were damaging the terrain. They sent men out in helicopters to shoot them, and word filtered through that the men were not doing the best job. Not all the kills were clean, they were leaving horses suffering and wounded, abandoning foals to die of hunger beside their dying mothers. Outrage grew until the locals were so incensed that they went and stood in the park themselves to protest and the shoot was called off. This happened only a year ago. Could the same thing happen here? Susan says that while Celia and Michael own Athenrai, nothing could happen to these horses. I hope she is right.

At the moment in this area the government is shooting donkeys. They have sent out two good-looking young guys in a helicopter with a battery of guns and ammunition. I've met the men, and they seem like nice enough fellows. We ran into them a couple of times when we were out bringing smoko to our road graders.

They have a strategic plan. First they go out, find a donkey and shoot it with a stun gun. They then land nearby and put a collar with a radio homing device around the donkey's neck. A little later they come back into the area, find the tagged donkeys who are travelling with a little mob of others, then they shoot all the donkeys from the helicopter *except* for the tagged one, letting him, the 'Judas' donkey, go free to lead them to others.

In the late afternoon I took the saddle and bridle down to the yards. I thought I should give Tatti a quick walk around.

The geldings are in a mellow mood at the moment. It must be the salt lick; between them in just a few days they've eaten most of a twenty-kilo block. Starsky walked up to the gate leading back to the wilds. I thought for a moment he was going to use his long teeth to simply unlatch the gate and then amble out, such was the purposefulness of his approach. Instead he just stood there, gazing out. As if that didn't make me feel guilty enough, he then turned and stared at me with a contemplative air, with almost a dreamy expression on his face. Maybe he was just thinking how nice it was to be safe and looked after instead of being chased from pillar to post by horny stallions staking their territories for their mini-herds. Then he yawned, about three times. Ron told us that horses go back to the place where they spent most time to die – I wondered if I would find any of these four lying motionless in the paddock before I leave.

Thursday 12 August

The latest is that the helicopter musterer can come on Friday afternoon, and work Saturday and Sunday mornings. Ben wasn't available, but Susan has tracked down an expert in this field from Fitzroy Helicopters at Fitzroy Crossing. His name is Grant. He is one of that rare breed, a pilot with the necessary skill and experience to muster horses.

Susan and Richard came back from visiting neighbours with extraordinary news.

They'd seen Sedna! She was galloping along beside them as they drove through the bush, only a couple of kilometres from our temporary yard, her tail carried high like an Arab, and her tall foal behind her, giving a few little light-hearted bucks as they travelled, and behind the foal, the chestnut stallion. 'She looked like she was teasing us,' Richard said. 'Flaunting herself – catch me if you can – and by God, I'll tell you one thing, she looks as fit as anything, and was she going *fast*.'

'So you think I've chosen a good horse?' I asked him.

'Oh yeah.'

I felt *so* proud of my wild horse.

Friday 13 August

It's almost midday, and Jeff and Gemma have just left on the mail plane. The plane was rather smaller than usual and heavily burdened with passengers, several rolls of carpet and other cargo. Peter, the pilot, brought his weighing scales out onto the tarmac and took a reading of the somewhat weighty ex-judge and his diminutive wife, then he fiddled with his calculator, making a few additions and subtractions on his clipboard. It seemed that Jeff would only balance if he sat in the front seat. Dodger, the young man already sitting there, was unwilling to relinquish his bird's eye view up with the pilot, but it was the only way they were going to be able to take off. It was a bit of an awkward path up the stepladder with Susan and the pilot pushing the judge from behind into his seat. Rose, the Aboriginal artist from Kalumburu, was sitting behind, hardly visible, squeezed in next to a large cage holding a blue heeler being returned from the Kununurra vet. She was making sympathetic noises: 'I know how hard it is, I'm an old person too, not easy for us flour bags.' She was referring to the judge's and her shared hair colour – white.

Meanwhile, Celia's daughter, Genevieve, has just arrived in the station helicopter, closely followed by a couple of her friends, Rachel and David, driving a big white Toyota Land Cruiser. They had been camping in the area. I don't know whether I have been in some kind of trance for the last few days, but either no one mentioned Genevieve's intended visit, or it has all been very last minute. It gives me the uncomfortable feeling that they have come to check up on us crazy people. Are we crazy? After an initial feeling of intimidation, I realise I am feeling rather relieved. It is, as it should be, that the family have someone here to see for themselves what is going on.

It's nine o'clock on the night before the muster and I am snatching a few quiet moments before the fray.

We're back in the house, supposed to go to bed early as we are getting up at five in the morning. I'm holed up in the smaller bedroom, but it's no longer the quiet house as Genevieve and her friends have moved in and I can't help overhearing their conversations, mostly about the frog in the loo.

A new frog has appeared, this time a big green one like an apple cut in half, with sinister glistening jet black eyes, and this time in the toilet bowl itself. This is bad news, because although a frog in the loo can be flushed away, the solution is only temporary and they invariably swim back up and resume readiness to leap up at you as soon as you are comfortably seated.

It happened to a friend of mine.

'You know how you imagine it would be, a frog jumping up and getting you, and how you imagine how awful it would be,' she paused in a reassuring way. 'Well, I want to tell you something, it's much, much worse, cold and wet and *tight*.'

Genevieve and Rachel are both young doctors and vegetarian. I have had two weeks of being told I'm a city sissy to steel myself against the physical risks, the possibilities of horses hitting their noses on the walls of the temporary yards, broken legs, stallions fighting, but these newcomers are still appalled at the possibilities.

Susan counsels not to think about whether a horse will be hurt because that is negative thinking. Not so the young things in the house, they are thinking about it. Genevieve is thinking about it all the time, and calls her sister in Melbourne to share her anxieties, and just at the point when I thought I had talked myself out of the same worries. It's a small house with thin walls and so I overhear phrases like 'stallions with broken legs' and words like 'carnage'. It is my project and I suppose at any point I can say, 'Enough is enough' and stop. I can command the wheels to stop rolling, but for tonight, I am just going to sleep.

In the afternoon we went up to the temporary yard – the only one that really exists as we haven't had enough iron gate, hessian or manpower to create the other two – and finished putting up the remainder of the hessian. Wire fences had been stretched up either side of the hill from the yard, so that any horses coming over the brow of the hill would find themselves galloping down into a funnel of hessian walls, and with any luck, into the yard before they knew what was happening.

Suddenly, standing there in the valley which looks for all the world as if the sculptor Christo has wrapped it as a work of art, I realised that it is all a possibility – more than that, it is actually going to happen.

I rode back from the temporary yard in the passenger seat with Ron driving, in a bouncing banging wreck of a vehicle, dragging a float behind us, my left foot wedged against the doorway of the car with no doors, so that any severe pothole encounter would not actually result in my being bounced out of the vehicle. We exchanged only a few sentences in the twenty-kilometre journey, but that was nice, it was companionable, to sit in silence and think, the tension of anticipation in the air. Ron does not feel the need to fill silences with strings of words, and nor do I. Anyway it took a good deal of effort to be heard above the rattling of the car.

He tried a couple of times. 'By this time tomorrow, we'll know if we have horses or not.' Ten kilometres later, he turned in his seat and smiled at me. 'Maybe we'll have horses in the yard. *Maybe…*'

So I sat there in my bouncing seat thinking over the events of the last three weeks, the experience of the Kimberley. I was thinking how I wanted to describe the red dust road, going through the bent white birch-like trees, with the vivid green leaves of the eucalypts, the creeks with their dark waters and fronds of palms all around, and how addictive it all is and how it reminds me of Africa, or at least the way people write about Africa: the space, the atmosphere and the huge skies.

One day many years ago, I turned on the radio and heard my godfather Laurens van der Post talking. He was describing a mountain in Africa that had hardly been looked at by humans; it still had its primitive power, because nature, rocks, mountains and rivers that have been looked at too much get used up. The idea stuck in my mind, and that is what I feel about here, the Kimberley. There is a force and an energy in the land here that it would be wrong even to try to describe because it isn't about words, it is about feeling yourself to be part of it.

What did I think this expedition was going to be? Mostly I thought it would be about a few of us rounding up wild horses on horseback, because I had forgotten about the trees that are everywhere and the difficult terrain. Really, I didn't think, I just dreamed. And now it is the night before and we are on the verge of it actually happening, and it's turned from this gentle dreaming plan to *Bridge On the River Kwai* meets *The Charge of the Light Brigade*.

TWELVE

The Horse Muster

Saturday 14 August

Today is the opening ceremony of the 2004 Athens Olympics.

Brumby is not a breed of horses. It is a name or a term used to describe feral horses breeding wild in the Australian bush, descended from domesticated horses that either escaped or were abandoned. This could have been from as long ago as the goldrush years of the mid-nineteenth century up to the present day. Brumbies do not conform to any standard type as with, for example, the New Forest pony or the white horses of the Camargue; their look is not even as uniform as the look of the American mustang. Their appearance is dependent on whatever breeds happened to be around that area but are usually largely based on Australian stock horse, a small, hardy, Thoroughbred type (until the 1960s more commonly referred to simply as station horses); they could also include Arab, Percheron, quarter horse, Welsh, or Timor pony. There were stations where the owners or managers took a real interest in breeding and importing good horses. I heard of a station manager in the Kimberley who liked quarter horses and so invested in a good quarter horse stock, another in Queensland who brought in Percherons seeking substantial bone in the breeding.

Brumbies are known to be clever, cunning and enormously tough. Natural selection in their breeding has taken care of that. A friend once told me a story. When he was in the army, stationed in Queensland, their commanding officer decided that the regiment needed a mascot, a drum horse, and what better horse for the Australian Army than a brumby, an appropriate choice because so many horses in Queensland are descended from Walers – the horses used by the Australian Army during the First World War. The soldiers knew that mobs of these horses were still around because when the men were up in the hills at their high-range firing area they could see brumbies milling in the area but there was never any need to move them on because by the time the gun batteries had unpacked and organised the equipment for live-firing exercises, they had all, to a horse, disappeared.

So the CO sent out six of his best soldiers, country boys who had grown up on stations and knew how to ferret out brumbies, in a couple of Land Rovers. Several hours later the gunners returned, sweaty and exhausted, the vehicles all beaten up by charging through the bush, but with no brumby. Obviously, the CO had to admit, he had underestimated the cunning of the target, the exercise would take more effort. Well, an airborne assault should do the trick! And so the CO sent out a Kiowa four-seater army helicopter, a vet and two sharpshooters with a stun gun, and an accompanying ground party. The horses seemed to be making themselves a bit scarce but eventually the men sighted an ideal target. (Or, as my friend described it, a grey blotchy one.) They swooped down over the cantering horse and the sharpshooter hit a bullseye on the brumby's rump almost immediately. But the horse just carried on cantering. The vet scratched his head and prepared another dart with an adjusted dose. The sharpshooters fired again, another bullseye. 'Any minute now the horse will fall to the ground in a deep sleep,' the vet told them confidently. An hour and a half later the helicopter returned to base having almost run out of fuel. No brumby. The horse had shown no signs whatsoever of dropping and no replacement had been found. The Australian Army had to admit itself outmanoeuvered by the enemy, and hired a professional brumby catcher.

'Are you sure the so-called professional found you a brumby, and didn't just go up the road and buy an untrained horse off a station?' was my immediate question.

'No, I'm not,' my friend answered, and laughed.

Grant, our expert musterer, had arrived the night before in a two-seater helicopter. He was too late for a practice run but in time to join us for a very jolly dinner outside under the stars. We barbecued beef and lamb chops, and pumpkin for the vegetarians, and ate it to the background music of Rod Stewart and the master of Australian country and western, Slim Dusty; we talked and laughed with the excited atmosphere of the night before a great adventure. Later we moved inside and showed Grant the videos we had taken from the helicopter with Dusty, and in particular, the footage of Sedna, while Ron discussed terrain, tactics and the placement of the temporary yard.

All alarms were set for 5 am and, as I slid out of bed into the watery sunlight and made myself a cup of tea, I was feeling surprisingly blank, a little like exam day at school, only pleasantly excited too.

By five-forty Susan and I were sitting at her table, just the two of us, drinking coffee. As usual we were talking sixteen to the dozen. I had dressed as Susan had instructed in as near as I could get to camouflage, desert khaki from head to toe, my classic LL Bean safari shirt (I've had it for about twenty years and I think this trip is the first time I've used it), over very ancient chinos bought about twenty-five years ago. Susan, contrary to her own advice, was wearing recently purchased bright pink linen trousers, gleaming white linen shirt and, of course, her Paspaley pearls.

First Grant set off in his helicopter to try to find and muster the horses we'd seen on so many occasions close to the road that leads up to the station: the two liver chestnuts and hopefully, the little group including the dark brown stallion and the tall dun foal that had so caught my fancy. We thought this would be the easy lead-in to the day's mustering, a plan with an almost sure-fire success and to those ends we had covered the fencing near the gate into the yard with hessian and built another wing of hessian sloping in on the opposite side. Ron thought we could run this lot straight down the road and into the paddocks as they were usually to be found hanging out quite close to the homestead.

After about forty-five minutes Grant returned. He'd had no luck; he hadn't seen a single horse in that direction, which was surprising and felt like an inauspicious start. My spirits sank. Was it possible that horses in the intuitive way of animals might have sensed the drama in the air and might have hidden in their most secret hiding places, or even left the area?

After all, it is a fact that animals can predict natural catastrophes and know where to go to keep themselves safe. We pulled down the hessian from around the cattle yard, loaded it onto one of the trucks, and then at 7.30, broke off for smoko and a conference.

While we ate Susan's fruit cake and swigged down coffee, I brought out my computer and showed Grant the photos of Sedna taken last year by Peter Eve. I was anxious that he should recognise the horse if he found her.

Richard emerged from the house and yelled, 'Mum? Have you put the rifle in the car?'

'Yes, darl.'

'And the bullets?'

'Yes, darl.'

'You sure we got enough bullets?'

'Richard!' I snapped. 'Could you just *cool* it?'

'Well, we have to take a gun. In case any of the horses break a leg, we'll have to shoot them.'

'We know that, Richard, we just don't need the song and dance.'

I certainly didn't need to be reminded, nor did Genevieve. I felt caught between the devil and the deep blue sea; I couldn't admit to the fleeting but haunting visions I was having of beautiful horses with broken legs. I was trying hard not to imagine Richard or Ron with a gun, even Susan holding the rifle to her shoulder. That is how it is out here in the outback, not for the squeamish.

At eight-thirty, we headed off in assorted vehicles for the temporary yard. Ron and Grant took off for a recce in the chopper. When we reached the site, we finished wrapping the fencing on the left side with the extra hessian we had brought from the home yards.

I stood and looked along the length of the enchanted valley and thought about how I might be taking a horse away from this idyllic spot . . . But that was the human way of thinking. I thought about a horse's point of view; horses would not just stand around admiring the view, they would judge the quality of life on a different basis, starting with a plentiful supply of food, water, security and safety from predators, followed by physical comfort and shelter, a surrounding of grass and space, and with four-legged company and the security of the herd coming very high on the list. While this valley could provide most of these items some of the time, so could I. I could promise even better returns on food, freedom from parasites and treatment of injury or disease.

As I stood in the valley that was now our horse trap, the sense of partial unreality returned. The next few hours would reveal the outcome of the weeks of planning and preparation. It was still not too late to say no, to stop the whole thing dead in its tracks. I saw the helicopter arrive and Ron and Grant step out. Of course, they all thought that I was mad, throwing all this effort and money into this round-up when for the sum I was spending on this adventure, I could buy myself an exceptional animal, already trained for dressage or show jumping. In somewhere like Kununurra or any small country town away from a city, I could probably find a decent enough animal for as little as four or five hundred dollars. Ron, who collects horses like some people collect stamps, probably has ten or twenty that I could choose from. But my fellow musterers were also intrigued and thrilled by what was going to happen, the adventure and the prospect of seeing these beautiful horses close up.

The men walked quickly over from the improvised heli-pad and met up with our little group. They were smiling.

'We seen a group of horses not that far off,' Ron reported. 'We think they'd be good 'uns to start. Didn't seem that worried by the noise of the chopper an' that. Just lifted their heads, took a look at us, an' then went back to grazin'.'

'Are they ones that we've seen before from the helicopter?' I asked.

'No,' he said. 'Them are different. If we can get hold of this lot, they look quiet enough an' that, might encourage other horses not so quiet to come into them yards.'

Grant took off again, this time on his own, lifting the red whirring bird into the sky, and we all retreated towards our posts, and checked our walkie-talkies. Ron and Maria were taking a tray-back high up to the other hillside, ready to drive in behind the horses once they were nearly in the yards, persuading them to keep on going. Richard and Andy lurked among the trees on the quad bikes, ready to whiz down and shut the gates behind the horses, and the rest of us waited in the shade up the side of the valley beside the horse transport vehicle, ready for the arduous work of watching, photographing and applying sunblock. It was amazing how it was all coming together, like when you are a child and you wait all those endless days and nights for Christmas, then suddenly there you are under the tree unwrapping the presents.

I had spent most of the time back at the temporary yard helping put up the hessian, and in vigorous silent prayer. Of course I was hoping madly that after this year of dreaming, we would be bringing in Sedna, her foal and even her stallion, but most of all I found myself praying for the safety of everyone, the wild horses and those involved in the front-line work, Grant in the sky and Ron preparing to throw himself into the midst of the wild horses. With the reality of the day was coming the reality of the dangers and the risks; nothing could be worth serious injury of horse or man, or even, God forbid, now that I was starting to really frighten myself, death. The truth is, my fear was back and this time probably with good reason. I was really scared, though I couldn't admit it to anyone, and all I could do was to take things five minutes at a time. I could call a halt to the muster now – in theory. I had the power to stop it now just by saying so. Or did I? Watching everybody running eagerly to their posts, I realised the venture had taken on a life of its own. I had come so far . . . I could not let fear of the unknown stop me now. I knew I had to trust Ron; he knows the country, he knows the risks, he knows the ways of horses, and he loves them, he would never knowingly do anything to hurt or damage a horse, though being the sort of man he is, he would probably be less careful with his own skin. I just had to let go.

I perched on the back of a truck, away from the others, and prepared the video on its tripod. I waited in silence with just the sounds of the bush and the cicadas. I felt I needed to be alone.

The others were chatting quietly, sitting with their backs against the wheels of the truck. Susan pointed out to me a few cattle grazing at the side of the valley, and at their head, a magnificent Brahman bull. At long last the sense of fear began to leave me, transmuting into pure excitement and anticipation.

After just thirty minutes or so, we heard the chopper returning, and then crackles and confirmations on the walkie-talkies that Grant was coming in, with horses it seemed.

It was happening.

I hardly know how to describe the magic, a line of equine heads, high in the air, their manes and tails flowing out luxuriantly behind them, appearing over the brow of the hill, running alongside the hessian. It was a heart-stopping moment. Real horses, no longer fantasies, that were coming in from the wild.

At the moment they saw the entrance to the yard, they slowed, swung around for a few steps, then saw the car and helicopter behind and turned around and carried on into the yards. Grant timed it perfectly, backing off with the chopper, so that miraculously they entered the yard at a trot, not a dangerous gallop. The horses came to a stop at the end wall of gates, swivelled around to canter back, but already the gate had been closed behind them.

We had our first brumbies, and we ran down the hill to survey them, approaching very slowly, quietly, and standing back from the bars so as not to stress them.

It was a group of nine, led by a tall, elegant brindled palomino stallion, mature and wise, we felt, a perfect gentleman of a horse standing in front of his group of mares and yearlings, assessing the danger of the human animals approaching the pen. He was not apparently distressed, just curious, and protective of his harem. The mares and youngsters immediately arranged themselves as far away from us as possible and with their hindquarters facing us, the stallion standing between us and his herd. If we moved around the sides of the pen, the horses would quietly rearrange themselves. It appeared to be a set course of action, a herd response. I was amazed that they seemed so unflustered, so calm, like this sort of thing happened to them every day. After all, these are horses that have never seen people and as the horse whisperers tell us, to them we are just other animals, the worst thing about us is that we are carnivores, so we smell bad. Apart from the noise of the chopper and the shock of finding themselves confined, the unusual sounds, the human voices, these horses have no experience of bad or frightening treatment from humans to give them reasons to fear us, only fear of the unknown and unpredictable.

Reluctantly, because we all wanted just to sit and watch, we left them to acquaint themselves some more with their situation, and headed back up the hill while Grant took to the skies again. It was important that we all be in position and away from the yards by the time he appeared with the next group, which could be at almost any time.

By the time he came back about forty minutes later with the next mob, the first lot were quite settled, adjusting to their new circumstances, and some of them even resting a back leg and dozing. Another thrilling line of heads and long sleek backs appeared above the hessian, and within minutes we had our next band: a rich dun stallion, chunkier and smaller than the palomino, with a couple of mares and youngsters. This was the most worrying moment, finding out how the two stallions would deal with each other. Everybody has heard stories of stallions in the wild fighting to the death and after a couple of beers, some of our menfolk had been quite liberal in the spreading of such stories, in true boy-fashion, the gorier the better. This second stallion, though, simply hid behind his mares and foals. Whether out of respect for the authority of the first stallion, or because of a wimpy nature, he certainly chose the path of least resistance. Again we ran down the hill to have a good look, but kept our distance from the rails so as not to frighten the horses, but after five minutes or so we were sent back to our posts.

The next mob Grant brought in I nicknamed 'the teenagers'. There were four of them, feisty and fun – the human equivalent would have been wearing leather jackets and chewing gum, and probably riding Harley Davidson bikes. They were young testosterone-packed males, thrown out from their herds because they would have been old enough to be considered rivals by their stallion, and ganging up for company until the moment came when they would be large and strong enough to go out and fight for their own mares – no different really to the human equivalent. There were two chunky bays, a skinny young chestnut with a white blaze and a dark dun who could easily have been the younger brother of our second stallion. As before, Ron waited ten or twenty minutes, and then in order to clear the outer yard for newcomers, he threw the teenagers in with the others. There was little a skirmish, horses charging around, a muddle of horseflesh and then the first stallion emerged from the centre, taking charge, sending a mare here, a yearling there, until he had things to his liking again.

The first stallion, the dark palomino, was proving himself undoubtedly the king, so I named him Rex, and the second stallion Mr Wimpy.

By the time Grant came back the next time, Rex had things well sorted. All the horses that were not from his herd were crammed into one-quarter of the temporary yard; Mr Wimpy was pressed up against the railings behind all the rest, while Rex's mares and youngsters were free to roam the remaining three-quarters. Then Rex dozed quietly in the middle, hindquarters facing the foreigners, and any horse from either side unwise enough to move from his position got a sharp nip or reminder kick. His self-appointed position as top of the hierarchy was achieved with minimum fuss, virtually a foregone conclusion.

There was still no sign of Sedna.

This next group brought a surprise, a tall black mule, with the body of a compact horse, the long ears a testament to the father (a mule being the product of a horse mother and donkey father). With such sterling stallions in charge of the mares in the brumby herds, it's a wonder that mules happen at all, but we had seen a couple from the helicopter. The donkey stallions, jacks, in the bush are tough creatures, willing to tear a horse stallion to pieces to get to a mare, and fighting to the death when vying with a rival jack for a herd of jennies.

The mule had come in cantering tight on the heels of a magnificent chestnut stallion with a crooked white blaze, tall and very muscular, probably about fifteen hands – a couple of inches smaller than Rex – but more solid in his build, which made him seem enormous. With him came a raggle-taggle group including a scruffy cream-coloured foal with a faint white blaze. It was surprising that such a beautiful and substantially built stallion as this chestnut should have such a motley bunch as a herd; it seemed to all of us that he deserved better. Now that we had two stallions worth their salt, pecking order in became more of an issue, and there was more charging around as they jostled for position, more dull *thwacks* of kicks, and the nips became more like bites.

After the ritual inspection and photographing of the new acquisitions, we retired back to the hillside to boil the billy. It was a strange feeling. We had horses. I have no idea what we talked about. I was spaced out.

The new chestnut stallion, it appeared, was causing trouble. Rex was searching him out to make sure he fully realised that Rex was boss. Rex was shaking his head, starting to rear and snort, and in response the bold chestnut, unlike the wimpy dun, was starting to demonstrate his own masculinity. Ron and Andy moved the chestnut to the narrow passage reserved for when we would eventually load the horses onto the truck. The new stallion made a couple of attempts to rear up against an eight-foot wall of metal, and then retired to posing, looking for all the world like a stud-book illustration, legs spread evenly, head held high on his deeply muscled neck, turning every now and then to watch us. Horses would come to visit him, one by one pushing their noses up to the metal bars to meet his in greeting, like Mafia members coming to pay their respects to a chief. Meanwhile, back in the main yard, Rex was making the most of the new situation and was busy appropriating the new stallion's herd. The sight and smell of a few untried mares was more than he could resist and so he took time off to mount one or two – how like a natural-born world leader to find time for that, even when the responsibilities of leadership were so pressing – while all the poor cuckolded chestnut stallion could do was look on.

I'd lost all track of time, and although I'd occasionally glanced at my watch, I'd hardly noticed what it said. I was high on the excitement, and the long periods of time in between the arrivals of the different mobs of horses seemed short. It was probably already two o'clock. We had sent Grant up once more to look for Sedna and he had been gone such a long time that we were becoming concerned. We tried to contact him on the walkie-talkie but he appeared to be out of range.

I was sitting on the hillside, alone with my thoughts, looking down at the yards and watching the chestnut stallion posing and occasionally pawing the ground. It was bringing to mind a new idea.

The crooked blaze, the striking bright chestnut, the angular appearance, powerful build, the obvious star quality – it was just possible that this statuesque creature was the horse that I had seen the year before on the first day, the horse that I had chosen and

Celia had given to me. The second day, when I had gone up in the helicopter with Dusty, Chris North and Peter Eve the photographer, we had found in almost the same place a horse that we had thought was the same one we had seen the first day, and immediately swooped down to photograph it. I remember being surprised at the time that the horse from the second day had long white stockings as I had no memory of them from the previous day – white socks, maybe, but not stockings. I also recalled the look of the first horse being rather more angular, with a higher tail carriage, and so thought the softer curves of the horse in Peter's photograph, the low-set tail streaming behind, had to have been a trick of the long distance lens. This was certainly a stunning stallion. A name for him sprang to mind: Pluto, another planet, not so far from Sedna, larger, better known.

The truth was beginning to dawn on me: who knows how many striking chestnuts with blazes and any combinations of stockings and socks are running around those many square kilometres that we'd flown over? They say that for every horse you see in this part of the Kimberley, there are ten more hiding, and the week before in the helicopter, we'd seen about forty. Chestnut with a white blaze seems to be one of the dominant colourings for horses of the area, and of the twenty or so we had just brought in we all had the feeling that they were horses we had never seen before. What I do know for sure is that Pluto is not the horse from the photograph on my computer, the horse that I have called Sedna. Sedna is the pregnant mare from the little family of three.

Finally Grant called in, and Susan walked over towards me holding the walkie-talkie, smiling. I could hear crackling down the line, she was relaying as much as she could hear on to me.

'Grant? Yes. Good. Three chestnuts... Good. Maybe Sedna,' she said aside to me. 'Yes. Grant? Duns and palominos? Sounds like a big mob, Grant... good. Well you just try. Fifteen minutes?

I'll tell Ron. We'll be waiting for you.' As she signed off, she was smiling. 'Three chestnuts, do you think it's Sedna and her family?'

'Who knows.' I hardly dared think, and at the same time, I was already making plans. Three horses: Sedna, her stallion and her foal with the flaxen mane and tail, what could I do with three? I'd have to take all three, I couldn't possibly break up the family, that would be missing the point, causing damage. I'd have to ask Celia but she would surely approve. She would see the point of not separating the horses. I was breathless with excitement. Of course it might not be Sedna but that was not the way to think. Think positive. Grant had seen the photos and video of Sedna. He knew what he was doing.

We could hear the helicopter getting closer. We returned to our waiting positions, then heard the helicopter retreating again, approaching, retreating, then stopping entirely. Susan yelled across that Grant had called in again that for the moment he had lost the chestnuts, but was still trying with a large group of palominos and duns.

Lost the chestnuts . . . There was not even time to take in the thought as a mob of horses came into view over the top of the hill, another moment of heart-stopping excitement. Ron and Maria swung out in their vehicle, but these horses were smart, they saw them coming and disappeared out of sight again, over the brow of the hill, followed by the helicopter. I could see the tail of the helicopter swinging and gyrating and then disappearing downwards, lower than the height of the hillside in front of us. I think the toing and froing went on for about half an hour, and then to my relief Grant called in to say he was giving up and bringing the helicopter back. No horse would be worth Grant risking his life with this low-flying battle, and it was clear that these horses had earnt their freedom.

Later, over a barbecue that night, Grant told us the story.

'Mustering horses is so different from cattle. With the brumbies, you're trying to muster such a large area and you can't run them all together and run them into the yard, like cattle, because they will split up into their family groups with their stallion and lead mares. What I have learnt over the years is that it's better to bring in a group at a time, pick on one mob, try to steer them in the direction of the yard, then sit back, letting them think they are going the way they want to go, not rushing them, not distressing them, though it's good to run them a bit of distance because then they will be tired and less likely to hurt themselves once they get into the yards. If you have two groups you go with the faster lot, otherwise if you are behind the slow lot then the fast ones will take the opportunity to head off at a tangent and the slow ones follow. So it's better to stick to the fast, then come back for the slow.'

He had gone further afield for the last search, nearly twenty kilometres away into one of the other areas we had planned for a separate temporary yard. He had found a group of three chestnuts and twelve duns and palominos, and started running them in but when the chestnuts had separated, he had stayed with the larger, faster group. He was unable to say whether the chestnuts had included Sedna. He had run them maybe twelve or fifteen kilometres.

Then, as he came over the brow of the hill towards our yard with the duns and palominos, the lead mare in front and the stallion behind, as is usual, the stallion saw the car at the side of the valley, realised what was happening, and came forward right under the skids of the helicopter, which at this point were only around fifteen feet from the ground. Apparently the stallion's head was snaking along the ground, his ears flat against his head, pushing in front of his mares and turning them back. What a star of a stallion. The one that got away.

By now it was three o'clock. We'd done all we could with this area, we had about twenty horses in the yard, and I felt it had been some kind of miracle, as they were all remarkably calm and organised. I stood in the middle of the group, Ron, Maria, Susan, Andy and Richard on one side and on the other side, Genevieve and her two friends. It appeared there was now a choice and it was up to me to decide. We could pack up and go home with the horses we had, or dismantle this yard and try one of the other planned areas, put up the whole caboodle fifteen kilometres away on one of the other sites.

We had spent all day in this one place, more than eight hours of helicopter time, and although Grant said that he was not tired and was willing to go on, this already represented a huge financial outlay. Grant told us that he felt we had covered the terrain around all three of the proposed sites. We had also covered almost all the areas that we had seen from the helicopter on the recce, and, interestingly enough, I don't think we had brought in a single one of the horses we'd seen that day, so one thing was for sure, there were plenty, plenty more out there. I looked at the group around me, Andy Susan, Ron, Maria, they were all game to go on, though no one seemed to be totally convinced we should. Genevieve was expressing the opinion that we had plenty of horses and should start choosing the ones we wanted and turning the others free.

There have been times in my life when my decisions have been informed by dreams – not wish-fulfilment dreams but night-time dreams. I had a recurring dream as a child. I dreamt that I was standing across from a giant playing a sort of ball game with those brightly coloured balls the size of small footballs that we used to have as children. Every time I won, I got to keep the ball, and the low rack of balls next to me was getting fuller and fuller. I had about fifteen but I kept thinking, just one ball more, and then I'll have enough. I had a strong feeling I was running a great risk, but kept rationalising the greed – what harm could one more make – and I kept winning, but each time I won the sense of risk grew greater. The rack was almost full and there must have been about twenty balls. Then someone said to me, 'What's that on your back?' In my dream, I twisted around and looked over my shoulder and there was some kind of creepy little figure crawling up my spine, a translucent figure, I remember, in bright colours, red and blue and some kind of tall black hat. I can see it to this day. I knew it meant that I was as good as dead. I had gone too far with my avarice and this was the punishment. I knew the dream was allegorical, it was my own private 'tempting providence' cautionary tale, to which I have adhered – often – in my life. So far we had escaped without injury to man or horse; no disasters, no broken limbs. We'd been careful and we'd been lucky. Would it be tempting providence to go on? But we had not caught Sedna. It was tempting, of course, so tempting, to try to go on, to continue, while we still had Grant. Then I looked across at the yard full of beautiful horses.

'I think we should take what we have and go home,' I said.

Richard pulled Susan aside; he was upset. I could only half hear snatches of his impassioned speech.

'Mum. You can't let Lizzie stop now . . . This is her dream. We have to help her follow it through . . . She has to find Sedna.' He was telling Susan, not me, so I let it ride, but I was impressed. It was so much a part of the two sides of Richard's character that, in the end, he was the romantic, the one fighting for the fulfilment of my vision.

I was still looking at the yard where Rex was arching his neck and shaking his head at his mares; Pluto posing at the side. There were enough dream horses there for any mere mortal. A feast of discovery. I was already in a state of shock. Having waited all my life for my own horse I was now living my Sir Lancelot moment where I could choose from a beautiful herd, just take my pick. Yes, of course I was feeling disappointed and sad that after all we had not found Sedna and to have lost that last herd, the duns and the palominos, but what were the chances of finding her if we pressed on? Not great. Brumbies are very clever and cunning, the last stallion showed us that, and they say you only have one chance with a brumby. If you miss the first time, then you will never succeed. If Sedna was in the area then she would have escaped us at some point during the day. Maybe that group of three chestnuts had indeed been her and her family. I believed in my heart it was time to go home.

Susan and I have discussed it since and, in retrospect, we think we might not have been thinking straight to have even considered continuing. The amount of work it had taken to put together that yard, to have dismantled it and built another with all the fencing and hessian and the limited man and truck power, would not have been possible. Anyway, we didn't really have the time to set anything up quickly enough to justify Grant staying on a day, and to have brought him back across the Kimberley would have been a huge expense and possibly days, even weeks, of waiting until he found a free day or two. As it turned out, Ron, Maria, all of us had our work cut out dealing with the horses we already had.

Ron had decided it would be better to get all the horses back to the station yards straight away. We did not have the facilities to feed and water so many horses so far from the homestead and he felt it better to get the added trauma of the truck journey over. We begun taking down the hessian from the wire fencing as Ron loaded the truck; I was half afraid to watch the main event – Ron, Richard, Andy and Maria loading the first twelve of the wild horses onto the beaten-up truck where they would have to stand together, hopefully not fighting too much, stallions mixed with mares and the mule and even foals for the ride back to the station, which in such an old truck, the weight of all the horses and the red gravel track would take a good hour. The loading seemed to go remarkably well; there were the thwacking sounds of hooves against ramps and jostling of horses kicking against old tin and wood, but in a surprisingly short amount of time the truck was ready and setting off. Once it was moving I knew that the horses would settle and simply concentrate on keeping their balance. Those of us remaining on the site set to work taking down the hundreds of metres of hessian sheeting, pulling out the wire strips holding the cloth on the fence and then dismantling the wire and posts, until finally that was done and the quad bike contingent left.

As the afternoon shadows lengthened and the light turned mellow, it was just Susan and me, left alone to wait by the yard with the remaining ten horses. We sat quietly watching the miracle of this little yard, discussing the day's events, observing the young horses, picking out our favourites, discussing them.

Even with only ten horses in the yard it was a constantly moving kaleidoscope of horseflesh, always rearranging themselves, pride of place being as far as possible from us; if at any time we moved closer to the enclosure, we would be presented with a row of multi-coloured hindquarters and long tails. At the other side of the yard, heads did occasionally come up for air and to get a closer look at us, with foals peeking through under their mothers' necks to see the strangers. Ron had taken both of the lead stallions in the first load, Pluto the chestnut and Rex the palomino, and so in lieu of a grown-up, fully qualified male, proceedings were now being dominated by one of the teenage contingent, a good-looking dark bay, a young stallion, whom I immediately named Cassius Clay because he was distributing kicks all around like Cassius delivering punches in the ring. Somehow it didn't seem to bother the remaining horses, but I found the constantly repeated thuds of hoof against horseflesh quite worrying. In the middle of the group and periodically coming up to the front as part of the constant rearrangement were two pretty dun youngsters who had come in with Rex. They had immediately caught my eye, not only because with their cream coats and black manes and tails they stood out from the crowd, but also because of an air of serenity that possessed them both, a calm eye, and the good-natured way with which they took Cassius's repeated punches, quite literally on the chest, without a murmur.

That night we had another barbecue under the stars. We told stories of the day's adventures, Grant relating the tale of the palomino stallion that got away, Maria describing the kick that went within an inch of Ron's head. We were all excited, and looking forward to getting to know the brumbies and watching Ron work.

THIRTEEN

Yards Full of Horses

Sunday 15 August

Our first day with our wild horses. I was awake at the crack of dawn, and couldn't wait to get onto the quad bike and down to the cattle yards. Once I was there, I sat on the ground protected by the heavy wooden fence, watching the horses, watching their games of dominance, watching them watching me.

Last night after Ron had brought the first load of horses down to the homestead yards, the ancient truck had coughed, expired and refused to start again, so we'd had to wait until the morning for him to fix it and fetch the other horses.

At about 8.30 he arrived back with the second load. He and Maria had managed to get all the remaining horses onto the truck with little trouble, he told me. They'd seemed easier to load than many so-called domesticated horses, and they had travelled comparatively calmly.

After a few nerve-racking minutes of the thunderous clattering of hooves against metal, the horses had started to come down the tunnelled ramp, one at a time, each one tentative, first walking, and then once on solid ground, trotting through the outer yards to join the rest, and each and every one with the free and floating gait that I associate with a well-bred horse. I sat watching: first the two dun fillies, then the young chestnut with his blaze, Cassius with his more rounded young stallion look, a young dark dun colt, and a few bays, Ron funnelling them all straight into the yard.

The gate was shut after the last went through and the truck lurched away leaving the horses to start on the serious task of sorting themselves out. Again I was struck by the churning mass of horseflesh that has become the trademark of this venture, the dull thud of Cassius' kicks, chipper after his night alone with most of the young fillies. Rex had disappeared into the centre of the fray, but suddenly my eye was caught by the most dramatic sight, Rex's head with its ragged mane rearing up from the centre of the churning mass and rising high in the air – looking for all the world like a horse sculpture of the ancient Chinese Tang dynasty – his ears back and lips drawing away to reveal jagged yellow teeth. Then, as I scrambled onto the fence to get a better look I saw his head plunging down, grasping the base of Cassius' neck just in front of his withers; from there he shook the young upstart hard, several times. I could swear poor Cassius was actually lifted a few inches off the ground. I was astonished that, in less than a minute, Rex had picked out the young male from the bunch that had started to get ideas of dominance, not that Cassius was doing any serious stallion posturing, just a bit of kicking. Rex must have picked up on a slight swagger in his step. It was astonishing that he had had the strength in those teeth to shake five or six hundred kilos of solid horseflesh. For the next week Cassius Clay was as good as gold, there was no biting and his back hooves stayed firmly on the ground. In no uncertain terms, he had been shown his place in the herd.

In all the imagined scenarios of events, who could have predicted that the first stallion we would bring in would instantly take control of the entire situation, assuming authority over the extended herd, organising all the horses and keeping them calm and unafraid, leaving us humans standing at the rails, mere onlookers. Rex, in spite of circumstances that could have had a lesser horse panic-stricken, fighting or running, just got on with his job. I was awestruck by his raw beauty. I've observed many stallions in my life, including spectacular Lusitanian stud horses, the very best champion pure-bred Arabs and star Thoroughbreds from the Kentucky racetrack, but never one with the authority, the nobility and the sheer common sense of Rex. But then I have never seen a wild stallion work a herd over which he has had total control without the interference of man.

I can hardly believe that we've done it, brought in wild horses, and not just a group of brown brumbies, with a watered-down stock horse look. I am more than ever convinced that I am looking at horses with exceptional breeding there, somewhere in their ancestry. To my mind, because of the way they move, this breeding has to be Arabian.

Monday 16 August

It is now forty-eight hours since the beginning of the muster and we're all a little shell-shocked.

We have twenty-two horses down in the cattle yards. Or at least, I think it's twenty-two. I've tried counting on numerous occasions, but they are all moving around so much, jostling for the prime positions, and the little foals are so hard to see, hidden behind the mares that it is difficult to tell.

I'm still tremendously relieved that all went so well. Admittedly some of the horses have scuffs and knocks from the walls of the truck and the rough posts around the yards, but nothing too serious, mostly just scratches or black patches of skin where the hair has been knocked off. This is not only a gift of divine providence, it is also attributable to the expertise and instincts of those involved: Grant, bringing the horses into the yards just tired enough, then backing off with the helicopter so that they trotted in; Ron, working out his yards and hessian tunnel, building them, planning with Grant, and then looking after the horses once they were in the yards, ever watchful, separating Pluto and Rex; Richard's help building the temporary yard; and Maria, tending the horses. And of course Susan, her planning and organisation had worked out perfectly. The eight hours of helicopter time turned out to be fifteen, including the travel to and from Fitzroy Crossing. I'd written out a huge cheque. Auntie Christine's inheritance was dwindling fast, but I know she would be smiling.

I went back down to the yards and leant over the railings watching Pluto. Ron has put the three lead stallions – Rex, Pluto and Mr Wimpy – in the same yard. Maria came and leant on the rails with me.

'See how they aren't fighting?' she said. 'That's because they don't have any mares or fillies in the yard with them to fight over.' She was right. They were standing around positively slouching, a back leg resting, indulging in the odd ratty snap at each other, but no masculine posturing.

The remaining horses, mares, foals and youngsters were still inter-mittently jostling around their pens with the dull thump of kicks, as they established their pecking order, but as they are not shod, they seem not to hurt each other. Otherwise they were quiet. Wild horses, as I read in Monty Roberts' books, are amazingly silent. Domestic horses start calling to each other when they are sepa-rated, the wild ones know better in case there is an enemy nearby.

With the yards full, the whole feeling of our venture has changed dramatically: it has gained a centre. No longer are we spread all over the property hardly catching sight of each other all day. Now we are trying to spend as much time as we can around the yards.

In the next few days, I have to think about which horse to take. In fact, I am talking to Susan about taking two. Any horse I took would need the security of a friendly equine companion from the Kimberley to survive the new experiences of the next few months. After all, I would be moving these horses across the Australian continent to start a new and very different life in the countryside near Sydney. Even the climate there would be dramatically different. I had left it to Susan to call Celia and keep her posted with the events of the muster, and it made sense to let her ask Celia about the possibility of my taking two horses instead of the one she had originally given me.

I'm endlessly leaning on fences and staring at the horses in the yards and then rushing up to Susan's house to have a discussion over a cup of coffee or glass of lime juice. This is such a big decision, and I want to get it right. Should I take Pluto, the big chestnut stallion, who could have been the original horse? Or would it make more sense to take a yearling, maybe the chestnut colt who is the clone of Pluto only young and a little frail? Would I dare take Rex, the beautiful king of the stallions? Or one of the bay mares in foal (almost certainly to Rex)? What about the two attractive dun fillies who caught my eye the first day? I've decided to take as long as I need to decide, whatever the pressures, after all I've waited long enough, thirteen months – or forty-six years – whichever way you choose to look at it.

The first step is for Ron to start working on the horses. That way I will have the chance to observe them in action and discuss the possibilities with him. The horses look calm enough, in their yards, eating hay, resting after the long distances they ran two days ago. I have no idea how they will react to his work with them.

In Broome last year, while sitting in the welcome cool of the

Kimberley Bookshop, I read a very moving story. I can't remember the title of the book or the name of the author, but the story (which was from the author's life) went from memory as follows: This man was an experienced horse-breaker, and on one of his trips out to a station he had been shown a few brumbies someone had managed to round up. He was particularly impressed by a tall roan mare and decided to work on her in the round yard. All went well and, after some preliminary work, he got to a point where the mare was standing at the side of the yard, comparatively calm, though still nervous, allowing him to approach. He got closer and closer to the mare until finally he was near enough to feel her breath on his arm, conscious of the steam rising from her vibrating body. Without looking at her, he slowly reached out to touch her on her neck. With this level of success so soon, in his mind he already had the saddle and bridle on, and was proudly taking this beautiful horse home with him. Very slowly, he stretched out his hand the last few inches and placed it on the mare's neck.

She dropped stone dead at his feet.

Whatever fears I had, Ron seemed to be taking it all in his stride. He was excited – not that his emotion was expressed in words, or in any way other than his evident concentration on the horses, the way he would quietly watch them, as we worked around the yards, giving them hay and water.

By the time I made it down to the yard this morning, well after eight, Ron was already working on one of the yearlings, one we had named Juno. He had a rope around Juno's neck and was doing the control pull, based on the technique of the original Australian horse whisperer, Kel Jeffery. She was a nice looking youngster of a very slight build, with that calm generous eye and rather pure look that seems to shine brightest at the yearling stage. She was bay, but the brown of her body had an elegant red tint. She had a nasty gash in her chest and a cut on her face.

Maria was sitting on the top rail of the round yard, watching.

'That's why Ron is working with her first. We need to get her treated,' Maria said. 'We think she was kicked by the mule.'

'We have two doctors in the house. Genevieve and Rachel are both trained doctors,' I told them.

'Ah, yeah?' Ron answered from his position the middle of the ring, not for one minute taking his eyes off the young horse circling him. 'Good. Couple more hours an' I'll bring her up to the house.'

I called up to the homestead on the walkie-talkie fixed to my quad bike. The doctors set about gathering their materials. Then I went to look in on the other horses.

Rex was now in a small enclosure on his own, or at least he had been on his own until early in the morning when the mule had fallen in love.

Mules are the offspring of a female horse which has been impregnated by a male donkey. In appearance a mule can be either male or female, although because of their chromosomal make-up they are not able to procreate, either with each other or with horses or donkeys. Mules can be a little confused . . .

The mule and the wimpy stallion had been put in the pen next door to Rex. Early in the morning, watched by Ron and Maria, the mule had attempted to jump an eight-foot-high metal fence – from a standstill – and had landed squarely on top. There, he had hung in the balance, stranded, swaying backwards and forwards, his belly resting on the highest rail, until he was able to tip himself forward, landing without a scratch at the feet of his king, Rex. What a fickle animal that mule was. He came into the yards close on the heels of the gorgeous chestnut stallion, and now has formed a passion for the more masterful and classy palomino, and even if Rex does occasionally kick or bite him – but most of all, ignores him – the mule puts up with it all without complaint. They make an odd couple.

By the time I got back to the round yard, Ron had Juno trotting calmly around him, turning in to him in total obedience. The transformation was nothing short of miraculous. Within the next hour, Ron was able to run his hands all over her body, pick up her feet and even persuade her to lie down. Within an hour and a half, she was in a headcollar and he was leading her the kilometre up the track to the homestead. She appeared to be enjoying the whole experience, loving being stroked by everybody, jauntily stepping along, stopping to sniff the quad bike, no longer worried by its noise. The only time she appeared to be the least bit agitated was when Ron left to go to his house to pick up pliers. I resolved to watch the next horse-breaking session more carefully. Maybe Ron had just chanced to hit upon the one youngster from the group that was naturally quiet and gentle.

Ron picked up her front leg and brought her down until she was lying on the lawn. We gathered around, Maria stroking her head with her leg across Juno's neck, Rachel's boyfriend held onto her back, while the girls prepared their suture equipment. Juno's skin was so thick that Rachel and Genevieve had to use pliers to pull the nylon line through, and apart from a couple of minor attempts to rise to her feet as the needle went in, Juno was a model of bravery. At the end of the hour long treatment, she lurched back up to standing and although limping a little, appeared to hold no resentment. Ron and Maria rigged up a small yard behind the Hilton, the size of a large loosebox, so they could keep an eye on her for the next few days and she could avoid the rough and tumble of the other 'teenagers', and to make it easier to give her the daily dose of antibiotics.

In the afternoon I went down to visit the old geldings, who have been woefully neglected the last few days. They followed me into the yard, expecting me to produce the magic silver bucket. Once inside, they did a double take at the sight that met their eyes. The yard – previously their yard – was now divided in half and the three big stallions stood in the first half. In the second part, now also divided, stood the mares and foals. Jester, Maria's light chestnut gelding, had walked in just ahead of the geldings, and if ever I have seen a horse drop its jaw in amazement, this was it. Starsky, Hutch and Tatti's heads flew up in the air, they took a good look, decided they had seen all they needed to see to make an assessment of the situation, and then headed back to the paddock at an urgent trot, cantering as they reached the gate in a rush to see who could get out first. I suppose because the wild horses had been so silent, only Rex allowing himself the odd snicker, the domestic horses had been blissfully unaware of events happening only a few yards away, hidden from sight. Why they hadn't smelt the strangers, I've no idea; perhaps they have lost some of a horse's keen sense of smell with age.

I led Tatti out of the geldings' paddock to give him a feed. The pony, Tonka, followed us and then refused to go back in. It would be easier to move a mountain than move Tonka when he refuses to go. His strength in stubbornness vastly outweighs his physical size; the stubby legs are planted firmly, if crookedly into the earth, the thick neck goes up from his body at a defiant right angle, head slightly sideways, and from this vantage point he glares with one glassy eye in glittering hatred. I found it distressing, trying to convey to Tonka that my intentions are good and being confronted with such unadulterated suspicion and loathing.

I thought of little Juno, a wild horse who had never seen a person and now was happily being led anywhere we cared to take her. From what I had read, and was beginning to see for myself, the joy of these wild horses, and also the responsibility, is that they are clean slates, full-grown yet not tainted by ignorant, cruel, or over-indulgent treatment. By the same token, their future behaviour and happiness will depend on the treatment they receive in the next few days, their impressions and the decisions they make about the best way to deal with us.

We let Tonka stay outside the paddock. By dark he was standing by the gate, but we decided to leave him out until the morning. I can't help feeling sorry for this horse, he is his own worst enemy.

Tuesday 17 August

Last night we sat out on the lawn under the stars, drinking vodka and tonics, and listening to Rod Stewart singing American songs of the thirties, perfect for cocktail hour in the tropics. Now that we could provide beef, Richard, Ron and Maria had joined us again. We were pondering horses' names. We have Rex, because he is the king of stallions, Cassius Clay the champion boxer, we've named Pluto and Juno after planets. The wimpy stallion became Mr Wimpy, and the coal-black skinny mare with jutting hips who arrived with Rex can have no other name than the Black Witch.

'And we have to name two of them Olympia and Athena, in honour of the opening of the Athens Olympics,' Susan said.

'What about the two dun yearlings?' I suggested, thinking of the two fillies that had caught my eye right away. They were both dun, or buckskin – a pale creamy gold with black manes, tails and points. One was slightly taller and the other, although probably about the same age, was of a more compact build and Arabian look. They had come into the temporary yard in the first group, with the stallion Rex. Ron calls them 'creamy-coloured', and he lights up when he talks about them. But he doesn't believe that they are sired by Rex. He thinks the duns are the offspring of some other stallion.

That seems to be the way out here – rampant infidelity and blatant cases of mares pulling the wool over their stallion's eyes. You can see a chestnut stallion wandering around with a bay mare

Ron Kerr. MARIA TOMLINS

Maria Tomlins with one of the youngsters. LIZZIE SPENDER

One of the Brahman bulls in the bush at Athenrai. LIZZIE SPENDER

The Caterpillar grader, a necessity on all large outback cattle stations. LIZZIE SPENDER

Taking the panels out to the site of the temporary yard. RICHARD BRADLEY

Grant in his Robinson 22 helicopter – the best chopper for mustering horses. LIZZIE SPENDER

The second group: Mr Wimpy and his band come into the yards. MARIA TOMLINS

Rex keeps watch while his family turns the other cheek. LIZZIE SPENDER

Cassius Clay in the foreground getting ready to take over lead stallion duties for the night. Just visible on the left is Mr Trouble. LIZZIE SPENDER

Rex the King and his harem, only five minutes after arriving in the temporary yards. Olympia's head is showing behind Rex on the left; Athena is on the right. MARIA TOMLINS

Top: Ron works for the first time with Olympia in the round yard and with Athena (*centre*). LIZZIE SPENDER

Below: Athena on her second day of training. MARIA TOMLINS

Kevin Collins and me in Broome. I'm wearing his
racing colours. SUSAN BRADLEY

The elegant Olympia is sprayed for cattle ticks at Derby. LIZZIE SPENDER

Olympia and Athena showing off their paces in Kangaroo Valley. LIZZIE SPENDER

The gentle giant Pluto.
LIZZIE SPENDER

Father Sanz's original Arab stallion, Summer Safari,
a few months after his arrival in New Norcia.
SARAH SMITH

and with them, a foal of some completely different colouring, such as a dun or coal black. You feel like saying to the stallion, 'Come on. Who do you think you're kidding? Move that fore-lock of yours and take a good look at Junior there.'

Perhaps this signifies a brisk trade in changing of partners, which would be good news as it bodes all the better for chances of limiting the inbreeding, because if that foal there is a filly, you can be pretty sure that the stallion will be into her as quick as Jack Flash the minute she reaches reproductive maturity at about eighteen months, be it his daughter or not.

We singled out the slightly smaller of the dun fillies and named her Athena, and the other dun Olympia. I prefer Athena's look, as I think she has a slightly better head than Olympia. Olympia's eyes seem high up to me, maybe because her head is longer.

Ron had begun working with Athena and she was taking nothing lightly. He had his work cut out dealing with her. Holding herself like a champion Arab, she stuck her top lip out, quivered her bottom lip and refused to show more than a passing interest in facing him, which is a crucial step in the early part of Ron's method of horse gentling. By the time he had the training rope around her neck and was starting the control pulls she was demonstrating rodeo-ring leaps in the air with every possible variation of mid-air twists and kicks that would have caused serious damage to anyone caught in their path. Admittedly Rex was leaning over the fence egging her on.

Now that he had recovered his strength, he was looking around for the wives and kids and becoming more vocal. By the end of the first day, just before we separated the stallions from our herd, Rex had been getting just plain narky and snapping at everything that moved. I had the feeling he was exhausted by his thirty-six-hour watch over the increased herd. When he wasn't putting his ears back, snapping and nipping, and delivering little kicks, he was stretching his head down into enormous, pink-gummed yawns. After he had been separated from the mares and yearlings, I dreaded finding him pining and fretting. Not a bit of it, he seemed relieved to be getting time off from his family responsibilities, some quiet time to himself.

Now he was quietly whinnying across the wooden posts at Athena, just one enclosure away from the round yard. I could imagine him saying, 'Good on you, I'm proud of you, don't give in. Don't forget that I'm the only male around here who gets to tell you what to do.' I feel sure now that with her courageous character, she must be Rex's filly.

Within two hours, Athena was happily following Ron around the yard, her body language now so much more relaxed. I was getting a strong sense that these young horses found it an enormous relief when they managed to figure out the demands being made on them, as if their intention had always been to fit in with us, to make friends with these strange two-legged animals. They try every variation of threatening postures out on us for size, and when these don't work, they move on to compliance. After a couple of hours in the ring with Ron, they would have a kind of jaunty air about them, as if they were rather delighted with themselves that they have figured out how to control *us*, the carnivores. Meanwhile they were totally fixated on Ron and watched his every movement, and I have the distinct impression they felt safe with him. He was their new stallion.

Ron works his own method, much of it based on what he had learnt over a fourteen-day residential workshop seven years ago on a station with a man called Kevin Wallace. They were taught to 'gentle' a horse, incorporating these new whispering methods and in particular, the not so recent techniques of Kel Jeffery. They also learned other important skills such as how to shoe a horse, and each of the students had their own unhandled horse to work with over the two weeks. From that workshop Ron has gone his own way, adding what he has learned from experience and from knowing and observing horses, breaking in, he estimates, about five hundred horses over the years.

He first silently observes the horse that he is intending to work on, clocking everything: intelligence, whether or not the horse knocks into gates, kicks other horses, or was kicked by others, breaks off for a quick flirtation, the horse's moments of quietness and moments of panic. He reads their body language until eventually he singles out the horse he wants to work on from its companions and isolates it in the round yard.

The horse might be left on its own for a while to take in its surroundings, maybe a few minutes, maybe half an hour, or even a couple of hours. Then Ron enters the yard with his chosen horse, with no tools other than the hat on his head. He strolls into the middle and quietly watches the horse as it charges around the edges of the circle, trying out a gamut of threatening gestures: furiously cantering, plunging, bucking, snorting, shaking its neck, making faces, stopping and swinging its hindquarters towards him, kicking or biting if he gets close, or even just throwing itself against the sides of the yard or making half-hearted attempts to jump the eight-foot fence.

From the moment Ron faces the horse in those first few seconds, and for the next two or three hours, his attention would be entirely focused on the animal as if he was not just training it but entering into its psyche, joining it in its horse-thinking world. Even if Ron turned his back on the horse and walked away, or went to the rails to have a drink of water, apparently relaxed and unconcerned, there was always that connection, that watchful part of him plugged in to the horse's state of mind and body, and the ability to react in a nano-second to the horse's sudden change of tactic, or violent movement.

After a while, the horse would calm a little and start running around the yard in a more concerted and connected circling movement. And then would come the signals that Monty Roberts talks about in his Join-Up technique, the slowing down, dropping of the head, chewing, all of which signify that the horse was beginning to think about what was happening, an ear pointing towards Ron signals that the horse might be ready to negotiate terms.

Eventually the horse would face Ron and take a few steps towards him. Ron would then approach the horse with his eyes down so as not to confront the horse like a predator, putting a hand very slowly on the horse's neck and then face. After a while, during one of the times that the horse would face Ron and appear calm, Ron would get the Kel Jeffery rope around its neck and from there could execute a couple of control pulls, which didn't seem to hurt the horse in the slightest, only instil a new-found respect for the power of the man as the horse found itself moving around at his will. But even then the horse might continue to try out old methods, bolting around the yard, swerving his hindquarters around, leaping into the air with bucks and swerves in an attempt to get the better of Ron. Sometimes falling over into the dust from the exertions, only now, with Ron tugging at the rope, the horse was feeling less in control.

At long last the horse would start to behave in a more consistently co-operative manner, as if having realised three essential details: that Ron was not such a life-threatening prospect as first suspected; that violent methods of self-protection were not going to work; and that the best way to control the human was to behave in a friendly manner.

I'm alone in the house for the first time in forty-eight hours. Genevieve and her friends have left, Rachel and Daniel in the Land Cruiser, Genevieve in the station helicopter to visit another of Celia and Michael's properties. It's just after lunch and I won't be meeting up with Ron and Maria at the yards until later this afternoon. I have time to think again.

We didn't find Sedna.

Everybody keeps saying what an incredible adventure it was, and they are right, although sometimes I can't help feeling desperately disappointed that we did not find her. I suppose the truth is that I bonded with the photograph on my computer screen, sitting at home in London at the kitchen table, or in hotel rooms around the world. I can talk myself into all the reasons why finding Sedna doesn't matter, that she would probably have been too old to train and too small for me to ride. Then there is the added twist to the story, that I could in fact have seen two different horses those first two days. The horse I chose from the helicopter, which we named Maia, and then the horse we photographed the second day who was eventually named Sedna, after the red planet.

I console myself with the thought that what lies ahead is thrilling. To choose from among these twenty-one horses the one that I will take home; a horse that is as beautiful and touching as Tatti has turned out to be, only young, trainable, and with a pace that floats.

Later in the afternoon I went back down to the yard. Ron was giving Athena a reminder session. She was high-stepping around the yard looking a million dollars. Maybe she would be the one I would choose, she looked so beautiful, with such a lively personality.

I went to the round yard and watched Maria as she worked with a very young colt, black with a white star, a tall baby, the fluff of some remnant brown young foal hair still on his flank. He was the offspring of the witch-like black mare. The Black Witch had been so quiet in the yards, walking up so close to me while I stood by a fence that I suspected she might have been born and bred on the station. The foal looked gawky and stiff standing around the yards with his mother, but now that he was moving, he was starting to show real class and enormous strength.

'I've called him Big Ears,' Maria said, getting close enough to pull the foal's ears.

My god – the same trait as Tatti. Was I imagining it or could I see the same slight Thoroughbred look? Is it possible that Tatti was bred on the station, from a mare or stallion that subsequently escaped into the wild, or even that Tatti started life as a brumby?

When I went back to Ron and the dun filly, he was sitting on the edge of the water trough kicking his heels while Athena drank. I sat on the trough next to him.

'Can I have a go?' I asked.

'Yeah. If you are thinkin' of maybe takin' this one, then she better get used to you.'

I took the lead rope from him. Athena trembled and sprung back into the air, almost pulling the rope out of my hand, not exactly fighting me, more just a demonstration of highly strung nerves. I was well aware that she was still large and heavy enough to trample me, even if only by mistake.

'Yeah, you's always goin' to have trouble with her,' Ron said. 'She's always goin' to be like that.'

'Oh, what do you mean, trouble?'

'Nah. Just a bit flighty, you know . . .'

I held the rope back out to Ron. 'Then maybe it's a little early for me to take over.' I was thinking of what I had seen this little horse in the round yard do only a few hours ago. That was no cute little Arab look-alike, at moments she'd been a wild creature with a flashing crazy eye, ready to fight to the death to protect her skin. She can't have changed that much in such a short time.

'Nah, take her.' He got up from the side of the trough and strolled towards the gate, leaving me holding the rope.

I managed to lead Athena a few steps before she leapt back again, this time at the sound of Ron opening the chain on the gate; the rope ripped through my hand.

'Look, Ron,' I said, 'I really think you should work on her more first. I don't know what I'm doing here.' I managed to get Athena to the gate and held out the lead rein again.

He took the rope from me and put his hand on Athena's face, she dropped her head, visibly relaxing. Then he turned, looked me in the eye and said, 'You take her, and work with her.'

There was no arguing. Ron's presence had an emotional power, and for a moment I was the subject of the focus that I had seen him turn on the horses. I was being compelled by a force greater than my fear. I was being tested. This was my adventure. I couldn't afford to be a wimp.

'Okay,' I answered. I took the lead rein and led her back into the ring.

I had to trust that after Ron's work she wouldn't kick or bite, but I couldn't be sure. She was still jumping back, but after a few minutes I could tell that she was starting to get used to me, showing signs of being willing to try. There was no real bile in the horse, no resentment or anger, just fear – of nothing more or less than the unknown.

I concentrated on being relaxed myself, breathing out through my arms, and within a couple of minutes she was leading easily, relaxing, taking time out to nibble at a couple of small spiky trees as we passed.

As I led Athena around I could see Rex just across the fence, staring at us with a mellow, thoughtful expression. Only when I noticed that his undercarriage was lowering and getting ready for action did I realise it was actually a lecherous look. 'But she's your daughter,' I squeaked at him. 'Or at least I think she is.' He wasn't impressed. It was the closest I'd been to Rex, his dark palomino head with its long wispy greyish cream forelock, and the calmest I'd ever seen him near a person. There he was, leering across the fence. For the first time I thought he actually looked rather sinister. I glanced back at poor, innocent Athena, so young.

Ron appeared back at the rails of the ring. 'She's horsin',' he said. I assumed he meant in season.

'But she's far too young to have a foal,' I said, stating the obvious.

'Yeah, but if she was runnin' around out there with one of them stallions an' that, she'd be made in foal all right – yesterday, today.'

I looked at Athena's little flank, still rounded, no imprint of a rib showing through the flesh, and then remembered all the young mares we'd seen, a foal and sometimes even a yearling still sucking, and another foal on the way. No wonder their ribs showed and their necks were thin.

I took Athena into another small yard, but she leapt and pulled back, being unfamiliar with the place. It was as if she associated what she had learned with the territory, and now we had to start again in this new yard. Ron showed me how to let her go to the length of the lead rein, have a little cavort, and how I should then pull her back, but release the pressure when she complied, reminding her that I was the one holding the power. I don't have Ron's muscles, but somehow he conveyed to me that if I just focused very directly on the horse with faith and goodwill, it would all happen.

After ten or fifteen minutes I took a break, stood back and looked at her. She was still breathing a little fast, getting used to me, alert and watching me with one big brown eye. Wary, but positive, not like Tonka's glare of sad mistrust. She was still young and small, too small to ride yet, but I felt sure that this little dun filly and I could one day be friends.

FOURTEEN

Athena and Olympia

The red dust gets everywhere, it's between the keys of the computer and all the camera equipment is coated in a thin red film. We change our clothes two or three times a day, wash them, hang them outside on a line, and they are dry in about twenty minutes, nice and crunchy and on the road to faded.

It is now exactly six days since the round-up, and it has been an incredibly busy time. We have decided not to turn any of the horses back into the wild until we have had a chance to observe and work with them all. That will also give us the chance to treat as many as possible for their infestations of cattle ticks, worms and parasites.

All the horses have to be fed and watered (some by hand as there are only three troughs), and constantly checked to make sure they are not getting into trouble. We have been moving them around, separating horses that are getting narky or leaving one or two on their own as part of the gentling process, putting them into the smaller yards that Ron and Maria have constructed out of heavy iron-gated panels joined with fencing wire. I helped them lift the panels and they are unbelievably heavy. Yearlings that have already been handled now need to be played with, and reminded of what they have learnt, led up and down, taken to the trough, groomed, turned, stroked, have things flapped at them, and occasionally pushed on to run around the yard to show that they have got it wrong when they turn their hindquarters on us, though I usually leave that to Ron.

Ron is still working a twelve-hour day. He spends three or four hours every morning and afternoon gentling the youngsters, carefully focusing on one at a time. He starts a new horse every morning, then uses the afternoons for reminder sessions. He also has the added task of dismantling the temporary yards that we built in the valley for the muster, hauling the phenomenally heavy panels, sometimes by himself, carrying them on his back, loading them onto the trailer and transporting them back to the homestead. Richard, now that the muster is over, is holed up in the morning from six to ten o'clock working on his novel and usually the rest of the day building a bird-watching shelter.

I help in the yards while Susan takes care of the station management. Then there is the everyday stuff of our lives: cooking, washing up, talking, drinking tall glasses of white wine and soda, and trying to catch the Olympics on the television.

Meanwhile I have made a momentous decision. After days of agonising and soul-searching, I have chosen the two dun fillies – Olympia and Athena – to be my horses. At one time I was seriously considering taking Athena with the young chestnut, Pluto's clone, whom I had named Caspar, but the more I watched Olympia, the more I found myself drawn to her.

Olympia is a little taller than the other yearlings, and her hindquarters are just slightly higher than her withers, which suggests she still has some growing to do. She is an enchanting concoction of youthful gawkiness and grace, enhanced by some kind of star quality because, when there is a bunch of them together, she is the one who seizes the eye – a combination of carefree sensuality and the magnetic pull of the charming narcissist. These astoundingly attractive qualities are only really evident to my infatuated eyes, to others she is probably just a funny looking brumby yearling with a slightly large head. Something about Olympia, perhaps it was her grace and her alert and generous eye, reminded me of Tamarillo's mother, Mellita. Admittedly it was a great leap of the imagination from the dam of one of the finest horses in the world to a Kimberley brumby, but for me there was a resonance. Occasionally the shape of Olympia's head and her short stubby mane would give her a rather primitive appearance, like that most famous of Ancient Greek horses, Bucephalus, the famed horse of the warrior Alexander the Great.

Richard had been the first to work on Olympia. He had worked with horses all through his youth when the family had owned Carlton Hill, the station outside Kununurra, and had followed that up with a Pat Parelli course at agricultural college in England. He was keen to help with the gentling work, but Olympia had entered into the spirit of kicking and biting with such heartfelt commitment that we thought it better to let the more experienced Ron take over before she could get hold of the idea that these threatening actions might actually work.

Athena had proved a handful in the round yard too, but I had chosen her all the same because of her brave spirit and her bright Arab qualities, and when I look back at all my diary entries, that image of the dun filly with the floating step and the Arab blood was always in my mind. The truth is that all the horses, however quiet they might have seemed from a distance, were wild and dramatic in the round yard.

It had become clear to me from early on that the sanest, kindest and most positive way to proceed would be to take two of the younger horses. They would be more receptive to training, not be too set in their ways, or too bonded to a life in the wilds. I felt they would adapt to a new environment, and accept new experiences more easily than the more mature horses. They would also be small enough for me to work with them without too much danger, and if fed well with nutritious feed and wormed on a regular basis, would almost certainly grow a lot taller, tall enough for me to ride, I hoped.

I would have loved to take Pluto. The more I thought about it, the more I believed that he was most probably my original chestnut horse, the one I saw from the helicopter the day before we took the photograph, the gift horse. If I had been experienced in horse breaking, and had a fabulous horse property nearby, I would have seriously considered doing so. Considered. The truth is, stallions, unless trained by an expert from a very young age, and handled by someone who really knows what they are doing, can be very dangerous. They can kill. Pat Parelli writes about seeing a woman have her oesophagus torn out by a stallion – one who seemed for the most part to be well-trained, friendly and co-operative. When you think about it it is logical. All the horses of a herd know they need to obey the stallion, and so could be willing to take direction from us humans, instead. But a stallion answers to no one. He is programmed to fight to the death, following his instincts of dominance and possession of mares. Even transporting or boarding a stallion is fraught with problems, they need to be kept separate from mares, geldings and especially other stallions; some transport companies refuse to carry them.

I could have chosen Pluto and had him gelded, or chosen Rex and had him gelded. That would have been more than half the battle, as without the male hormones coursing through their bodies, they would definitely have calmed down – most of the time – but ideally, gelding should be done when a colt is young, some say about six months old, otherwise they can have flashbacks. Susie

Little told me on the phone of a horse she had owned that had been gelded late and would every now and then forget and start behaving like a stallion, usually when she was on his back in the middle of a showground. Gelding any of them would have meant flying in a vet and getting close enough to give the stallion a shot to knock him out, and I would have felt sad, gelding such magnificent males as these. Then there would have been the difficulties of transporting such a large and wild animal, or spending months on the property training the horses and, quite frankly, I did not have the expertise. I would need to ask for help training whatever horses I took. I was eager to find out all I could about it and to get it as right as possible, and to train horses that would be happy, and that I could ride without fear.

So I chose Olympia and Athena; they were beautiful and, once whispered, as gentle as one could hope for with wild horses.

There was another crucial reason behind my decision. In my view, contrary to Ron's opinion, they were almost certainly Rex's offspring, or at least had lived with him, so not only would they have his keen intelligence and sparky spirit, but they were also well brought up! They had grown up in a well structured family, with lots of discipline. We knew from watching Rex with the other horses that he was a disciplinarian and kept a tight ship. He worked as a team with his lead mare the Black Witch, who would have been responsible for disciplining youngsters and making decisions for the herd on grazing, and as a result Rex's mares and foals were obedient, secure and relaxed, and not inclined to fearfulness. I felt sure that the two duns would know from their horse-childhood that life has rules that must be followed. I just needed to convince them to follow my rules instead of the lead mare or stallion, to convince them that I was their lead mare. Choosing young horses from a wild herd with a good stallion, I had an extraordinary and almost unique advantage over choosing one of those millions of horses worldwide brought up in domestic circumstances. If there is one thing I have learnt from this experience it is that there is no substitute for another horse's example for teaching a horse how to behave.

Once I had made the choice of my two duns, I bonded with them. Within a few days I was totally enraptured by them, which mostly took care of any risk of my changing my mind, something I usually do a lot. So the choice made, I settled into a routine of spending an hour or so twice a day working with my two fillies, to consolidate the whispering Ron had done with them. The whispering was a truly miraculous start, instilling principles that they would never forget, but it became apparent to me from very early on that this was just the first step, and needed to be followed up with patient and consistent work. I asked Ron to give me some pointers. He suggested just repeating the basic work he had done, bearing in mind that it would take them a couple of weeks of daily repetition to get something firmly in their minds.

I discovered that when you enter the paddock, you zone in on your horse and after a couple of minutes if there are other horses around, or almost immediately if they are alone, they should look right at you and come towards you. I did notice Athena and Olympia were both bobbing their heads up and down; I asked Ron what this means.

'Probably telling you to piss off,' he said, and laughed.

Once cornered in a contained space, they allowed me to approach, or they even turned and trotted towards me with a bright expression, as if pretending that this had always been their intention. Then they stood stock still, but vibrating with charged energy. I raised a hand slowly to their neck and the instant I touched them, they let out a tiny fierce snort and a jump as if fired by an electrical volt. The jump can be anything from about two centimetres in the air, hooves hardly leaving the ground, to about ten feet away, and it is done at the speed of light, far faster than any human reaction. Once I managed to put a hand on their neck and then face, they relaxed visibly, especially if I remembered to breathe out and relax as well. Their starting away can recur at any moment of surprise, if they see me from lower down or higher up than expected, or for no apparent reason, as if they have simply forgotten that there is a tall blonde person standing next to them.

Once caught, with the lead rope snapped on and after they have sniffed my shoulder or my chin again and reassured themselves that they know me, they appeared to settle down and really enjoy the attention: leading, walking, grooming, turning, and even just being talked to. I felt that playing with the yearlings was going remarkably well, until this morning. Athena's hind leg was still swollen from a kick that she must have received very early on, probably from Cassius Clay that first night, so I left her to Ron's attentions with the water hose and the penicillin shots, while I focused on Olympia.

When I went into the yard, the group of yearlings did their usual trick of running up and down trying to hide behind each other, but then Lympi separated from the others and came walking calmly towards me. I always find this to be an amazingly gratifying experience. I put the rope slowly around her neck and next put on her headcollar. From this point on she was all sweetness and light. We did walking on a loose lead rein, the horse virtually following me where I went. Then we practised standing still and being groomed, followed by a bit of a hose bath on her legs, which she was not too sure about and she pawed at the puddles. I noticed she was baring her teeth in the air, like a half yawn, but I was getting too cocky to remember to read the warning signs. In the interest of getting her used to noise and people, I tried jumping up and down a couple of times, which she found not nearly as amusing as I did, but she was prepared to overlook it, or so I thought. I was thinking that she was actually more relaxed and good-natured than most domestic horses I had worked with. I was thinking how astonished my horsey friends in England would be to see this scene: Lizzie and her wild horse, getting on like a house on fire. I went and sat down on a red rock in the corner of the yard in a nice shady place to have a bit of a rest and to carry on thinking these pleasant and self-congratulatory thoughts . . .

When suddenly out of the corner of my eye I saw the beautiful blonde Olympia, with her ears flattened back against her head, swooping down from a height to attack me. Four hundred kilos of cream-coloured horse, teeth bared, dive-bombing and heading straight for my left arm.

Before I had a chance to move out of the target zone she hit her mark. She landed close enough to deliver a hefty and toothy bite straight into the muscle, and then retreated, leaping in the air and cavorting backwards. I jumped up, shouting reprimands at her, and pulling back on the lead rein, but it was too hard to be angry with her, as written across her face was the most sincerely apologetic expression she could manage. I had never been attacked by a horse before, so it gave me a fright, but as Monty Roberts says, forget about us teaching the horses, they are here to teach us. It's crystal clear that I had gone too far in too short a time and committed the cardinal sin of forgetting that she is a large wild animal, under pressure, and at any moment likely to exercise her instincts for survival. I had been seduced by the notion that she is my new best friend rather than an animal still experimenting with ways to deal with me. After all, if she had really wanted to hurt me she would have struck with a front hoof, or turned and kicked. This was more a mare-to-mare negotiation. How could she resist the chance I gave her to try to establish dominance over me? She got away with biting for a short while on that first day with Richard and might have been trying an experiment with me to see if I could be intimidated. Ron had warned that letting her get away with biting that first day could be dangerous. Apart from feeling very sorry for myself, quite shocked and in need of a strong cup of tea, I was worried that I might mess up the progress of her training, so I went straight to Ron, who said to move her to the small round yard and he'd have a look at her later, commenting that she might be a bit sour.

In spite of the extraordinary success of the venture so far, I still had tremendous highs and lows. Today was definitely a trembling low. The image of a horse coming at me at speed from above, ears back and teeth bared, is not one that I will easily forget. Will these horses ever be anything other than wild at heart? And romantic as that sounds, will I be able to cope with it in the real world? The feral factor?

Later, I asked Ron how to proceed with her training. He didn't seem the faintest bit worried and told me just to go on as before. So I did. Then I found that Lympi had another problem, a habit of backing away from me if I moved back much beyond her girth area. Ron realised it was because he never did the last stage of the treatment, working on her hindquarters and back legs, rubbing a cloth over her, dropping a rope around her hindquarters and back legs, lifting her hooves. After he'd done that extra work, she was fine.

Ron and I do a lot of leaning over fences like characters in some farming soap, mulling over the merits of various horses.

'Reckon that chestnut stallion's got good bone,' Ron says as we watch Pluto. 'If I was you I'd turn him out with them mares, then you'd get a brood of foals with bone an' that.' As if we were talking about some domestic herd and not one that we just happened to have picked up less than a week ago.

'Yes. He looks like he could have some heavy horse in him.

Percheron, d'you think?' I ask, hoping I have some idea what I'm talking about.

'Nah, got them fine legs. They all got them fine legs.'

'Quarter horse then,' I hazard. Quarter horses are much heavier than one would think, it's just the size of the saddle they wear that makes them look comparatively normal. I consider myself a bit of an expert on the size and weight of quarter horses having had that one fall on top of me in Steamboat Springs about twenty-five years ago. I remember thinking exactly that as the horse landed on me: My god, this horse is much bigger and heavier than I expected.

The three stallions, Pluto, Cassius and Mr Wimpy, have palled up quite well and don't fight (much), as there are no mares in the vicinity for them to compete over. The mares are in fact only a few yards away but somehow a fence makes all the difference. Every now and then, when I am standing in the mares' field, I see Pluto peering across at them, Rex too. I feel sorry for poor old Rex, he had quite a collection of mares before and now all he has for company is a sycophantic gay mule.

Ron told me about the brumbies in the Northern Territory being nearly wiped out in the '80s. 'They shot 'em, brought in the pet-food buyers, left horses to die of their wounds, foals runnin' around without their mothers, left 'em to starve to death.'

'Who on earth would want to do a thing like that?'

'The government – say they doin' damage to the land – say they not indigenous an' that, them's feral, horses that used to be domesticated – now breedin' in the wild.'

'Were they great-looking horses like these?' I asked him.

'Ah yeah . . . Beautiful horses. They turn 'em horses out in the Wet to fatten them up, then muster 'em back at the beginning of the Dry, never get all of 'em back, so some of 'em good 'uns stays out there and breed.'

I went around to the yearlings' yard to look at Athena and Olympia – my horses. *My horses.* After all these years, I can finally say those precious words, and it is such a thrill. I look admiringly at their hooves: both of them have two white hooves on their hind legs, to go with the white socks, and two black on their front legs to match their black 'points', the black on the lower part of their forelegs. They are probably half sisters with their similar colours and markings. Both have such perfectly formed, neat, well-shaped hooves. I'm as proud as any mother counting the perfect toes of her baby. And I have two horses. I'd always thought that must be the ultimate luxury in life, every time you wandered up to the stables to go for a ride, to have two mounts to choose from. Admittedly neither of my horses is in show-room condition. They both have a few scuff marks, even on their faces. But you cannot bring suburban sensibilities of well-tended and beloved horses that travel in nicely padded trailers dressed in a variety of travel boots to the outback of Australia. You can't compare horses in England for which a little scratch or patch of black skin showing through on the face or flank is a major drama with this little band with their battle-weary scrapes. (Maria reassures me that the hair always grows back on these marks, that they won't scar.) The truth is that I cannot save the horse population of Western Australia from the dangers of herd life and the ever-present spectre of government culling programs, or even be responsible for the fate of these twenty-one horses and a mule. But I can do my best for my two duns.

Saturday 21 August

I can't believe that it is only a week since the horse muster. I'm becoming quite used to the idea that we have all these gorgeous and interesting horses, no longer regarding it as a miracle that we caught them. When I talk to friends on the phone in Sydney,

England or America, and they express astonishment that we pulled it off, I feel surprised that they are so surprised. It is no longer an impossible dream, because we have done it, and even if I do not have Sedna, I have my two wonderful duns, and we still have Pluto, there in the yards.

This morning Ron handled the last remaining of the bunch of seven yearlings, a bright bay mare, and so now we have a fairly contented yard down there. They are, for the most part, not so panic-stricken to see a human holding a lead rein approach them across the yard. They look up and then there are just a few moments of alert head-nodding as they try to remember the new rules.

Ron says that if my two fillies were out in the wild, they'd be in foal by now, or at least Athena would be. He's looked at their teeth and says that Athena is nearly two, but Lympi is much younger, she still has her milk teeth, she's probably only about eighteen months. For a horse that only has milk teeth, she sure knows how to use them. Since Ron mentioned that Athena is 'horsing', I have noticed that she certainly spends time flirting.

Mr Trouble, the dark dun colt – called 'Trouble' because out of all the youngsters he had been the most difficult to handle – found himself to his great good fortune standing near her. Being one of the group of teenagers that had come into the yards together, he was still rather polite and finding his hooves stallion-wise. Very unlike our stallion Rex, who no doubt because of the pressure of domestic responsibilities and keeping so many mares satisfied, is of the 'Fling-yourself-on-top-get-a-grip-on-their-necks-and-go-for-it' school of lovemaking. I suppose the years of controlling a comparatively large herd has taught him these time-saving approaches. One would think, looking at Rex with his majesty and beauty, that he would be inclined to approach the matter with a little more finesse.

Mr Trouble sidled up to Athena in a kind of deliberately cool way, and after a brief nose to nose greeting, he moved along a little, towards the nose to tail position, shielding the front of her body from us with his body. From there, he commenced languorously licking the side of Thena's flank with long strokes, starting a couple of inches behind her girth area and working back towards her hindquarters, as if he had all the time in the world. Thena was alert and rapt, her ears were pricked forward, and she was all but smiling a coquettish smile. Then I saw her head bob down, disappearing briefly from sight, reappearing under the colt's belly, ears still pricked, her eyes wide with delighted curiosity, having a closer look at the sixteen inches of dark grey tube that had recently appeared out of his sheath. She stretched out her nose and gave two very delicate sniffs, registering complete approval with everything she had found so far. The tube stiffened and swung around, Thena's ears wavered, and she pretended in a sort of ladylike way to back off, but after a few seconds had returned enthusiastically to her anatomical investigations.

At this point the spoilsport humans put a stop to proceedings, not wishing to have an unwanted teenage pregnancy sapping Thena's strength during her essential growing years. But there was no stopping Thena's feminine guiles.

Whenever she was in the outside yard, she would stand by the fence closest to the young macho stallion Cassius, who had now been turned out with the geldings in the big paddock. Athena would pretend to be staring out nostalgically at the view while Cassius pranced and cavorted and did everything he could think of to gain her attention, all the time exhaling breathy whinnies. Thena would then sigh, as if the beauty of the landscape was just too much to bear, and glance at him quickly. At that point Cassius would reel back in ecstatic joy, joining all the whinnies up into one heartfelt neigh, an expression of passionate longing, but before he had time to leap forward and press his nose against the rails, she would nonchalantly swing around in a half circle, and, carelessly leaving her hindquarters pointing towards him, put her head down and nibble at a few stalks, relaxing a back fetlock to give her pert haunches an interesting and attractive slant. Cassius, meanwhile, in a frenzy of unsatisfied lust, would be trotting up and down by the fence in short sharp bursts, frantically shaking his head up and down, snorting and groaning, his fathering equipment already lowered, stiffened, and ready for action. Thena was apparently entirely unaware of the passions she had aroused, while the serene Lympi – the innocent sister – would look on with wide-eyed curiosity at poor Cassius' tortured antics.

The truth is that Thena is capable of being a real 'madam', and I pity any stallion unwise enough to take her on. He would have no idea what lies behind that flirtatious, light manner. She is as manipulative as hell, and if I didn't know better, I would think it possible she could be . . . a pony. A naughty little pony.

This morning I was standing outside the yards with little Brody, when suddenly Brody pointed into the bush and said, 'Look.' Coming towards us out of some tall dry grasses was the little figure of our pony Tonka, head very low in a gesture of submission. He was coming in from the cold, asking to be allowed back into the herd, true to all the principles of horse whispering. He looked so sad, even more mournful than usual, and although he allowed me to stroke him, he wouldn't go into the paddock in spite of the magic bucket being held in front of his nose. I got him halfway through the gate, and the other geldings, although now all gathered around, held back from thrusting their noses into the bucket, as if conscious that a delicate operation was taking place that involved Tonka's security. At the last minute Tonka ran back out and so received my thoroughly pissed-off words at the disappearing plump hindquarters, 'Well, to hell with you. Live out in the bush all alone if that's what you want.'

He obviously spent quality time thinking over my wise words because, when I went back to the gate half an hour later, Tonka was standing there looking as contrite as a very small and bad-tempered pony could manage, and this time he came straight into the paddock, where he stood looking at his old team. Tatti looked less than delighted to see his companion and just turned away and put his head down, swishing his tail around, which of course I now understand to be a horse's manner of acceptance without threat.

I went back to my work with the duns. Ron is with a bay mare called Gita, Maria is bonding with Gita's foal and I am working with Olympia. We are all chatting away to our charges in that idiotic way you do with animals but hoping that they find the sound of our voices soothing, and if they don't, well, the truth is at least we do.

'For God's sake, Lympi, it's only a body brush. Look, it's really soft. No, you can't eat it. God, what a beautiful dappled gold you are . . . There, isn't that nice? So why are your ears back? By the way, Olympia, if you ever bite me again you are really going to regret it . . . So what about a rope over your hindquarters? What do you think of that? Huh? Not nearly as bad as you thought, is it?'

I overhear Ron, sitting on the edge of the trough just a few yards away, Gita on the end of a loose rope.

'Don't have to stretch your neck out like that, could just get nearer, you know. Just move that leg. Yeah. That one. No worries.'

His concentration when he works with a horse is just extraordinary. It's as if he was plugged in to the horse's consciousness from the moment he goes into the round yard, tuning in to the horse's mood and state of mind. And that is where his focus stays, for several hours, or even a day or two, after which the horse appears to be calm and happy and enjoying the attention. And he's right, because every now and then a seemingly calm and happy horse will suddenly go berserk. Several times I have seen Ron nearly get kicked in the head, or standing in one of the yards, a haltered horse charging wildly around the edges, driving the horse on to remind it that in the centre of the ring with the man is the only safe and comfortable place to be, or judging the exact moment he can throw himself in the horse's path to grab hold of the rope.

Sunday 22 August

Time is running out in a big way. I'm not exactly sure when Ron is leaving, it could be Tuesday, it could even be Monday, but it will be very soon because he has another job to go to, mustering cattle over towards Kununurra. I hate to think of Ron leaving. We could not have done what we have without him, and when it comes to horses, this man is pure genius.

He has now handled all the mares and foals as well as the yearlings. The only ones not to have been gentled are the three big stallions and the mule. We've also treated all the handled horses for worms, parasites and tick infestations, and Susan has sent to the pharmacist in Kununurra for human worming tablets, just in case any of us has picked up some unwelcome internal visitors. When I go down to the yard, I cannot get over the change that has taken place in these horses. No longer a case of fight or flight, this lot seem to have relinquished panic for more simple grumpy avoidance.

I just rang Barry in San Francisco. 'Have you caught the horse yet?' he asked me. I wondered if he's heard a word I've said for the last week.

'Well no, unfortunately we didn't manage to catch the horse on the first day – that was a week ago – and it was too big a set-up to go ahead into a second day. But we have caught twenty-one horses and a mule, and I've chosen two out of –'

'Yes, yes,' he said rather impatiently, 'I know all that.' Maybe he was just repeating the question without thinking. Funny to remember that there is a whole other world out there.

When I got back down to the yards at 5 pm, Ron and Maria were shuffling horses around, separating the ones that are to be set free.

We had decided that for now we would keep the best mares, those which had been in Rex's original herd, but to turn Rex loose with the two others mares and a couple of youngsters.

First we moved the two mares and youngsters into the yard next to Rex. One of the mares is horsing, so Rex started prancing around, playing the stallion, showing off to the mare on the other side of the fence, chasing the mule around, and then turning the other way and giving plunges and threatening looks to Pluto, just in case he was unwise enough to consider making a move. Then came the moment Rex had been waiting for; he was put in the same yard as his new mares.

He couldn't believe his luck. No longer the large mournful figure that has been moping around, suddenly he was 100 per cent the male leader again. He arched his neck, pranced, gave a couple of throaty snorts, a few neck wriggles, and was immediately back to his old self. He mounted the bay mare, then very suddenly and dramatically plunged over the water trough and through a wooden fence, breaking a large heavy pole, to try to nab his old wife, the Black Witch, from Pluto. He disentangled his front legs from the splintered wood, apparently unhurt, then mounted the bay mare once more before mounting the black mare again, just for good luck, one presumes.

Maria reckons he mounted the black mare four times in the

space of half an hour, but in his excitement and hurry, lost his aim and kept doing that thing to her that would not make her pregnant.

We loaded Rex and his mares into the truck, first running them along the tunnelled cattle run and stopping them one at a time. We had built a small fire and had heated the station horse brand to glowing red to try to brand the horses on the way out, with the idea that if the government shooter came in, they can't kill a branded horse. Rex, however, found the experience so upsetting, having his back to his mares and being contained in close quarters, that he was shaking all over, so we hardly got a chance to get the mark on him and we let the others through unbranded.

We drove them up to a creek near where we had found Rex, about twenty kilometres from the homestead. Maria and Ron climbed along the roof of the cabin and then let down the ramp of the truck from above. We saw Rex sniffing the ramp then walking slowly down.

We watched as Rex, followed by his new family, trotted majestically through the long grasses and between the silver-trunked eucalypts until nearly out of sight, then slowing to a calm walk. I had expected him to gallop wildly, chasing the womenfolk ahead of him.

Rex was always the one who had to go back into the wild. had known the wild and we could never take the wild out of him. Rex had brought us in all our best horses – including my two – and we sent him back out with a couple of ratbags. I'm certain that during the next few weeks Rex will increase his herd, nabbing mares from the less clever young stallions, and probably find himself some lookers, even babes. I dread the day his strength starts to fail him and a younger stallion drives him away, because without his mares he would be a forlorn figure.

Just knowing Rex has been a real gift. We have been in a

privileged situation to see how a stallion from the wild interacts with his herd and other horses. His charisma and star quality are such that it was hard to let him go. It was like losing a good friend.

Next we loaded up Mr Wimpy with the gay mule for company. We drove them down to just beyond the billabong at the back of the homestead, on the edge of a huge paddock, and let down the ramp. Mr Wimpy trotted off quietly into the bush with the mule a polite distance behind him.

A shot has just rung out. That is the pig gone. I can smell the gunpowder and there is the squawking of the geese.

Monday 23 August

This evening we turned Pluto loose in the paddock with the remaining mares and foals. For the moment at least, he will remain in the station orbit, but free to roam a large area as the paddock is about two hundred acres in size.

We were standing around the field at intervals so as to discourage him from making a run for it and so taking the risk of hurting himself on the fences at the other end, but there was absolutely no need. In spite of his spectacularly statuesque appearance, he seems to be a gentle soul who believes in a quiet life.

As he walked with his mares around the edge of the fencing, he was alternately sniffing the ground and then raising his head high, looking around, not at us but beyond us.

'He's lookin' to see if there's any stallions he's goin' to have to fight to keep his mares,' Ron said. 'I bet he'll be mighty relieved to find there aren't any.' We laughed.

FIFTEEN

Fate and the Piglet

Last night, Andy and Ann had a party over at their place.

It's really hard to write this, but we ate Wilhelmina. I felt like Hannibal Lecter. I should be vegetarian because I love animals, but I'm not.

I'd been worried about the poor pig's imminent fate for days and had kept driving my quad bike past her pen to check that she was still alive, and then feeling like a traitor as I cheerfully cooed at her through the wire of her cage and she snuffled and grunted back in a comradely way. I kept hoping she would win a reprieve, but the truth was Wilhelmina had become impossible and too large to handle, and so her days had been numbered.

The whole event had had a somewhat ritualistic feel. It had been talked about and planned for days, and when the actual moment came all the menfolk went off and took part, down to the initiation of the two small blond boys. I think Brody was the first to announce that the deed had been done, and that his mum would be serving up Wilhelmina for dinner.

After Ron and Richard had done the butchering, they erected a spit beside the vegetable patch, skewering the pig with a star picket fence post, then placing her above the flames, which to my eye looked far too high to do the trick – glowing coals would have been more effective. They'd started in the morning, then took her off early in the afternoon because they reckoned she was done. The pig on the spit looked no different from so many of the *porchettas* I've partaken of in Italy, although the ring still in her snout was a little much to take. I had to make a few detours on the quad bike to avoid the sight. I'd tried to think of an excuse to get out of the dinner, but Susan told me that I was the guest of honour and to pull myself together – now that I was a fully-fledged outback girl . . .

Andy and Ron had wrapped her in wet hessian, only it turned out she wasn't cooked at all, so late afternoon they put her back over the flames. We rolled up for dinner at about seven and started on the red wine while we waited for our main course to be ready, sitting around a large table on Andy and Ann's porch, Brody at one end looking rather pale and silent.

When Wilhelmina was finally taken down and carved, all but the outside bits were still pink. By this time, the men had had more than a few beers, little Jack had fallen asleep and been put to bed, and Brody was inside watching a video. Ann had made us pumpkin, potatoes and her special baked courgette slice. The courgette slice was delicious, and I ate mostly that. I hardly ate any of Wilhelmina and even then went to bed feeling sick. The size of my portion did not warrant the death of the pig. Wilhelmina had had her revenge and I had to take Alka Seltzer before I could sleep.

Over dessert and Nescafé, we told snake stories.

Richard told a story about a two-foot-long tree python he and some friends had found when the family had been living at Carlton Hill. The small (but ambitious) snake had been found lying prone on the ground while in the process of swallowing a one-foot-long goanna. They had placed the snake in the middle of the table between the candles and left it there while they ate their dinner and by pudding-time there was only the tip of the goanna's tail still hanging from the snake's jaw. Richard quoted statistics that say in Australia you are never more than seven metres from something that can kill you. Susan added that eighty per cent of people who quote statistics make them up on the spot.

I dread seeing a snake, especially at night, and not only do I walk around with a torch, but sing opera arias loudly with the hope that that will frighten them away. I alternate Gluck's *Orpheus and Euridice* with Mozart's *Marriage of Figaro*, and Susan, good friend that she is, claims to enjoy my impromptu recitals which she hears from her kitchen as I walk tentatively towards her house, two torch-lights focused on the ground ahead. The snakes come out to bask on the paths warmed by the sun during the day, apparently relishing the heat. It is now almost chilly at night, down to twelve degrees. People around me are always saying, 'Look, there's a snake'. But somehow I can never see them. It seems that Andy is another who never sees snakes, although their last dog was killed by a big brown.

As the candles burnt down low and we finished the last dregs of the Margaret River Merlot, Ann turned to me.

'Lizzie . . .' she said loudly and firmly. I could tell she was about to ask me an important question. 'You're having a great time playing with your little horses down in the yards, right?'

'Yes,' I answered.

'But tell me something, why didn't you just go out and buy yourself a horse? You got beautiful horses coming out of your arses in England. Haven't you?'

We all laughed. 'Yes, Ann. You're right. We do, I suppose. Well, it's a long story. I guess you could say the horse chose me. Thank God. Or else I might never have had the courage . . .' I looked at Ron; he was sitting back in his chair, his hands locked behind his head, smiling his warm and broad smile. Of the people sitting around the table, he would probably understand the best. That connection with horses is so hard to describe. It seems you either have it, or you don't, and once you open yourself to it, it can take you on an incredible journey, as it had me.

I dreamt all last night about searching for stables to keep the two duns, then finally in my dreams finding somewhere in Richmond, just west of London, where you could ride through Richmond Park jumping logs. I also dreamt that Pluto had a problem with his eyes because of inbreeding, and that I should leave my two fillies somewhere for a year or so to see if any problems develop before I ship them three-quarters of the way around Australia.

I still have not found anywhere to keep them near Sydney. This is turning out to be harder than I imagined because New South Wales has been suffering a drought for the last few years and apparently no one wants to board horses.

There is no plan in place either for the fillies' transport and I am beginning to panic. Ron is suggesting that the fillies leave with him on the truck and that he takes them to Kununurra. At the moment the Kununurra yearly race meeting is on. From there we would hope to get them onto the one and only truck carrying racehorses going back to Katherine, or the other sole truck heading for Broome, from where we could ship them on to Perth. Ron says they could stay with someone called Jeff in Kununurra, who has the use of the paddocks around the racetrack.

Jeff's place sounds a rough and ready solution. The problem is, they could get stranded there for months or even years, or stranded further along the road, in Katherine. And as it is Ron's last day this means my little horses would be leaving tomorrow.

Still, every day, I'm amazed by the miracle Ron has created with the horses. All our remaining horses are now more or less friendly, apart from a jumpiness at first approach, so that not even he can ever afford to rest on his laurels. Today I saw him dragged around the yard by one of the youngsters that Maria had whispered, losing his hat. All he was trying to do was put on the smart new rope headcollar that arrived on the mail plane, in a box full of five assorted colours.

I went out to the field to check on Pluto and his mares. They were grazing quietly, way out in the middle, but still in sight of the yards. As I climbed up onto the gate for a better view, Pluto threw up his head in his imperious Roman general way, gazing straight at me, and then high-stepped over in my direction to take a closer look. If he can't tell the difference between a rival stallion and a woman in a sun hat and 'Ski Colorado' shocking-pink T-shirt, then his eyes definitely need testing. Ron says that horses are colourblind, which I suppose is half an excuse. He stopped about a hundred yards from me. His crooked blaze, scarred from fights with other stallions, gives him the appearance of an old heavyweight boxer whose nose has been broken many times. He watched me for a couple of minutes and then floated back over to his mares, his surveillance duties fulfilled. I love to watch Pluto. I feel happy that he is still here by the station and so he is still in my life, my original dream horse. I hope that after I leave, if he is still around, Susan will be able to email me pictures of him and stories about how he is getting on.

Yesterday, using the two quad bikes and four of us on foot, we rounded the group up and brought them into the yards and fed them some hay, kept them in for an hour or so, then let them out. We wanted to see if we could get them into the habit of coming into the yards of their own accord. At five o'clock today, there was a little line standing at the gate waiting to come back in, the two mares with the foal standing between them, and behind, pretending to sniff at the ground in a nonchalant way,

Pluto. The girls had turned up for tea and Pluto had felt obliged to follow, however unmanly this might seem. Is it possible that this great big stallion is henpecked? Or just sensitive and thoughtful of others' needs?

This morning we made a decision over Cassius Clay. Cassius has an interesting physical feature: his testicles are so enormous that soon after we had brought the horses down to the yards, the men were to be seen staring at him in a speechless way, until Richard broke the ice. 'If we're thinking of keeping him, we're not going to geld him are we? I mean couldn't he just have a vasectomy?'

He is so wild, so much the young tough stallion. Susan decided we should let him go free, back to the wild. At four o'clock we gathered to watch. We took our positions, waiting as Maria and Ron walked behind him through the yards chivvying him out. Ron had told us that Cassius would follow the fenceline of the paddock until he found the gate that we had left open for him, and from there, would make his way back to his original home in the bush. Horses have a phenomenal sense of direction and are able to find their way home from anywhere.

Cassius came out into the entrance to the paddock reaching forward into a magnificent extended trot, gobbling up the ground in front, his mane and tail streaming out behind him. What a striking vision of a horse returning to the wild! He started off down the fenceline, then suddenly swerved back between the onlookers and the rails of the cattle yards and disappeared around the back. A little later he reappeared, again chased back by Maria and Ron. He passed us and instead of turning right into the paddock and thence the open spaces, made a sudden sharp left, trotting straight up to the heavy iron gate behind which Ron's horses and the four pensioners were picking at their hay, pressed himself up against it, and refused to budge. It seemed that he had no desire to head out into the bush. The call of the wild was passing him by. It appeared that the call of regular meals, water and available horse companionship was more compelling, even if it meant putting up with the proximity of us humans.

We took the four geldings from the further yard and put them in with Cassius. Tatti immediately gave Cassius a thorough kick with both hind hooves just to establish who was boss, while Tonka ran around at a safe distance with his ears back and head down in a pretty good imitation of a stallion, before all five headed out of the gate best of friends for a good old graze in the big paddock on the far side of the yards.

With the plan in place for my horses to leave on the truck with Ron, I am already suffering withdrawal symptoms, separation anxiety. They are so sweet, those two, that it is like leaving two puppies to fend for themselves. They are like mythological creatures, wood nymphs, somehow not real, with their gold hair, slim legs and delicate hooves. Thena, with her prancing Arab look, graceful Lympi who sighs contentendly when you rub her forehead, and her breath that smells of hay.

I am trying to introduce the fillies to hard feed: Rider Mix, a mixture of nutritious grains to help them grow and gain condition. They do their very best to please. They stand there quietly while I hold handfuls under their mouths, sniffing a little, and then finally blowing out, so that the whole lot scatters. I show them the bucket and they stand patiently without comment waiting to see what we're doing next. Lympi ran her mouth around the rim, chewed at the wooden handhold and then started absentmindedly sucking the metal handle. It's frustrating that I can't persuade them to eat. When I tried to introduce them to the salt lick, I held up the paper from the top of the lick hoping to entice their heads down to the ground and salt lick level with the delicious smells. Lympi sniffed loudly and then dutifully ate the piece of paper. Thena, knowing something was expected of her, put her head down and started licking, only when I looked down, she wasn't licking the salt at all, she was licking one of my red-dust-encrusted white leather trainers.

Wednesday 25 August

The heavy truck has finally rumbled down the drive carrying Ron and his horses. They have been here exactly three weeks and a day and it feels like so much longer; with what we have achieved, it feels like months. Ron has taken a couple of the yearlings to train. Also in his truck are his own horses, who appear rested and in better condition after their pleasant holiday at Athenrai. As for Olympia and Athena – they are not in the truck, they are still here, with us.

We all got up just after dawn at five to say goodbye as Ron and Maria were planning to leave early to avoid the heat of the midday sun. Then we heard that the dawn departure had been rescheduled as an 8 am departure. At ten, the projected departure went into a hiatus, progressing into Ann cooking them bacon and toast, and finalising 'Kimberley time' as a midday departure. Maria drove behind Ron in the red Nissan with the saddles and several spare tyres on top, and the dog and her two pups inside enjoying the luxury of air-conditioning.

We kept Thena and Lympi here. It turns out that the truck we'd hoped to put them in from Kununurra to Broome and on to Perth is now fully booked. At the last minute I had cold feet and simply could not bear to see them go into the unknown. We will find some other way of looking after them rather than risking them being stranded for months in Kununurra, where it would be hard to me to visit.

What with breakdowns and flat tyres, that was the last anyone heard of Ron and Maria for a couple of days. We found out later they had called in to other stations to unload, feed, water and rest the horses.

It has been a very emotional twenty-four hours. Suddenly the stable yard is almost empty apart from three foals, Juno and my two duns. I feel like I've been holding my breath for a month.

I feel emotionally drained. I chastise myself for not feeling deliriously happy; after all, here I am at the top end of my own barometer of personal fulfilment. I suppose that the intensity and changing circumstances of the last few days has taken its toll. And I guess that we are all just plain tired.

Now that it is almost all over, at least the catching and the initial gentling stage, and I have signed some hideously large cheques, enough to buy at least one, even two fully trained horses of quality – thus bequeathing not just half but by now almost my entire inheritance from my Auntie Christine to this cause – I am wondering what I actually thought was going to happen.

To begin with I had no idea, but if I forced myself to think, it was along the haziest lines; something to do with us riding up into the hills on stock horses, finding where Sedna hangs out and then luring her into a yard with delicious feed.

And what were my hazy imaginings on the subject of taming wild horses if by that miracle we were able to capture them?

I reckoned that the only way to win a horse's trust would be through intercepting the path to the thing that I believed a horse values above all else: food, even water. I thought that I would put Sedna into a small enclosure with a bucket of feed at one side and another containing water, and over the fence, I would sit patiently, reading a book, or writing in my notebook, just sitting there for hours on end until the horse became accustomed to the sight and smell of me and no longer able to resist the temptations of the stomach, would approach. Soon after which the horse, over-come with gratitude for the fodder and realising what a kind and loving person I am, would agree to become my friend and work with me.

This was a somewhat optimistic plan as, apart from the fact the brumby might well decide to starve to death rather than approach me, I am not the most patient of people and would prob-ably have lasted no more than a couple of hours in the heat on my seat next to the rail. I would have felt so full of remorse depriving a horse of food and water that I would have cracked way before the horse.

Something has happened to the geldings. They have grown sleek and enormous, and most puzzling of all, their legs seem to have grown longer and they seem considerably taller. I find them quite intimidating: Tatti now resembles a racehorse, Starsky is like a battle-ship, Hutch looks comical, as his ribs still show in spite of his increased girth (and height), his hips still jut, and his coat is tufty like that of an old and much-loved teddy bear, and Tonka is just Tonka. They no longer qualify for the title, the pensioners.

Tonight, for old times' sake, I gave the geldings their favourite feed from the bucket.

I noticed Olympia watching them, her eyes on stalks as Starsky and Hutch argued about who got to thrust a muzzle first into the Rider feed and chaff mix. I climbed through the poles of the fence and tried Olympia with the bucket again, and this time her head disappeared into the depths and when it reappeared, she was chewing delicately on a few oaty morsels. She'd refused to eat them before because the smell was unfamiliar, but after she'd seen the other horses partaking she must have realised the grains would be safe to eat after all. Then she must have decided she liked the taste because she eagerly tried again, her head descending into the bucket so fast that the handle clanged. Starsky, Hutch and Tatti had their noses down in the trough next door having a long draught of water, but at the sound of the bucket, all three heads shot up in unison, all three necks twisted around and, water still dripping from their muzzles, they stood glaring at the slight figure of Olympia as she crunched tentatively on a few grains of the feed. Tatti came over, thrust his nose through the fence to investigate this parvenu, and then the three of them stalked off, thoroughly insulted at the nerve of the new creamy coloured favourite.

I am finding huge differences with these wild horses. They are more alert than their domesticated cousins; they look around in a lively fashion, obviously taking in their surroundings, they sniff the air, they listen, their ears constantly moving, and they act on the information received from all their senses. They watch each other carefully, and learn, like Olympia learning from Tatti that it is safe to eat grains. And because they pay great attention to other horses, they pay great attention to us humans. Horses brought up in domesticated circumstances seem to me almost dozy and incommunicative in comparison with my experience of these Kimberley brumbies.

Thursday 26 August

I've now been in this little paradise for exactly a calendar month.

A stark possibility is that I may be outstaying my welcome. Susan has thrown herself into the project heart and soul in the way that she does, as she is an exceptional friend and one of life's great enthusiasts, but she must be getting a little sick of the sight of me heading across the lawn towards her house, even though I am a good breakfast and coffee-maker and do lots of washing up. The fact is, there is nothing that can be done about it, as the horses can't move from here for ten days and anyway they need more handling. Some days I despair. I went down this morning to give them some hay and Lympi jumped backwards when I touched her as if I were an axe murderer in disguise. As Pat Parelli says, they are panic-aholics and it's also possible that the three oats she ate yesterday have gone to her head.

Starsky was lurking by the fence. I went up to stroke him and he had wild lavender caught in his headcollar and in his mane.

Friday 27 August

It turns out that getting a horse, or rather two little dun yearlings, out of here is not only hugely expensive but almost impossible. Surely we can just rent a float and car, I asked Susan, but apparently a normal horse float would be destroyed within twenty miles on these roads.

Any vehicle taking on the roads around here has to be a super-tough, well-built four-wheel drive, and drivers need to be prepared for several flats or blow-outs. It is dangerous to travel alone after dark, or without a satellite phone and large quantities of water. Tourists are continually rolling over because of their inadequate vehicles. Now when I see mothers delivering their tiny tots to nursery schools in giant four-wheel-drives, jamming the streets of the suburbs, I laugh because I know the country that these robust cars were built for.

Susan has been on the phone every evening, as have I, chasing up contacts, friends of friends of friends who know about shipping cattle, polo ponies or racehorses. I've even had friends from England going onto the net and emailing me lists of livestock transport companies. After ten days of research we have finally put together a plan. The horses are to be picked up by a truck driven by Dusty's brother Jo, and driven to Derby on 5 September, a mere 750 or so kilometres and still only a fraction of the full way to Perth, then put onto a horse transporter with racehorses the remaining way to Swan Valley on the outskirts of Perth, which is still thousands of kilometres from Sydney on the eastern side of the continent. By the time they reach Sydney, Aunt Christine's legacy will have gone.

Yesterday Susan and I went for a little drive in the home paddock. We drove out to see our original three yard sites and caught sight of about a dozen wild horses, most of them very curious about us and our car, including a group of small duns who watched, fascinated, as we set up the fire and boiled the billy. The little stallion was quite compact and reminded me of Athena. Could he be her father? Mid afternoon we found the most idyllic place for horses, a slightly raised plateau between some hills and hidden by trees, with two or three pools of creek water, surrounded by the greenest foliage. I saw three magnificent golden palominos canter away, their long flaxen tails swishing behind them. Could they have been part of the herd of twelve that got away?

As we crossed the billabong next to the homestead on our way home, Susan turned to me. 'Do you realise that we have just driven 124 kilometres and we haven't stopped to open a single gate. People really have no conception of distances up here.'

I was beginning to get a very clear sense of distance, feeling a very long way from finding a safe haven for my surrogate children, feeling stranded with no way to get them home.

SIXTEEN

Blue Moon

Sunday 29 August

In just five days Jo will be arriving with a truck to pick us up, my horses and me. We are still awaiting confirmation about the rest of the way to Perth; we are trying to get them onto a truck taking some racehorses from Broome back down to Perth, a journey of more than 2,000 kilometres.

It feels strange being here without Ron and Maria and with so few horses left in the yards. It's so quiet, almost deserted. But it's also wonderful having my horses to myself. I'm settling down into the routine of working with them every day, trying to get them to the stage of development where they can handle the travel and we will be able to load and unload them safely. I am aware that anything they learn now they will never fully forget.

Monday 30 August

Now the horse carrier taking four other horses down to Perth is threatening to leave earlier, on Friday, and apparently there is no way whatsoever we can get them to Derby by Friday. We are sending emissaries to try to persuade the owners of the other horses to keep them in Derby another three days. This is planning Kimberley style.

This morning I walked Lympi and Thena up from the yard to the station buildings, a walk of about half a kilometre, and mostly I had to take one at a time, in relay. The beautiful lawns, houses, music, bougainvillea all came as a complete surprise to them and they held their heads high as they took in all the new impressions. I let them graze on the outer edges of the back lawn, and I don't think I have ever seen horses eat grass faster. Now they are standing on the edge of the bush, eating, I suppose, what they usually eat in the wild, which seems to be everything from the ends of the long grasses or any tall plant or bush to hoovering up quantities of dead leaves.

Lympi has a new bad habit, a way of pushing boundaries, experimenting with me, I suspect. Lately she had been refusing to be led. I'd tried 'request–response–release' but that didn't work, nothing was working, so now I was facing her, staring up at her muzzle pointed stubbornly towards me, bottom lip slightly protruding, her ears back, and therefore elongated. I was thinking, well, she can be extremely contrary, even stubborn and her forelock is very short and tufty, and her ears are so long, really quite unusually long for a horse. Is there any chance that she could be a mule? But can a mule turn out a golden, dappled dun, and are mules known for their affectionate natures? Lympi is certainly beguilingly, heart-rendingly affectionate. It's unbelievable really, for a wild horse, that once upon a time not so long ago used to bite.

Or do mules have frilly tails, like donkeys, or devils?

I brought the two fillies back to the yard at five, they loved their day out, but I also got the feeling that they were pleased to be home. They immediately tucked into the hay as if I had been starving them all day. Outside the fence to the yard, facing me and staring gloomily in, are the four sleek and aged geldings, resentment radiating from their now portly figures. They want to know why their yard has been taken over by two cream-coloured youths, *female,* with apparently unlimited access to the oat bucket.

Tonight is a blue moon – two full moons in the space of one month.

I sat at the table outside by myself in the light of a single candle, and watched the moon rising through the trees. I would swear that up there in the inky outback sky it really does look blue, with mottled shadows across its face and surrounded by the glowing dots of stars.

Once in a blue moon you catch wild horses in the outback and tame them, and once in a blue moon, does one of them turn out to be a golden mule?

Tuesday 31 August

In the last few days the whole atmosphere has changed. The weather has been almost cool and breezy, with clouds – fluffy things, like pieces of candy floss lying on their sides. At night, after dramatic sunsets comprised of all variations of blues, reds and oranges, it is positively cold.

Last night we watched the closing ceremony of the Olympics, which led me to think about how far I have come with Athena and Olympia in the fifteen days since their namesake event.

When I go into their yard morning and evening, nine times out of ten they approach me, which I find astonishing. I can groom them, feed them, let them walk around untethered and catch them again easily; pick up their feet (oh all right then, I've been a little nervous myself about the back feet and not wishing to convey my nerves, simply not attempted that); put on a saddle cloth, including flapping it around their backs a bit, leave a rope resting over their hindquarters or just above their hocks; I can lean my weight on their backs and all is fine, and in the last two days, put on and leave on a bridle, even a saddle. Remarkable progress for horses who are probably less than two years old and barely two weeks out of the wild. They seem, if anything, to enjoy the attention and the diversion.

This morning, when I arrived at the yard, Lympi was still flat on her side, fast asleep. I have never seen horses so willing to lie down to sleep, and even sleep in as these two. It was already eight. Thena gave her a nudge and she scrambled to her feet. I brought them up to the house.

On the way up, Athena took fright at the silver metal water tank, made of corrugated iron, the exact same one that we have passed twice before without incident. Thinking of Ron's ways, never missing the opportunity of getting a horse used to the sort of noises and things that happen in the real world, I decided to chuck a pebble at the metal just to make a little tinkling sound. I reached down and picked up the nearest pebble, which was more like a small jagged rock formed in some kind of red stone with holes, and without thinking I threw this miniature meteorite. It clanked loudly at the base of the tank. The two horses almost simultaneously rose several feet into the air, returning to earth way down the path facing in the opposite direction and heading back towards the yards at an impressive gallop, leaving me choking in a cloud of red dust with a nasty rope burn where the ropes had ripped through my right hand and the unwelcome prospect of a long and very hot walk all the way back to collect them.

Fortunately they had stopped not so far away. They stood there looking a little embarrassed trying not to catch my eye, Thena nibbling at a few tall grass stalks at the edge of the path. Then as I approached them, Olympia turned to face me with such a beseeching expression – don't be angry – written all over her face. Ron had said that Athena would always be flighty. Would both of these yearlings turn out to be too flighty for me ever to ride?

This morning we ate a passionfruit straight off the bush on my balcony. Sadly it looks like most of them will ripen just after I leave, along with the mangoes on the tree which is heavily laden with them, and the tomatoes which have remained obstinately small and green since I arrived and are now covered with a fine netting hanging on black metal arches built by Andy to prevent the birds from getting to them first.

I can hear a bull bellowing in the distance, and a butcher bird nearby imitating the sound of the new puppy crying, all against the constant reassuring chirp of the cicadas. It's 10 pm, the generator has been off for half an hour – it's time to turn out the oil lamp, crawl between the navy blue sheets and go to sleep.

Wednesday 1 September

Last night was the coldest September night on record in this part of the world. It was definitely chilly.

I fed the wood nymphs their breakfast, trying to sneak some molasses into the mix which didn't impress them at all. Lympi swung her head up high and curled her top lip to reveal gums and teeth, which is what she does when confronted by a new confusing smell, like eau de cologne, then she commenced trying to eat her way through the bucket from the outside as if this clever trick might reveal some oats uncontaminated by the syrupy and sweet molasses. 'But it's so good for you, full of vitamin B,' I wailed, like a harassed mother at breakfast with her toddlers.

The other wild horses are still in the 200-acre paddock but spending most of the time and often the nights in the yards as we have left the gates open on one side to give them access. Gentle giant Pluto is such a sweet horse. This morning I saw him nuzzling the Black Witch who was lying down, politely and with affection to suggest that she gets up when I appear, or maybe he is just checking that she is okay. I've decided that he is not henpecked, just a perfect gentleman of a horse.

Thursday 2 September

There are, of course, mornings when I wake up thinking, what on earth have I done? I've captured horses, brought them in from their life in the wild, in this idyllic place, endangering both horse and man in the process. This is no chocolate box story, no children's fairy tale. This is the realisation of a dream, with all the inherent risks, twists and turns of real life. I come from a world where horses travel in padded floats wearing bandages on their legs, and after talking on the phone to Susie Little in Hampshire this morning, I feel it has been irresponsible of me not to have sent to Sydney for leg bandages and travel boots.

Would I have the courage to turn them back into the wild, is that the answer? Or at least leave them here in a huge paddock, with the possibility of them escaping or even being turned loose at some time in the future? I have learnt that their life in the bush is not quite as idyllic as it might seem, not exactly the dreamy notion of the horses galloping free as seen from a helicopter. The grass is only lush and green a few months of the year, the rest of the time they have to scratch around for adequate feed and they all suffer from the effects of malnourishment in early life. In some areas research has shown that the average lifespan of a brumby is no more than six or seven years, because the feed is so coarse that their teeth are unable to break it down sufficiently to be digested after that age. Although they always have some water, in the dry season the places to drink become more scarce and they have to travel some distance to reach them, and so if injured are left to die of thirst as the herd travels on to a watering place. They suffer from hideous tick infestations, parasites and worms. We have seen large and very alive worms crawling out of the backsides of a couple of the foals. Flies lay eggs on the horses' legs which are ingested as part of their grooming process and then grow into large yellow larvae in the linings of their stomachs. Except for the stallions, the horses have thin necks and prominent ribs because of parasites and the lack of food. In the case of the mares they are usually pregnant from the first day of sexual maturity, their strength sapped by yearlings still suckling when a new foal is born. They can't even afford to grow fond of their stallion and little herd because at any moment they can be stolen by another stallion.

In the case of the stallions – and even the teenage colts – there can be violent fights between them for the control of the mares. The day of the first helicopter recce with Ron, we saw a lovely stallion, chestnut with flaxen mane and tail, limping across a clearing. 'That'd be a broken leg,' Ron said as we hovered lower to see. The stallion was unable to put any weight at all on one of his forelegs. With a broken leg from a fight with a rival, what will happen to him? I thought to myself. A lonely death lying in the relentless sun, unable to limp to water, his carcass picked to the bone by giant ants or torn by dingoes. Then there are frequent forest fires in this area. I have heard reports about brumbies in other parts of Australia being so badly burnt that they have to be found and put out of their misery.

Well, that is how they live, that is nature. Then I remember that they shoot horses. There is always that risk too. Someone in a government department somewhere decides that it is time to do something about protection of the bush, and then signs a proposal to start culling the brumbies.

How would I feel, turning my two loose and never knowing

what happened to them, or even worse, hearing maybe even years later that the government shooters have been sent out there?

I imagine Lympi, staggering to her knees, her beautiful gold coat stained with blood from a shot in her shoulder that has missed her heart. I imagine Thena lying dead, covered with flies and ants as a young foal, with the chestnut markings of Pluto, stands by, a pack of dingoes approaching ready to attack and kill her foal.

These thoughts are inescapable because some of our horses are already out there in the wilds, including the beautiful Rex. We will keep Pluto, our gentle giant, with his new herd of mares, close to the yards as long as we can, but when fences are knocked down by trees during the wet season they will have the opportunity to return to the bush.

This morning the travel plans are falling into place. A truck going to Port Hedland from Perth to collect a load of racehorses has been persuaded to go on further to Broome and pick up my two. A friend of Susan's from Broome, Doug Milner, has volunteered his own vehicles with a friend driving for a small fee to fill in the extra 200 kilometres between Derby and Broome. Once we get them to Perth, Doug and his girlfriend Jane have a business boarding horses, mostly racehorses, and so I will be able to leave the two duns there for a few months to build up their strength.

I spoke to Susan about the leg bandages. She didn't laugh at all. I got on the phone to the chemist in Kununurra and ordered a quantity of crepe bandages, medium weight, padded gauze dressings and surgical tape to create make-shift horse leggings, all coming out on the mail plane. To that we added Combantrim, which is human parasite or worm medication, a family-size pack. Susan is adamant we all need to take it.

This afternoon it rained. Not just a few drops, but a proper, heavy summer shower of big wet drops against a stunning sky, all slate and blue-greys, still peeking out patches of bright baby blue. Susan came flying down to the paddock on her quad. 'In all my time in the Kimberley, that is the first time I've ever known rain in September.'

'First a blue moon, then rain in September,' Richard said. 'Next we'll be finding hens with teeth.'

. . . Or a dun mule.

Friday 3 September

Only two days to go.

Every time I go down to the yards on the quad bike, I think about how much I am going to miss this place; the balmy air, the big rustling trees, the red earth, the blue sky. Most of all the sense of space and serenity.

I spoke to Susie Little last night – she'd received the emailed photos and doesn't think Lympi is a mule at all. She thinks she is a very nice-looking horse, with quality. I couldn't have been more pleased than a mother who has just been told her child is a genius, a great beauty and nice to boot.

It's night time and I'm writing by the light of the oil lamp. I can hear a cuckoo. Or maybe it's a butcher bird pretending to be a cuckoo. It could even be the same one that usually imitates the puppy crying at this time. This morning there was a crescendo of birds chattering, and up in the tree between the two houses I saw a mass of the green parrots with reddy orange breasts, like a ladies' morning tea party, all talking at once.

Saturday 4 September

Already my last day . . .

Susan baked a birthday cake for smoko, as it is Jack's third birthday. He has been in a state of excitement, running around all morning with a wooden sword and shield painted silver and black that Andy made for him.

I'm so dug in here that we'll need the fork lift truck to get me out. I can't imagine leaving, and find it so hard to pack. I checked on the horses early as usual. They were munching hay like it is their last chance, and it will be, more or less for the next few days. I'm excited about setting off on the road with my two blonde companions. This feels like the start of another adventure. It's all very well picking up the Holy Grail but you still have got to get it home, run the gauntlet of those who would have it off you. I'm hoping the horses will still be able to eat and drink on the road and not be put off by the trauma, as I've heard sometimes happens. Apparently horses when they travel don't even like to drink the water as it tastes different from the water they are used to back home.

Funny to be packing for my horses as well as myself.

PART III

THE RETURN

If you want to make the gods laugh,
tell them your plans.

Chinese proverb

SEVENTEEN

The Journey

The night before we left Athenrai there was a birthday celebration on the next door property, Drysdale, only about ninety minutes drive away. I dressed up in a festive Indian flowery top that I had bought in Byron Bay.

We arrived at about seven. It was a real country and western-style party, with a long table for about thirty laid out under the trees in the growing dark. People of all ages in hats and plaid shirts were milling around with cans of beer or lemonade in hand and kids were running around playing. Susan went to the bar and ordered gin and tonics for us both, and then introduced me to a slim, pretty girl, Joanna, whose twentieth birthday it was. Jo who has come to collect the horses, was standing under a tree, beer in hand. He is taller than his brother Dusty, with a lankier frame, but the same air of watchful serenity about him, and while Dusty has a smooth, short beard, Jo prefers a shapely bushy moustache, an unnecessary camouflage for such a nice-looking young man, in my view.

Annie and John, the owners of Drysdale, had prepared an astonishingly lavish feast, considering they were just as far from any shops as we were at Athenrai. There were plates of fried calamari, bowls of exquisitely fresh king prawns and even platters of oysters flown in that morning under refrigeration on a charter plane that brought in tourists to stay on their property; and fish they had caught at one of the coastal fishing camps 100 kilometres away. I was surprised to find that the sea was so near, as I had assumed it was much further.

We went home on the early side, at ten, to be ready for our dawn start. Susan offered Jo accommodation in 'The Hilton', but he seemed to prefer the idea of throwing his swag in the back of the truck. No one in the outback seems to worry about sleeping rough, they just throw a swag wherever they happen to be.

I walked into the little house that feels like my home, now looking so sad and empty, my bags packed and ready by the door, and crept between the navy sheets for the last time.

Sunday 5 September

Before leaving this morning, I went down to the yards with a box containing crepe bandages and thick padded lint in lieu of padded travel boots, but the horses absolutely refused to have anything to do with all that sissy stuff on their legs. They'd seen the truck, it was six in the morning (way before their normal getting up time), they were thoroughly suspicious and on edge. Whenever I went to touch their legs they would snatch them away. Jo was wonderfully patient with them, and because he behaved as if he had all the time in the world, it took him only ten minutes of prancing and backing off before they allowed themselves to be led up the cattle loading ramp straight onto the truck. Athena went first, of course. In spite of her highly strung temperament, she is by far the more courageous of the two.

The vehicle was very large, six tonnes I was told. I could see that the crate area was about twenty feet long and eight feet wide. It was a rough cattle truck with no roof and slatted wooden sides, very like the truck Ron had brought to Athenrai. On the driver's side near the front there was a horizontal gap in the slats, so the driver could check on the cattle. Jo had portioned off a quarter of the truck at the front for the horses so they would feel more stable as the truck swayed and bumped along, jarring relentlessly against the corrugations in the road. The horses were fantastically stoical and braced their legs on the 'mesh' as Jo called it, whereas I would have called it uncomfortable metal ridges. Thena travelled with her head pointing towards this rudimentary window so she could look out, and Lympi facing the other side with only a thin gap very low down in the slatted sides, so whenever we stopped the truck and I went back to see them, she was standing with her head down, trying to see out. They were not tied up, as is local custom, and she did turn around for a bit and join Thena looking out, then for some reason turned back. It could be that they were keeping the nose-to-tail formation so as to have eyes at either end, watching for the enemy.

Meanwhile, the three of us sat up front. It was supposed to be just Jo and myself, but at the last minute Susan had picked up her handbag and a tiny overnight bag and jumped in the truck to keep us company.

When we stopped for lunch at Mount Barnett, far from refusing to eat and drink Athena and Olympia plunged their heads into the bucket of water and drank half each, and then appeared to be thoroughly put out that I hadn't brought hay and only gave them handfuls of dried grass from the roadside. I think they thought the whole thing was a plot to keep them from their fodder. It was ten hours over corrugated roads and potholes, but they seemed fine in the legs. As Jo said, they're used to walking all day over hard, stony ground.

After we'd checked on the horses, Jo boiled a billy on the roadside while Susan and I went and bought food. We sat at a round table outside the shop with an English couple, both doctors from York, travelling with their small children. They had been warned against such a hard journey with young children but had decided that life was too short not to seize the moment in spite of the risks. Susan gave them tips on where to go and where to stay, highly recommending a couple of nights at Home Valley which just happens to be managed by her other son, Nicholas. I stocked up on chocolate and after drinking billy tea, with sugar but no milk, the traditional way, we hit the road again.

In the entire journey of 600 kilometres, the equivalent of London to Edinburgh, we only passed twelve vehicles, including the three or four we overtook on our side of the road. Two of the vehicles were 'road trains', huge jointed, two-storey cattle trucks, these ones painted bright blue and yellow. Every car and truck prompted a few minutes of conversation.

'That's the Tula road train.'

'Yeah, so Tula must have nearly finished their muster.'

Coming into Mount Barnett we had passed an open four-wheel drive, laden with Aborigines on a day out, spilling out of the sides, all the passengers smiling and laughing.

'On their way to Kalumburu.'

'Yeah.'

There was a silence. I sensed a subtext but didn't ask.

We saw crashed vehicles abandoned in the scrub by the sides of the road there seemed to be one every twenty or thirty kilometres.

'I remember that one,' Susan said as we rumbled past a tinny and rusted white hulk only about forty-five minutes out from the homestead. 'By the time I got there they'd taken the driver and passenger to hospital; another car had stopped and a young couple, nicely dressed, were rifling through the contents of the car, taking everything. I asked them what on earth they thought they were doing, and they made some lame excuse, like they thought the car had been abandoned.'

The next crashed car we passed had been stripped of everything including its wheels. Picked bare like a carcass after the birds of prey and the ants had finished.

'They never learn, do they?' Jo said.

'I know. These tourists come out here, economise on the rental and don't get a four-wheel drive. I don't know what they could be thinking.'

'Yeah, or else they get a Land Cruiser but don't know how to drive it.'

'Yes, and they *all* go too fast.'

I thought rather uncharitably of the very speedy drive back from Kalumburu the week before at 110 kilometres an hour. 'But Susan, you say you have to drive fast to avoid the jarring of the corrugations...'

'Yes, Lizzie, but you have to know exactly what you're doing. What the tourists do is they take the corners too fast, get the wheels caught in the gravel and then they're out of control and skid off the road. There is a real art to driving on this gravel.'

Then there followed a clutch of stories about people who set off through the outback knowingly ill-prepared, believing that they could extort help from the stations.

'They seem to think you'll just rush to their aid and give them a spare tyre or a tank of fuel...' Susan said.

'... and they never seem to have the money to pay, do they? They just expect you to give it all to them.' Jo laughed.

'Yeah and it's not just the money, it's the time it takes sorting them out.'

'So what do you do?' I asked.

'Well you have to help them out, you have no choice. They are stuck without our help.'

'We tend to send 'em on to Drysdale or one of the stations that cater for tourists.'

'Remember that guy who set off from Kununurra on a moped with only three litres of petrol and no money?'

'What happened to him?' I asked.

'Don't know, we patched his tyres and he just went off and we never heard from him again.'

All around us, the ever-changing scenery of the land, trees growing sometimes more dense, occasionally almost disappearing to produce flat dry spaces with just scrub. Now and then we slowed to drive through the shallow water of a creek where it crossed the road, prompting further comments.

'This was a hundred metres wide in the Wet.'

'Yeah. Went right up to there.'

Looking down along at the creek I could see flat stones and lush foliage, a sudden oasis of fern-like plants.

'That's the pandanus palm,' Susan told me. 'They have the most beautiful bright orange nuts. Aborigines always know where to find water because of that plant. Even if the water is underground.'

As we travelled west, we glimpsed the odd spectacular boab tree, shaped like a giant bottle with a jagged arrangement of branches above, and occasionally, the road climbed a slight hill from where we could look down over the endless sea of terracotta earth, stones and green trees stretching out to the horizon.

'Lizzie, you know what the Aboriginals call the boab tree? They call it the upside-down tree. Myth has it that sometimes when the Wandjina spirit gets angry with someone, it grabs them and then throws them headfirst into the ground leaving their legs waving around in the air, and they become the boabs.'

In the afternoon we reached the most stunning scenery of all as we moved into the King Leopold mountain range, the trees became more varied, the rocks more dramatic and the colours changed into the greys of the limestone. The road was now intermittently becoming bitumen. Every jolt caused by a pothole brought my attention back to the poor legs of the patient horses quietly travelling in the back, so the bitumen came as a relief, if only temporary.

'They put the bitumen in this side of the mountain 'cause there've been so many accidents here.'

'Yeah, you'd think where the road climbs and bends, people would slow down a bit, wouldn't you?'

They pointed out the massive body of a crashed road train lying at the bottom of a valley beside the road.

'That was ten years ago, wasn't it?'

'Yeah. The Dromoland road train.'

'Empty, thank God...' Susan added.

'Yeah.'

'The flying doctor had to land on the road here.'

'Yeah, and it wasn't even bitumen in those days.'

'Things are a bit different now, aren't they?'

'Yeah, wouldn't get that happening now. Those were the days, when the pilots used to land on the roads when they had to.' They laughed.

'What do you mean?' I asked.

'Well now they are unionised, counting their hours and flying by the book.'

'Got that much gold braid on their epaulets, more than a 747 pilot...'

'The trouble is, Lizzie, the flying doctor service wanted better planes. They got better planes which is good, except that now their planes are so sophisticated that they need the best airstrips to land on, and a lot of the stations can't afford to upgrade their airstrips to a level to accommodate such hi-tech planes.'

In the late afternoon, after we had passed through the King Leopold Ranges and the landscape was flat again, we stopped for more tea and the last of the chocolate. I strolled around next to the road, pulling up handfuls of spiky foliage for the horses. Then I wandered away from the truck, surrendering myself for one last time to the magical outback serenity, enjoying the bleached appearance of the pale green and yellow grasses sprouting from between flat grey stones, feeling the gentle heat, the light breeze on my arms. I was beginning to attain a sense of achievement; we were on the road to a more controlled environment where Lympi and Thena could not escape back into the wild over a broken fence. I peered into the truck. The horses seemed content. I had the distinct impression that Thena was enjoying the journey; I felt sure that the constantly changing scenery was feeding her highly tuned curiosity. I pushed more handfuls of grass through the slats to them.

As we drove, Jo rolled himself skinny cigarettes using just one hand and driving with the other. By now we were close enough to civilisation that fences and gates began to make the odd appearance. As we approached some dramatic red rocks sticking up out of the plateau, we came across a man feeding his horses only fifty metres off the road. We screeched to a halt and set off on foot to investigate.

He turned out to be the owner of the property, a friend of Susan's of course, a tall and handsome John Wayne/Jack Palance type complete with cowboy hat. We admired his horses, mostly ex-racehorses, though to my view, after the time spent with our herd, they all looked rather sway-backed and ungainly, and their heads seemed heavy and jowly. We told him we had brumbies in the back of our truck and he seemed astonished that they were so quiet.

We were now on the home stretch, only a couple more hours to go before we reached Derby; the first stage in our trip. Soon after this last break, the sun set, fast, as it does in this part of the world, and we were driving along the road in the dark. Jo and Susan, spurred on by this chance meeting, chatted intensely about the people on all the stations nearby, and about a tragic helicopter death the year before. Jo took his hands off the wheel and waved them about eloquently as he talked, while I had my eyes firmly glued to the road in the classic way of a nervous passenger, ready to alert him to snakes, cattle, kangaroos or rocks. In spite of my best efforts, Susan, with her trained eye, was always the first to spot the cattle wandering loose, their eyes reflecting the head-lights as we drew closer. At least horses are bright enough to canter off the road away from the enemy, I thought as yet again a cow appeared from nowhere in front of us, loping out from the shadows onto the road. Somehow we reached Derby in one piece, exhausted but happy to have arrived.

At eight, we unloaded the horses into the rodeo grounds, rather a scary place in the dark, full of little yards closed in with high steel post fences. We let them loose into the first of a chain of connected enclosures covered with soft sand. They shot off together, disappearing deep into the darkest corner of the furthest yard, showing us only their hindquarters, herd behaviour. No doubt in their minds they were letting the stallion deal with the problems, though they did re-emerge pretty fast when the top quality hay made an appearance, and then both had a good long drink from a murky old trough. We left them in peace. Jo went off to his wife and his home, while Susan and I checked in to the local motel.

After my experience at Kalumburu, I had my fears that it could turn out to be 'basic', but not at all, it was a good travellers' motel, with a large bar and dining area, and it even had a swimming pool and a few tall but ratty palm trees in the middle.

We were about to settle down to the Sunday night buffet when a message came through on Susan's mobile phone. There had been a horrific accident near the gates of Athenrai. From what we could gather, the open car that we had seen coming out of Mount Barnett, filled with people, had attempted to overtake one of the road trains, but in the clouds of dust the driver had not spotted the curve in the road ahead and had ended up running into a tree. Miraculously nobody had been killed, though some had been seriously injured. Andy and Richard had been the first at the crash site and with instruction from the doctor at the base, had taken the injured back to the station, done what first aid they could, and put flares on the runway for the flying doctor. From the accident to getting the injured people onto the flying doctor planes took more than eight hours, and two of the women had to be airlifted 3,000 kilometres to Perth to intensive care.

Monday 6 September

As usual, we were up at the crack of dawn. Susan had found herself a lift back to Athenrai with some friends and left early, while I had breakfast at the hotel and waited to be picked up by the stock inspector, who needed to see the horses before they could leave for Perth. On Jo's advice we had made the appointment before we left the station.

As I was in my hotel room preparing to leave, I noticed a little sign on the little travelling salesman's desk, printed onto cardboard:

Dear Houseguest,
Although smoking is permitted in the rooms it would be appreciated if you could smoke outside as it is a constant

dilemma for housekeeping to wash the curtains and the bedspreads.

Thank you for your understanding.

The Management.

I had visions of the housekeeping staff standing around for hours, suffering agonies of indecision about whether or not to wash the bedspreads.

The neat and youthful figure of Christie, the town livestock inspector, was waiting in the hotel drive, standing by her Land Cruiser, which was laden with plastic storage boxes. I gathered from the young man helping me carry out my bags that she is a familiar figure around the hotel, responsible for inspecting the hotel swimming pool. We squeezed my three bags and camera equipment into the back of the vehicle, between a couple of giant tubs of tick spray.

'What about the brand?' Christie asked me.

'Oh yes. Well, Susan says she's very sorry but we forgot to brand them. And then we meant to bring the station brand with us, but we forgot . . .' I was hoping she'd let us off this formality. After all, they weren't old cows, or rough old station horses, they were my sensitive little babies.

'You mean they're not branded?' was the somewhat icy retort, the words I dreaded. 'Well.' She considered for a weighty minute. 'I'll let you off this time, but they have to be branded before you leave Perth and go interstate to Sydney.'

'Oh, you mean I just find someone who has a brand . . . and brand them?' Visions of the glowing red-hot metal coming out of the fire and being thrust onto the shoulder of Athena, she who always goes first.

'Oh no,' Christie continued. 'It has to be *your* brand.'

'My brand? I don't have a brand. I'm not even Australian. I live in central London. It's not something we do much there.'

'Yeah, but you register for one, at the agricultural office in Perth. Choose two letters and a number, check they're available, and then have one made.'

I was shocked. My precious horses having their coats singed and delicate flesh burnt by red hot metal? I thought of poor Rex in the metal pen, his hindquarters sinking and his entire body shaking while we tried to brand him. It was done with the best intentions, thinking we could be saving his life.

'It's proof of your ownership. Don't worry, they do it with dry ice nowadays,' Christie said. 'Not so bad.'

When we reached the rodeo grounds, the whole place was alive with sulphur-crested cockatoos – white cockatoos with curved feather top-knots which fan out into a bright yellow crest. There must have been a couple of hundred perched on the railings and trees, chattering and flying around and making a hell of a racket. These were no cooing, warbling birds staking out their territory with a pretty tune, this felt like a major parrot convention and sounded like a ladies' lunch for five hundred, all yacking away at the top of their voices. I believe a sulphur-crested cockatoo holds the *Guinness Book of Records'* title for the most accomplished imitator of the human voice.

The horses were fine and the pair of them floated over to check in with me, the nearest thing they have right now to a lead mare.

Christie opened the back of the Toyota and started unloading equipment. We both dressed up in blue paper suits with heavy gas masks and bright turquoise household rubber gloves, and I climbed over the metal barrier and stepped into the ring.

After the initial few moments of the two horses trying to pretend they couldn't see me, Athena walked a few paces in my direction, I clipped on the lead rein and handed her over to Christie.

Christie held her by the end of lead, and sang to her as she sprayed. The two horses were astonished, probably more by the singing than the spray, as I had been practising water spray on them for several days, but had only ever sung to Rex. I couldn't help thinking how elegant Olympia looked dancing around on her lead rein, even when she decided she'd had enough and retired backwards − drenched in the tick spray − and put on her mule act. The whole exercise only took a few minutes and then we went back to the car and peeled off the protective suits.

'So how are they getting to Broome?' Christie asked.

Right on cue, a battered float appeared in the yard, pulled by a small cream-coloured tray-back with a heavily sunburned and tattooed arm hanging out the window. A beaming face leant out and flashed an almost toothless smile in our direction.

'That's Kevin,' I said. 'He'll be taking us the next leg of the journey.'

The tray-back came to a halt right in front of us and Kevin climbed out of the front seat. He was of stocky build, with a rather rectangular, cheerful face crowned with very short salt and pepper hair, and wearing a dark olive green singlet with matching shorts and thongs. He walked up to the rail and cast a knowledgeable eye over my two waif-like, and now soaking wet, horses.

'Them's going to load okay?'

'Hope so,' I answered.

At least he didn't ask if one of them was a mule.

EIGHTEEN

Broome

It was almost ten o'clock by the time Kevin and I set off from the Derby rodeo grounds. He drove along steadily, eyes fixed on the road ahead while we chatted.

'You married, Kevin?'

'Nope. Like I was, but horses and women – they don't mix.'

Kevin Collins was the friend of Doug Milner who had been requisitioned to drive us from Broome to Perth. The conversation moved onto 'his bloke', which was confusing until eventually I surmised that by his 'bloke' he did not mean a same-sex partner, he was referring to one of his racehorses, his favourite, his grey 'bloke'. Bloke turned out to be west coast vernacular for racehorse.

'He's called May Man, he's sired by Danehill. He's a good horse that Danehill. He's in Ireland States now. They're sending mares over from here to get them serviced, they wait till they have a plane load, and then they send the lot – forty at a time.'

We sat in silence for a while, both mulling over the vision of the stallion with his forty brides, exhausted by his conjugal duties.

'An' they charge 140,000 dollars service fee for each mare.'

We sat in silence for a while longer, mulling over 140,000 dollars times forty.

'So May Man must have cost you a fortune?'

'Nah. He belonged to a syndicate, out of Singapore, it was. They was havin' a problem with him playing up at the starting gate, so they had him cut, then turned him out for a year. After twelve months, they decided they didn't want him no more, they'd moved on to another horse. So I got him cheap through a fella up at Melbourne that owed me a horse.'

We drove over a narrow bridge. In the Wet one year, the water had come up so high, he told me, that they had found a twelve-foot-long crocodile sitting right in the middle of the bridge, blocking the traffic. Kevin was a font of information. He told me that deserts in Australia are actually filled with water, because there is an underground artesian well, a table of water, which starts in Indonesia and continues under the sea halfway down Australia. This means that Broome cannot run out of water for at least forty years. When we stopped for petrol I bought ginger beer and almond and honey bars but Kevin refused all offers for refreshment. As we drove out of the service station, he pulled out a stubby, a can of beer, from a canvas bag on the back seat and said that's what he was waiting for at the end of the drive.

When we drew up in the red sand of the Broome racetrack, it was exactly one o'clock. I climbed into the float to find that the horses had finished the small amount of hay I had managed to balance in the broken orange string haynet, and I suspect had started on the haynet itself because there seemed to be even fewer pieces of forlorn orange string hanging down than before. They greeted me with pricked ears and alert interested expressions. They were not so enthusiastic about the idea of backing out into the unknown and Kevin standing directly behind them voicing gravelly words of encouragement made it even worse. Eventually I banished him out of earshot, and first Olympia and then Athena made a somewhat jumpy backwards exit from the trailer.

Here, in the quiet breeze only a sand dune away from the Indian Ocean, they stood out on the road, heads held high, sniffing the sea air with rapt attention. We led them to Kevin's favourite yards, deep soft sand with shade at the back and sheltered from the sea breezes. They plunged their muzzles into the red plastic tub of water before giving urgent attention to the hay that we had provided. I left them to recover and went off into town to check into my lodgings, unpack and throw a few dusty clothes into the washing machine.

Just before sunset, which the person at the front desk informed me would be at 5.55, I went back down to the racetrack, following the extended sand dune to the end of the point where, carved out of the red dirt, was the Broome racetrack.

Kevin was pottering around, watering a few plants. He'd built a little home up at one end of the small yards. A lean-to formed the sitting area, furnished with a fridge and basic gas cooker, and in the middle a long wooden table and several cast-off armchairs; behind was a darkened room that appeared to have no windows, which I surmised must be the bedroom. Out back was a caravan, a rotary hoist and a twenty-foot boat on a trailer. We sat down at the long table under the awning, Kevin made me a cup of tea, while he opened a stubby, and we talked horses. Or at least, I talked about Olympia and Athena and he talked about his grey bloke.

'Had some fireworks here the other night. Over on the beach there. My bloke, he ran around kind of scared, then he came over and stood next to me.' Kevin laughed indulgently. 'Came and stood right next to me. Think he thought I was goin' to protect 'im.'

Tuesday 7 September

I've been up since five-thirty this morning, God only knows what I've been doing. Susan recently bought a house in Broome but was letting the previous owners stay in it over the dry season when she would be up at the station, but her new car had been waiting at the airport for me to use during my Broome visit. Broome is considered crowded. In other words it is a town with a population of 12,500, which can swell to 35,000 in the high holiday season. Now is fairly high season as it is winter down south and comparatively cool. But to a person from Europe, Broome seems extraordinarily deserted for a place boasting tens of miles of white beach, constant sunshine and a refreshing light breeze. In the shops there was only a sprinkling of shoppers, although the cafes and restaurants appear pleasantly full. The only bottleneck appears to be the Broome Juice Bar in Jimmy Chi Lane, a pedestrian lane in the middle of China Town.

'Yes?' the young woman intoned crisply as I appeared across the counter of the deserted stand.

'A mango and raspberry smoothie, please.'

'That'll be four dollars and . . .' her eyes moved upwards and along the inside top of the window where a line of orders on Post-its were stuck '. . . twenty-five minutes to wait,' she said, followed by a harassed sigh. It seems that this bar supplies all of the several cafes and restaurants in the area on an individual order basis.

I am staying out at Cable Beachside resort, which is set back from Cable Beach, a spectacular white sand strand stretching 25 kilometres along the coast. I have a small holiday apartment with a bedroom, a comparatively roomy living area, kitchenette, and washing machine. In the centre of the complex there is a swimming pool and a barbecue area.

It never ceases to amaze me that even in very small towns in Australia, there is almost invariably a great little restaurant or cafe just around the corner where you can order innovative, delicious and very reasonably priced food in a modern setting.

Last night I had an excellent meal all on my own with only

my notebook to keep me company at the Zoo Cafe, just the other side of the crocodile farm from my hotel. I ordered Moreton Bay bugs (a kind of chunky freshwater scampi) served on crispy rice noodle and courgette pancakes. They were delicious. I felt calm and happy sitting there looking out over a small garden of water-lily-filled ponds, coconut palms and flowering shrubs. I moved on to half a grilled lobster with butter and garlic. Everything was going well, I thought as I sipped my chilled wine. I was even complacent; nothing could go wrong now, the plan was very simple and foolproof. The horses were to spend from Monday night until Wednesday under Kevin's care at the racetrack and then travel by truck with a few racehorses down the coast, arriving in Perth about twenty-four or thirty-six hours later, while I would stay an extra night here before catching up with them in Perth. The trip for them would be far less arduous than the trip from Athenrai. And it would be no hardship for me to pass time in the pleasant warmth and sunshine of Broome. All appeared to be going smoothly, they hadn't seemed at all fazed or damaged by the first leg of the trip and the drive down to Perth, although long, would be on smooth roads. Life just couldn't be better. I drank my coffee and paid the bill.

After a breakfast of granola and honeyed yoghurt with a carrot, celery and ginger juice at the Zoo Cafe, I wandered down to the racetrack. Kevin was with a friend, a jockey born in the north of England, called James. They were sitting under the awning knocking back stubbies. They made me a cup of tea and we fell to talking.

'I must try to make it down to the beach for a swim,' I said.

'Uh, mmm' they answered, variously. I realised I was sort of hoping that the two of them would give me permission to leave them, encourage me to abandon ship and go down to the beach for time off. I have a thing where I get stuck. I can be sitting with friends in a cafe or someone's house, or even sitting with people I don't particularly like, and find it hard to get up and leave. Not that I wasn't enjoying sitting there in the sea breeze only a few yards from the wood nymphs, drinking tea and flipping through old racing magazines, having various blokes pointed out to me.

'Look at that,' Kevin said proudly, jabbing with his crooked, deeply tanned, blunt finger at a blurred picture of a jockey in blue crouched over a blur of chestnut horse's neck. I wasn't sure what it was I was supposed to be admiring, other than the horse he was pointing at was definitely the one winning the race.

'Ah, I see. One of your blokes –' I commented with enthusiasm.

'Nah,' he replied, somewhat impatiently. 'It's Jimmy – winning the Gold Cup at Kununurra.'

'Oh.'

I tried to steer the conversation to the subject of the beach and for a while we chatted about the unspoilt beauty of the golden strand.

'Any crocodiles?' I asked. I knew the answer. Of course there weren't any crocodiles, or nobody would be allowed to swim. Though I remembered that several years ago, after I had been commissioned by *Harpers & Queen* to write an article about the Barrier Reef, I read a tourism brochure covering the whole of Australia and had not managed to find in any of the sections about beaches a single mention of deadly jellyfish, crocs or sharks.

'Any crocs?' Kevin repeated. 'Nah.'

'Nah,' James added.

'Nah,' Kevin repeated. He took another swig from the stubby and looked thoughtful. 'Well, there is one,' he said.

'One?' I squeaked. 'What d'you mean, one?'

'Yeah. There is one,' Kevin continued in a conversational tone of voice. 'But you'll be okay if you want to go for a swim because he don't come till October. That right, Jimmy?'

'Yeah. October.'

I remembered once when Barry and I were staying in Port Douglas on the east coast, we had rushed down to the beach in swimsuits to find a sign telling us that swimming was forbidden between the months of November and April because of the presence in the water of stingers – jellyfish whose sting can be fatal, allegedly causing the victim to have a heart attack from the pain.

'Oh, so what about the other months?' Barry had asked the muscled, blond young man handing out towels and umbrellas.

'Well, I reckon it's safe to swim, box jellyfish don't come in these waters those months.'

'Yes, but do *they* know that?' Barry asked. 'Can they read the sign?'

With this in mind I said, 'Hang on a second, Kevin, what do you mean October? Supposing this year he decides to come early?'

'Nah.'

'Why should he limit himself to October? It's already September now.'

'Anyway, he ain't looking for meat,' Kevin said. 'He's lookin' for his creek.'

'His creek?'

'Yeah. No worries. He swims along the beach lookin' for where he goes to get into his creek.'

'And he never feels like a little snack on the way?'

'Nah. I was out there last October swimmin' my grey bloke. There was my friend Tony with me, swimmin' one of my other horses, the one's called Boussac. We was crossing over the sand bank and we saw this black thing in the water there, like a log it was. Then Tony asked me, when we got back to the beach, "What was that? The black thing we saw?" "Oh that, that's the crocodile," I told him. But the crocodile didn't come near us,' Kevin added, as if entirely proving his point.

We moved on to my favourite subject, those extraordinarily beautiful gold creatures munching hay twenty-five yards away.

'You going to ride them, Liz?'

'Yes. I hope so. I mean, I'm hoping they'll grow if I feed them really good stuff with lots of protein.'

'Yeah. No worries. Should get a bit of height outta them,' Kevin said cheerfully.

'Yes, the taller one maybe,' James said. 'She's younger, isn't she? She should grow, well there's a way we work it out, us jockeys, measure up the top of the leg, then double that an' . . . Well, course, depends on how old she is.'

'Are you good at telling age, James?'

'Well yes, I suppose so.'

'Why don't we go and look,' I suggested. We trooped around to the yard, I snapped lead reins on both horses and then handed Olympia's rope to James. He let the rope go slack and standing in front of her, pulled her lips back to see her teeth. She put her head high in the air and moved backwards. James tried again, moving forward after her, reaching up and pushing back her top lip.

Wham, a gold front leg curled out a forward punch.

James leapt backwards just in time. I was straight on Lympi's case, pulling at the lead rein. 'Lympi, no. No, Lympi.' Her head went up in the air, and she gave me one of her graceful misunderstood looks. I was very surprised that Olympia, such a gentle soul, should deliver her first ever strike this far down the road of her training, in the direction of a not so diminutive jockey who knows his way around horses. Then James turned towards me. 'Caught off my guard. Of all people, I should have been prepared for that,' he said. And it all fell into place. For Lympi, with her inordinate sense of smell, the surge of beer breath hitting her was equivalent to a physical attack. My heart went out to the poor little yearling, exhausted by her travels, striking out with an elegant golden front leg to save herself.

We arranged to meet down at the wharf for dinner, which suited me fine. I had quite a few dishes on the menu there still to try, like the chilli mud crab, the mussels, except that once there, the barramundi – grilled or fried – with chips was always so irresistible.

In the afternoon I had a sleep and woke late.

By the time I made it down to the wharf the wind had come up. James and Kevin were huddled over a couple of drinks in a corner of the patio garden where the lurid glare of fluorescent lighting wasn't so strong. I bought a bottle of white wine at the counter and joined them. We ordered fish and chips. I sensed from their subdued manner that they had something important to tell me.

'Murph. He's the fella taking your horses in the truck down to Perth,' Kevin started.

'Yes?'

'Jimmy says he's stopping at the racetrack at Carnarvon,' Kevin continued.

'Yeah. He's goin' to the races,' James confirmed.

'Oh yes, I know that, he has to pick up a couple of horses.' I felt relieved; was that what was worrying them?

'No, he ain't, he's goin there cos he's goin' to the races,' Kevin said.

'So?'

'He's going to the races for two days,' James added.

'Two days!' I echoed.

'Yeah. Maybe longer. Leavin' your brumbies out somewhere there in them racing stables, with them other big horses. An' what we want to say is, we don't think they'd survive that,' Kevin said.

'They're too small, your yearlings, don't have enough condition on them.'

Just when I thought everything was going so well. My horses. Were they suggesting this would kill them? This couldn't be, it had to be sorted out, of course, but it had been difficult enough finding this Murph character and getting him to agree to take them. Nobody wanted to transport brumbies, we'd already had to pretend they were hacks. Everyone thought I was mad, that much was evident. Now what? I could be stranded on the race-track at Broome for weeks?

Then James and Kevin started talking between themselves, and there was a lot of mention of names like Bones and Rags. Finally Kevin spoke to me. 'Tell you what, Liz, think I can borrow a float from a fella owes me a favour. I could drive 'em down. Don't really want to, but I could. If Doug agrees to me taking his Toyota down. Think he wants his daughter's car brought back up.'

'Oh that sounds great, so it could all work out.'

But they weren't giving in that easily.

'Well, I don't know, I'd have to ask Doug, and as I say, I don't really want to, but I would hate for anythin' to happen to those two little brumbies,' Kevin said doubtfully.

'It's a long way,' James added glumly. 'I mean even the petrol is gonna cost you at one dollar a litre.'

'I mean there's nothing in it for me, then I'd have to ask Doug, I mean it's wear and tear on the cars.' Kevin's voice was positively depressed.

'I'll pay you of course, Kevin,' I said quickly. The Broome to Perth section of the trip was already going to cost me an arm and a leg using the truck, this surely would not be much more. 'And if, as you say, Doug *wants* the cars transported . . .'

'Yeah, but for a couple of hundred dollars he could get them transported in a truck that Rags is takin' down next month.'

I was getting the strong feeling that I was being manoeuvred into a position of need, tangled in a web of intrigue, caught up in the intricate workings of the Western Australian turf; a maverick racing world kept separate from all others because of the distances involved. It reminded me of my early years in Ireland, how after the Galway Races Anjelica and I would sit in Paddy Burke's, the famous pub outside Galway town, eating oysters with brown soda bread and thick butter, listening to all the horse characters around us plotting over a Guinness. 'By the way, who's Bones?' I asked.

'He's a jockey we know,' James answered.

I'd heard Ron talk about someone else with a funny nickname, someone called Cockatoo, he'd mentioned him often, asked Susan if she knew him, said that he was a horse trainer and a bit of a Mr Fix-it on the racetrack. He would surely be able to help sort out the horses' transport, if this plan of Kevin's fell through. 'Do either of you by chance happen to know a fellow called Cock-atoo?' I asked.

'Cockatoo? That's me,' Kevin answered, and smiled his broad smile in which he reveals no teeth.

So Kevin was the famous Cockatoo. 'Oh, what an amazingly small world,' I said, peering as discreetly as I could at the tattoos on his arms – obviously the origin of his name. 'But, Cockatoo,' I said, 'I'm a little confused. I hope you don't mind me saying but that tattoo down your right arm looks much more like a peacock than a cockatoo. And isn't that a mermaid with an anchor on the other side?' I could also see a palm tree, a dolphin, a couple of naked ladies, but no cockatoos, at least nothing visible.

'Cockatoo got nothin' to do with them tattoos,' Kevin said.

'Kevin's second name is Collins,' James said. There was a pause.

'Yes?' I was none the wiser.

'Cockatoo Collins,' James said, as if I was being particularly dim-witted.

'Who's Cockatoo Collins?' At the risk of seeming a complete numbskull, I needed to find out.

'You ain't heard of Cockatoo Collins?' Kevin said with amazement.

'Sorry.'

'He played for Port Adelaide,' Kevin continued.

'Footy,' James added.

'O-h-h,' I said, expressing my relief. At least I knew what footy referred to.

I talked to Doug on the phone later and got the same somewhat doubtful tone of voice and the suggestion that they were doing me a great favour, which probably meant they would want something in return, but they wouldn't say what right out, except that Cockatoo would do it for Doug because Cockatoo owed Doug a favour. I'd fallen into a world that revolved around favours. Was that just a euphemism for money? It was like the riddle of the sphinx, I would have to guess where I fitted into the great patchwork of favours, apart from money of course. I kept feeling that I had fallen into a network of agendas, mainly because everyone kept reassuring me that I hadn't.

Eventually, I came to three conclusions.

The first was that while there was no favour they wanted from me right now, from habit they liked to think I was just slightly beholden in case that came in useful later in the form of a return favour, another form of Kimberley or racetrack currency. Why do something just for money when you can also extract a future favour as part of the deal?

Second, that Kevin is a man who loves horses. Not always the case on the racetrack, where big money is at stake and horses sometimes represent no more than a commodity, valuable but expendable when they do not perform. I don't think he loves all horses, but something about my two waif-like brumbies and my obvious commitment to them had touched him and he genuinely feared for their survival.

Third, I was paying, and although I checked with Susan and their charges were perfectly within reason, people on the racetrack always seem particularly short of the readies, and particularly enthusiastic about readies from some crazy English sheila who looked like the type who might actually pay up, even better, pay up on time.

Wednesday 8 September

It's 9.30 pm – I'm so tired. I have just enough energy to write an email to some friends.

> To cut a long story short, I am disappearing for three days onto the road between Broome and Perth, plunging deep into the darkest Pilbara mining country, the stuff of Tim Winton's novels. I am, however, hoping to reappear north-east of Perth about Saturday afternoon. I'll be travelling with a horse trainer called Cockatoo. I have no intention of sleeping under the stars in a swag (despite the kind offer from Jimmy the jockey to lend me his). I'm insisting on a motel, which isn't necessarily any safer than pitching our tents in the wilds, as we will be going through some rough country where many of the motel windows are barred, not to mention the shops, especially shops selling booze.

The following afternoon, I went out to the racetrack. James and Kevin were at their habitual place – sitting at the long table. They made me a cup of tea.

'Hey, Liz, we think you should have some photographs of the brumbies on the track,' Kevin said. 'That'd be a laugh.'

We set off down to the yards and collected the horses. In the last couple of weeks my initial impressions of Athena have changed, and I have grown to admire her. She's a brave little soul, she will always go on ahead of Lympi even when quivering with trepidation, her head up and alert, her tail carriage high, always prepared to venture out and see what the world has to offer, be it the back end of a float, a new stable, or as today, the finishing post of the Broome racetrack.

Jimmy led her, keeping a safe distance from the boxing Olympia. It was interesting to see the two old racetrack habitués respond, both watching Athena, having eyes only for the horse that had go and pace. Of the two, she was the one that cavorted along, pricking her ears forward and looking down the length of the sand track towards the ocean as if measuring it up for size, while Lympi moseyed along behind, gazing longingly at tufts of green grass.

Thursday 9 September

I was up at the crack of dawn, packing for the trip, and more or less set to go by eight, with the ominous sense that it had all become too much.

I was agonising over an inner conflict. Part of me strongly believed I should go with Cockatoo and the horses. It was my responsibility to see them through the next leg of the trip and to be on hand to tend to Lympi and Thena, load and unload them and be a reassuringly familiar face. The other part of me said, no, I didn't have to play the good girl, always exceptionally conscientious, I should relax, and put my confidence in Kevin, trust that he could handle things and thus release me from the obligation of a very long journey (estimated at two twelve-hour days) sitting on the hard front seat of the small cabin. It was possible that I would see some interesting scenery but would that compensate for the relentless hours of flat bush and monotonous bitumen? The world would not fall to pieces because of my absence, and it would be sheer arrogance to think so, or to believe that the horses wouldn't be perfectly happy with Kevin, whom they knew and liked.

I rang Kevin and leant on him to find another travelling partner. I tried to put this change of plan in a positive light. He would be better off with a hardier companion, someone who would not demand to sleep in a motel, one who would be more fun and less inclined to complain about bed bugs and rowdy pub noise, then slow to wake up and get going, not to mention expecting breakfast other than a slab of silverside. Of course, I was exaggerating. If necessary I would sleep anywhere in any old swag and would take my own supply of nut bars to eat, but Kevin seemed reasonably agreeable to the revised and improved plan. By about ten o'clock he had found another travelling companion, at a price, but it was worth it to me. After all that, Kevin's departure has been postponed till the next day, because the new travelling companion was down at the doctor's getting a medical certificate.

We went out shopping for petrol and hay bags, but on the way back into the yards, we had a shock. There was Lympi, running loose on the dirt track, her long legs and slightly higher hindquarters carrying her along at a sort of camel's lope, more tentative than her usual confident extended trot, head nodding up and down a bit.

'Did you forget to shut the gate?' Cockatoo asked me, comparatively mildly I thought under the circumstances.

'Well, I don't think so,' I muttered. 'But I guess I must have.'

But when we reached the yards, we found Athena in the pen staring over the fence, the gate still firmly chained, watching her wayward stable companion with evident curiosity. I caught Lympi easily enough; she appeared a little embarrassed at her adventure and came straight towards me, bobbing her head down in submission.

I felt she was grateful to get a friendly stroke. It seemed that she had simply figured out how to escape. I'd noticed her the day before, looking around, investigating the gaps in the simple metal gate – a rectangle of hollow metal poles, with only one pole diagonally across the middle – putting her head through the top triangle, testing it for size. Kevin was searching the ground, reminding me of the cowboy movies of my youth – like a native American studying the tracks. Then he came up with the theory that she had managed to roll under the lowest rail, only about two foot six above the ground. It seemed impossible that she could have got her large body under such a low rail, but he showed me a small dent in the sand at one side where he said she would have rolled, and then evidence of where she had wandered around in the next yard, taking a walk up towards the sea and back, faint marks I would never have noticed.

I had seen her rolling in the sand, tipping over the other way to propel herself to get up after she'd been lying down. She must have tucked her hooves in very close to her body to have managed to roll through such a narrow space. I couldn't help but be enormously proud of her. It shows she has initiative, although I suppose if she'd been lying down close to the rail and rolled, it could have happened completely by chance.

We practised bringing the horses into the trailer, using hay in a bucket as a bribe, then I took them for some fresh grass; Kevin was keen they not eat too much or he'd have a mess in the trailer the next day. He always takes a great interest in their droppings.

'That buffel grass, best thing for 'em, goes right through 'em, cleans 'em out. Should have seen their droppings this morning, bew-di-ful, they were wet and just lovely.' Other people get up in the morning, make a coffee and then go and pick up their mail or check their email; Kevin makes a coffee and then goes and checks the horse droppings. Susan had questioned my memory later, as she said Kevin couldn't possibly have called them drop-pings he must have said horse shit. So I asked him. As I had suspected – he had called them droppings on this occasion, he reassured me with a smile – presumably to be polite to this woman who comes from England and speaks in that 'proper' way.

The yearlings were eating prodigious amounts of hay and grass and were constantly looking over the rail for the next snack. When I tried to take Lympi back into her yard after only ten minutes of green grass, she was incensed. Her nose went flying up in the air, her front hooves dug deep into the sand, an expression of bewil-derment combined with mild rage was written across her face. I could almost hear her saying, 'Are you out of your mind? There's great grass out there, long luscious tufts, and any fool knows we're just coming into the last two months of the dry season, won't see stuff like that around any more.'

I watch their ears move backwards and forwards faster than ordinary horses, their sense of smell and their hearing undeni-ably sharper, their entire body language more alert. They are more tuned in to the dictates of their instincts and so I'm sure that on some level Olympia is perfectly aware that the big Wet is still two months away.

Creatures in the outback know more about weather predic-tion than man, in spite of all his clever scientific instruments. Female crocodiles lay their eggs before the Wet, building their nests on the banks of the shrunken creeks and rivers. They build them at exactly the right height, so that when the river swells with the rains and the baby crocs crack out of their shells, the babies are at the right level on the wall of the river bank to slip directly into the water. Somewhere in the internal weather barometer of that prehistoric female reptile, she knows what kind of wet season it will be each year, and how high the river will rise. Or at least this is one of Cockatoo's stories.

Lympi's manners are getting the tiniest bit frayed, a touch of impatience, a small shift but one that has to be watched. I am on the borderline of having to be more than just firm with her. In other words, she's a wilful horse and she's on the edge of getting spoilt, knowing how to handle me better than I know how to handle her. I know that's Kevin's opinion and I've had a sneaking suspicion myself.

'Not now, but you'll have to teach her who's boss,' Kevin says. 'I don't mean you have to be cruel...'

I agree, or at least I know what he is saying, though for the moment I'm just glad that they are both trusting and calm. He didn't see them three weeks ago, and from the way they are now, it's hard to believe they were ever different. It's as if I managed to pick the only two horses wild in the outback who are completely tame. All that matters now is getting them down to Perth and then we can see how they are there when settled into the next phase of their new life. There is a line in Hitchcock's film *Marnie*, when Tippi Hedren looks at an image of a wildcat that Sean Connery has told her he trained himself.

'Trained to do what?'

'Trained to trust me,' Connery replies.

'Is that all?' Tippi asks.

'Yes,' Connery says in a way that suggests that's all that matters.

That's the way I feel about the horses. It is the most important thing about my relationship with them and it is the great challenge. It is the foundation for everything that happens from now on, and it is infinitely precious to me. I want to do everything I can not to undermine or shake their trust, which is such an enormous compliment, coming from them. All the same, at some point soon I will have to start to let them deal with their new life without my constant doting presence.

Friday 10 September

I was up with the kookaburra at 4.45, ready to go down to the racetrack, give Kevin the petrol money and cattle tick paperwork, and load the horses.

Kevin was buzzing around, packed and ready to go, or at least he'd thrown his swag, hold-all and an esky containing a slab of silverside and a few stubbies, into the back of the tray-back, but the latest news was that his travelling companion had bailed out. 'Just been up here in a taxi to tell me he can't come. Says he's been subpoenaed to act as a witness for some court case. I got someone down at Newman who'll held me unload and load in the morning. No worries. Give him a carton.'

A carton – what Susan calls Kimberley currency – a cardboard box (sometimes called a slab) containing twenty-four stubbies of beer.

The horses were leaning over the rails wide awake, curious about the early activity and whether it might signify a prompt break-fast. We loaded them up into the trailer. At first there was resistance – hooves firmly planted, noses up in the air – but when the yellow bucket containing breakfast appeared, noses came down and legs followed noses into the float. Once they were in they were fine.

And so the tray-back pulling the trailer headed off into the dawn light against a vivid orange sunrise for the start of the long journey. I was left waving goodbye and wishing I had brought the video camera down for the early morning scene.

I have one regret.

I wish I had taken the horses down to the beach and shown them the sand, the same pale gold as their coats, and the sparkling azure sea, the edge of the Indian Ocean. I would have loved to see their reactions, although I have a pretty good idea what Athena's reaction would have been.

We might just have made it down to a few feet from the water's edge; Athena, her tail held high, with a bouncing, edgy stride once there, would have trembled a bit, sniffed, snorted loudly, pranced, put her head down for a closer look, and then at the sight of a bubbling wave a couple of inches higher than the last, leapt into the air with all four legs straight, and disappeared at the speed of light in a cloud of sand to land somewhere way down the beach. I would have been left with chronic rope burns on both hands as I ran along behind calling her name in an idiotic way, to find her eventually cavorting amongst the umbrellas five miles away in front of the smart Cable Beach Club Resort, or even taking a short cut through the middle of the Sunset Bar. She votes with her hooves. And Lympi would have rushed along behind in her usual apparently vague (but not so vague because it is lightning-quick), copy-cat way.

One of Kevin's 'gallopers' took a short cut through a Broome beach bar once. Kevin was sued. 'It was all the fella's fault,' Kevin grumbled when he told me the story. 'My grey bloke would never have thought of biting that fella sittin' there havin' his drink in the bar, if the stupid fella hadn't hit the horse on the nose.'

My wood nymphs were in the best possible hands. It would be a long trip for the little horses, but they would be well looked after cocooned in the back of the float with a plentiful supply of hay, and once in Perth they would be safe. I sighed a big sigh of relief. Nothing could possibly go wrong now.

NINETEEN

The Road to Perth

So Cockatoo and his precious load headed off into the morning, while I drove back into town for breakfast.

As the day proceeded, I filled my time with pleasurable activities such as choosing books for Brody, then trying without success to buy moleskins in the feed supply shop in order to be prepared for the cooler weather in Perth. Broome shops sell nothing resembling warm garments, however, so I settled instead for a fishing waistcoat with thousands of pockets, which I bought from the camping shop, for next time I decide to go fishing or make a video film. Every now and then I would glance at my watch and run a parallel check with the progress of the float and imagine my uncomfortable experience, had I been sitting in the car.

Only later did I discover that in fact the journey would have taken me at times through spectacular and beautiful landscapes. Somehow it had been hard to get that sort of information out of Kevin and Jimmy.

By the evening I felt sure things were fine, or I would have heard. At five-thirty I went down to the beach and had my first swim of the week. The beach was about as crowded as England's

Norfolk beaches in mid-winter. Here and there a few young people were playing ball, taking photographs, or just sitting on towels and watching as the sun sank lower and lower, glowing a luminous scarlet. Up on the shallow cliff, three bus loads of senior citizens had their cameras and videos lined up ready to catch the magic moment of sunset. I dipped into the glinting surf between the safety flags in the company of a few other bathers, careful to keep two muscled youths playing frisbee in the water between me and the open seas in the hope that passing crocs or sharks would find them a tastier snack than me.

The parallel check with Cockatoo and the horses was getting vaguer as I couldn't quite pinpoint an image of the Newman motel, in the heart of the Pilbara mining country, where we would have spent the first night as it was the only town within several hundred kilometres equipped with a motel. Bars, singlets, beers, lino, noise, meat pies, all came into my imagined picture.

Susan, Richard and a friend of theirs, Marsha, had arrived in town. They had stories from the bush. The mare we called Lizzie, which had come into the yards with Rex's herd, has given birth to a beautiful filly, a dun, and therefore all bets are on that she is the child of that wonderful stallion Rex and a half or even full sister to one of mine. Pluto who had been separated from the others for a couple of days has now been given back his two mares and is incandescent with joy, rushing around with his tail high, making up for lost time mounting them. He's also been given the four youngsters: Ronny, Sonny, the black foal and Juno, and as an afterthought Tonka, the pony. The Black Witch immediately took Tonka in hand, achieving what we had decided was possible for the merely human, teaching him some manners.

Richard has backed Cassius. He was heard murmuring as he climbed into the saddle for the first time: 'If I had half this animal's balls I guess I wouldn't be feeling quite the way I'm feeling now.' That said, Susan observed that in this moment of tension for the horse, Cassius' balls had shrunk to a fraction of their normal impressive size. We wondered about the biological significance of this – perhaps so as not to aggravate passing stallions. 'Hey man, you don't have to worry about little old me. I'm no threat. *No way* am I after your mares.'

At eight-thirty the following morning, my mobile phone rang. I was finishing my first cup of tea and working at my computer.

'It's Kevin.'

'Oh great. Good to hear from you. How are you?' I got up and wandered the few steps back into the kitchenette to make myself another cup of tea. 'Everything okay?'

'We's at Newman, got in a bit late last night cos we 'ad a couple of flats on the road,' Kevin continued, while I flicked on the switch of the kettle. 'Had to buy a couple of new tyres though, got them receipts for you. The horses . . . they went out all right, last night, into the paddock, ate their hay, but this morning . . .'

'Everything all right?' I yawned and dropped a tea bag into the mug.

'Nah. Got a problem, a real problem –'

'What?' I interrupted, my anxiety level just starting to twitch in response to his tone.

'Well, got the little one up into the truck. It was difficult, cos they didn't want the hay no more, but then the other one, Olympia, well she wouldn't go in, couldn't get her in, tried, and then she broke her lead . . .'

At that point everything went into a blur . . . because what I thought he'd said was, 'She broke a leg.'

My beautiful Lympi, her elegant straight legs, one broken, having to be shot. Had she already been shot? And now all was over, and all because I was too selfish, too worried about my personal comfort to follow it through and go on the road with them, because they would have been all right with me. No legs broken. A beautiful horse dead, and all my fault. Only, to my surprise, Cockatoo was still talking, something about running around in the bush.

'So I can't catch her, see,' Kevin was saying. 'Dunno what to do, can't catch her on my own. She's in there somewhere, gone onto the track and then into the bush behind, won't let me get near her, just runs away.'

'You mean, she's okay?'

'Yeah. I was loading 'em, got her almost the whole way into the float. Athena was already in, good as gold. Then I tied them both up and went round the back to close the tailgate, but Olympia wasn't having any of it, so she pulled right back an' broke the lead rein.'

From then on, whatever he said was only good news because they were both okay. Not hurt, not dead. And whatever the problem, however bad, it could be surmounted somehow.

'Only I can't catch her and don't know what to do . . .' Kevin was saying.

'Just catch her, Kevin,' I shrieked. 'You can't imagine what we've been through to get these horses this far, and . . . she's my horse! You can't just lose her.'

There was a short silence. Then Kevin said in a cool, matter-of-fact voice, 'You ever been to Newman racetrack?'

'No.'

'Then you have no idea what it's like here. I can't catch her. She's in the bush.'

'So Kevin, what you do is you take Athena out and tie her up outside the float.' I was trying to regain my serenity, speaking in a voice that, while pleasant, I hoped would leave no room for argument. 'Or lead her around and she will act as bait to get Olympia back, you see?'

'I'm not taking the other one out of the float, now she's in,' Kevin said firmly.

'You'll have to. It might take a bit of time, you might have to tie Athena up and pretend not be interested and just . . . just wait.'

'Wait?' It was a heavily gravelled squawk. 'Wait? I can't wait. Got to get to Perth, because I got to come back to Broome by Monday.'

'Okay, Kevin, don't move. Stay exactly where you are. I'll come there to Newman. I'll drive down . . .'

'Ain't time for that. Got to get back to Broome,' he said.

'I'll fly down and I'll catch her. She won't have gone far, she doesn't like being alone.' But I had my doubts – with a horse you can reach the moment when you have crossed the line of tolerance and the horse resorts to extreme measures. By now I had visions of Lympi, having passed her point of tolerance, streaking into the wilds, or even just drifting deeper into the scrub in her vague way, searching for the perfect tussock of grass, and thus destined to spend the rest of her life in the bush outside Newman, a bush that extends for millions and millions of acres without fences, the nearest fence somewhere outside Sydney, the other side of the great continent. I'd heard that there were plenty of feral camels in that part of the world, but horses? Would there be a herd of horses she could join? A stallion who could look after her? A stallion good enough for my graceful Lympi? Or just some common brumby stallion who would father little colts with coffin heads. But first I would spend weeks camping out in the Newman motel, or in a swag under the stars if necessary, looking for her. I owe Olympia a life, and anyway more than that, I love her. But Cockatoo was still talking . . .

'After all, we still got *one* horse . . .' he was saying in a consoling manner.

'What?' By now I was back to bordering on the hysterical.

'Ain't taking Athena out, won't get her back in,' he snapped.

'Ain't got time for that. Got to get going. Don't see what we can do about the other. Never going to catch her. She just runs away when I get near to her.'

Was this what Kevin would be saying if it was his galloper out there in the bush, his dappled grey bloke that he loved so much? Would he just shrug his shoulders, open another stubby and drive away?

'Kevin? You can't leave. You're not leaving without Olympia, that is your priority now. That is your only task. To catch her.'

'Yeah,' a sort of disgruntled, grunted noise.

'Don't move. I'll ring you back in ten minutes.'

Then we rang off. We'd reached the end of the road with that conversation. I was just praying he would stay put. I rang Susan. She concurred. Take Athena out and lead her around and even if Kevin has to spend all day there and the next day, then turn around and go straight back to Broome . . . We agreed. Well there must be some way of getting us there. Susan was thinking to herself, drive Lizzie twelve hours to Newman, having driven eight hours from the station yesterday . . . ? Yes. Could be done. I was thinking, there must be a bus, or I could rent a car, charter a single-engined plane, it can be done, or at least attempted. Suddenly time was unimportant.

I rang him back. 'Kevin, whatever happens you are not to leave Olympia until I get there . . .'

'I caught her,' he said before I had a chance to continue.

'*What?*'

'Yeah. No worries. Managed to corner her and drive her into a small yard.'

'But it was only five minutes ago you said –'

'Yeah. Well now I caught her.'

'Oh Kevin, that's fantastic. I'm so relieved I can't tell you, I'm so happy . . .'

'Yeah. No worries. And now I'm gonna look for someone gonna help me load her cos I'm not doin' it on my own.' His voice was firm. He'd moved on.

Very suddenly, all seemed to be hunky dory, or at least, a horse in the hand instead of disappearing without a trace into the bush. I sighed a sigh of enormous relief, unhooked my shoulders from up under my ears, and plugged back into Cockatoo's immediate concerns.

'What happened to the fella who's supposed to be helping you for a carton?' I asked.

'Him? He had to go to work.'

'Oh.'

Half an hour later, Kevin rang again. He'd loaded the horse with the help of a trainer he knows who owed him a favour, and a strap held behind Lympi's hocks, and was about to get back on the road. 'Don't know when I'll get there, down to Doug's. About ten, eleven tonight,' he grumbled. I tried to sound sympathetic, but I was so relieved it was hard to concentrate. We'd caught Lympi and now both horses were safe and on their way, that was all that mattered.

Sunday 11 September

I'm on the flight to Perth from Broome. Qantas has upgraded me to business class so I have the luxury of space and am able to spread out enough to open up the laptop and write.

We're flying over the endless expanse of red earth. On the way up, seven weeks ago, it meant no more to me than very interesting and impressive landscape. Now, on the way back, it signifies roads that my horses are travelling along with Cockatoo at the wheel staring ahead at the unrelenting vista of bitumen and scrubby bush. I look eagerly out of the window hoping to catch sight of the long, pale, geometrically drawn line that could be the road they are on but see just the endless sunburnt country. I've looked at the airline map. Newman is a long long way from Perth; 1,018 kilometres as the crow or jet flies, and therefore almost two-thirds of the entire distance of 1,677 kilometres from Broome to Perth. Although I gather Broome to Perth by road is more like 2,300 kilometres. Almost the entire length of the west of Australia, north to south, from the place where it is the dry season, with intense heat and all-day sunshine, to the rain and chilly winter weather in Perth.

I'm nearly two hours into the flight and there's still an hour to go to Perth, where I will pick up a rental car and drive on for 40 kilometres. I could be flying over them now. I look out the window again. The landscape is more or less the same, only more wooded, interspersed with what look like small hills and salt flats. I can see the occasional road down there, but they all seem to be heading in the wrong direction, west to east, some even petering out before reaching the horizon. (Only later do I find out that these visible roads are, in fact, tracks for taking machinery out to the mines.) I don't see how Cockatoo and his precious cargo can get there tonight. I am winging over the distances propelled by jet and it is still taking so, *so* long.

TWENTY

Swan Valley

Sunday 12 September

When I arrived in Perth, contrary to all the dire reports of freezing cold and rain, it had turned out a beautiful warm summer's afternoon. I picked up the rental car I'd booked and sat in the car park for half an hour, playing James Taylor on the CD player, and getting my thoughts straight, making the emotional leap from the space and peace of the Kimberley, to this return to urbanisation. Then I started the car and headed north-east towards the hills.

There had been a great deal of toing and froing, trying to find a place to agist the horses for a year while they grew and matured enough to be broken in – a 'horse boarding school' – where I could visit and work with them whenever possible. Eventually we had decided initially to leave them for a few months in Perth to fatten up and gain condition before the long trip to Sydney. It turned out that Susan's friend Doug Milner, whom she had rung for advice about travel, was now living in the Swan Valley, about thirty kilometres north-east of Perth, with his girlfriend Jane, and that one of Jane's professions, apart from being a midwife and a race-horse trainer, was running an agistment centre on their property. This was my destination – in the heart of horse and wine country.

It felt strange to be driving past small fields with wooden rail-ings. Inside the neatly contained fields, there were horses and ponies of every colour and description, more horses than I'd ever seen anywhere in the world in such a small area, half of them bundled up in smart, if muddy, rugs. In addition, it seemed that every quarter of a mile there was yet another sign advertising a cafe or restau-rant and cellars with wine tastings, at yet another boutique vineyard. Every now and then there was a larger spread of uniform vines, and I would see a name I recognised, such as Houghtons. The green of the abundant grass and high trees shocked my eyes after weeks of the dusty reds and ochres of the outback.

As the sun started to set, I arrived at a rickety white gate that marked the borders of Doug and Jane's property, and drove up half a mile until I reached a bungalow. At the end of the drive I found the slim figure of Jane standing next to a trailer. She'd just that minute arrived back from stewarding at the racetrack and her white breeches were streaked with mud. She introduced herself and suggested I come on up to the top paddock while she unloaded the horse she had been riding that day.

I jolted up the rough track behind the float. The trailer appeared to be housing something closer to a rugged-up whale than a horse. I was impressed; here was this slip of a young woman riding a horse that was a substantial 17.2 or even 18 hands high, at least. We came to a halt by a gate to a paddock. I opened the car door and stepped out and was met by an astonishing sight – lumbering around behind the gate were a couple of heavily clothed dinosaurs except, of course, their heads were not small, they were gigantic, with heavy curved jowls.

I was beginning to get the uneasy feeling that my eye could have become somewhat distorted by my time with my wild horses and by my attachment to the wood nymphs. It was just possible that these horses of Jane's were not actually freaks; more that mine were particularly small, let's not use the dreaded word, p*** size. Technically, any horse under 14 hands (or 14.2 hands in England) is a pony, but I never hear people refer to the ponies of the Camargue, they're the 'white horses of the Camargue', although they are no bigger than mine, and Arabs who vary in size but rarely achieve a height of more than about 15.2 hands are always called horses. These wild horses of the Kimberley are mostly descended from Thoroughbreds, Arabs, quarter horses, and Australian stock horses. Their smallish stature, I believe, comes from the hard life in the bush, the lack of feed in the dry season, the parasites and worms, and in the case of the mares, the back-to-back pregnancies starting from when they are little more than babies themselves; I'm told that a mare's height remains the same from the birth of her first foal. Pluto seems to me from his build to be at least 15.2 to 16.2 hands high. In reality he is probably less than 14 hands high.

Doug was waiting for us back at the bungalow. He was not at all as I had imagined him to be from his strong and assertive voice on the phone. For some reason I had envisaged a burly type, instead of which he was slim and finely boned, his wiry frame crowned with a mop of light red hair. They made me a cup of tea. Doug had heard from Cockatoo, who was stopping over another night on the road, snatching a few hours sleep and then leaving before daybreak and would now be arriving early the next morning.

'Not unloading the horses?' I asked.

He laughed. 'I don't think he'll be unloading the horses, not after last time.'

•

At eight in the morning Doug knocked on my bedroom door. 'They'll be here in fifteen minutes.'

I threw on my clothes and we jumped in the car and headed out to the main road to meet Cockatoo. Jane had decided the horses should spend their first couple of weeks on another property, where she had lived before moving in with Doug. The horses would have some time to get used to the big wide world before being put in with the Tyrannosaurus Rexes in her top paddock. Doug or Jane would visit them every day with feed, and meanwhile there were people around to keep an eye on them.

After only a couple of minutes waiting on the side of the main road, Doug's cream tray-back with Cockatoo at the wheel came into sight. We led the way the eight or so miles to the other property. I almost felt I was back in England when I saw the green paddock filled with clover, well-fenced with wooden rails, probably only two or three acres in size, and at the end just over the lane, a railway line. A railway line! This would be an insane introduction to the real world for the two little creatures from the wild.

'Don't worry,' Jane said. 'The trains are very slow and only pass through about twice a day.'

As soon as we had come to a standstill outside the gate to the paddock, I climbed into the back to see Athena and Olympia. It was only a couple of days but I had missed them badly. To my surprise, they seemed calm and unchanged, still wearing the same rather solemn expressions on their faces.

We backed them out of the trailer and after a glance around their heads went down into the grass to see if it tasted as good as it looked. We turned them loose in the paddock, Jane insisting on taking off their headcollars, telling me it was dangerous to leave them on as they could get caught up in branches or fences. I did know that from my early training, but I had just come from a world where not only did we leave their headcollars on, we left the lead rope on too so that they would get used to treading on it, having their heads being pulled down and not panicking. 'Much better to teach 'em that,' Ron would say. 'That way, they tread on their reins by mistake, they don't break 'em. Saves on reins.'

At this point we heard a heavy rumbling as a large engine slid into view at the end of the field pulling a seemingly endless train of goods. The horses raised their heads, watched for fifteen seconds and then, instead of fleeing, cantered off in unison to have a closer look, stopping just a few yards from the fence and watching for a few minutes before resuming grazing. It was an astonishing sight. These two horses know no real fear. I have Daddy Rex to thank for that.

I felt a great sense of achievement. With the help of my friends and all the new people I had met, I had safely brought the horses to a place where they could not run away and with any luck would not be hurt. This was a great place for them to rest and regain condition, get used to domesticated horses and people, as the first steps to their new life.

Kevin came back to the house for breakfast. Doug cooked bacon, eggs and tomato on toast for the three of us, but Cockatoo refused to eat, claiming that eating gives him indigestion so he claims he subsists on a diet of stubbies and evening meals. The conversation turned to a set of golf clubs he'd been given.

'So, do you play golf, Kevin?' I asked, thinking he appeared a somewhat unlikely figure to make it up to the golf course, as he seemed to prefer to either get on with stuff or potter around his house.

'Me play golf? Nah.'

'Oh. So why are you keeping the golf clubs, then? You could sell them.'

'Well, cos someone might want to borrow 'em.' Someone to whom Cockatoo owed a favour?

After breakfast Cockatoo set off back to Broome. He was in a hurry because he had an appointment to meet up with a man in a pub in Paynes Find whom he'd run into the night before and who had promised to give him some muran tea.

'What's muran tea?' I asked.

'It's a cancer cure. Amazin' stuff. The Aboriginals use it, call it the medicine bush, an' this is the only place it grows. You pick the leaves and boil 'em up into a tea.'

'Oh, Kevin. You don't mean you have –'

'Nah, I ain't got cancer. But someone might. Might come in useful.'

We went out to the car to see Kevin off. He was heading up the road to visit his daughter who lived nearby, before the journey back to Broome.

Cockatoo bounced down the drive at the wheel of Doug's daughter's car. It turned out the car was too light to pull the float, so that would have to be shipped back later. I waved, and a tanned and tattooed arm hanging out the window waved back. He'd been a good friend and I was hoping I'd have the opportunity to find him again down that red dirt road on the racetrack, or if he moved on to a different life somewhere else in Western Australia, he'd keep in touch and let me know.

'Want to come for a ride?' Jane asked.

'Yes, sure,' I answered with alacrity. After all, I had brought all the kit and now finally I was going to have the chance to ride a proper, grown-up horse in the real world.

We went down the lane to the garage. There was a corrugated-iron room where Jane kept her equipment, but my tack was still in its turquoise giant holdall, sitting parked in an outside sink.

'Do you think that we could put the tack into the . . . ?'

'Oh yeah, later, and by the way, if you're going to be riding in

Australia, this stuff is called horse gear,' she said, pulling a maroon bridle out of a bucket, 'not tack. And these things are great, I swear by them. I've had this one twenty years, none of that saddle soap cleaning nonsense, you just run it under the tap.' I was gazing in barely disguised horror. She was holding up the most basic of bridles with very thin reins made of some kind of PVC, somewhat cracked by age. I was deeply shocked. Where were the days of the beautiful leather bridles? Always a light tan at time of purchase, mellowing to soft dark brown after months or years of proper care. Tack cleaning was one of the disciplines of horse riding. First you had to rinse the bit, then clean the leather parts of the bridle and the bit with a damp sponge to remove the grease, and then use translucent saddle soap to clean the bridle again, rubbing it in so that the saddle soap would work to soften the leather of the saddle or bridle. Every few weeks you would be required to take the bridle completely to pieces and clean it with some kind of nourishing leather food.

We loaded up the back of the quad bike with buckets of feed and 'horse gear'. I climbed on behind Jane and we headed up to the top paddock. Slowly, I had been making the adjustment to normal-sized horses. Jane's no longer looked to me like dinosaurs, although their breeding was without question on the heavy side, even to the untrained eye, and I fancy myself as having a good eye when it comes to a horse.

'Are they Irish draught?' I enquired, as I pulled the heavy blanket off my mount.

Jane looked at me aghast. 'They're racehorses.'

'Oh,' I answered. 'Gosh,' I added for good measure.

As I rode along behind Jane, watching with morbid fascination the Rubens-esque haunches of her racehorse waddling on in front of me, I was trying to keep my lumbering gelding somewhere under control, afraid to canter, feeling the narrow PVC reins inadequate for such a substantial mount.

I was beginning to feel like a complete stranger in the horse world. I was coming in from the cold myself and the brumbies had been my somewhat unusual re-introduction. The truth is, my benchmark of perfection was now the delicate and fine-legged Olympia, with Athena coming a close second. I was more or less a clean slate myself with my out-of-date riding style and tack, and my memories of how things used to be. Athena and Olympia and I would be learning together, which was an exciting thought. I felt I had so much to learn from them, and I was in such an enormously privileged position to have them willing to teach me, with the true generosity that is the mark of most horses. I was looking forward to riding my own horses that I could train to respond to a whisper of a command.

After the ride I drove out to the other property and spent time watching Olympia and Athena in their new home. It appears my little horses have a routine. They eat a little hay, after which they walk down to the trough and drink a couple of short draughts of water. They both have a particular drinking style: they lift their heads and hold the water in their mouths, as if considering it, for as long as fifteen seconds, doing a sort of horse gargle, possibly checking for stray baby frogs or tadpoles, after which they swallow. After eating and drinking in this fashion, they then stroll down to the end of the field and look over the fence, one of them takes a good lungful of breath and lets rip an ear-shattering neigh. That bit I find almost unbearably touching, because I imagine that they are looking at the great big bay gelding in the field next door, the one with the crooked blaze, and asking whether he is Pluto, because they are used to Pluto looking over the fence at them back at Athenrai, used to Pluto watching over them. They are accustomed to having a stallion around to protect them. They don't seem to mind much which stallion – after all, they showed little signs of pining when Rex was turned back into the wild. It seems that any stallion will do, so long as he is strong and male and there for them. Somehow in the big wide world my two seem just a little lost.

When I went into their paddock, they sort of shimmered towards me at a 45-degree angle, more like aquatic creatures than horses, their bodies and heads close together and a rather earnest expression on their faces as if they were coming to investigate a being recently arrived from outer space. I caught them with ease and put on their headcollars and lead reins. They resumed grazing, with their heads close to my feet, to the point where I was having to move to let them get at the grass underneath my feet. I thought about the qualities of my two horses.

Lympi is possessed of the gift of grace. So what is it about 'grace' that is so attractive beyond just the fluidity of movement, of form? The same thing that is so magical about a horse, especially a wild one: that in the heart of them is a kernel of wildness, there is a sense of the unobtainable, a sense of a dream existence. And then with Olympia there is a clarity in her manner, which is almost limpid and makes her nickname of Lympi all the more appropriate. Athena is brave: even when quivering with trepidation she will always go first, stepping out with her light step, into the unknown. How strange this world must seem to these two innocents – us two-legged carnivores with our cars and trains, music and breath reeking of beer or garlic or peppermint or other strange substances.

I have a strong sense that when they were with Rex they were not often afraid. They trusted him, let him do the worrying, they just bounced around within the herd and got snapped at and kicked, but with him in charge they didn't have to think beyond him. Even living with Rex, there could sometimes have been moments of great fear: other stallions stealing them away, terrible storms with lightning, members of the herd wounded by falling trees.

I heard a few weeks later that back at Athenrai there had been appalling forest fires raging through the area and coming up to the edge of the lawns of the homestead. Some of the wooden posts of the cattle yards were destroyed. I imagined all the animals and particularly the horses out there in the wild, running through the bush, frightened, not sure which way to turn, getting separated, getting burnt as they tried to dive through flames, foals separated from their mothers. I was glad that Olympia and Athena were not among them.

Monday 13 September

Today it is exactly seven weeks since I left Sydney to start on my great adventure. Only seven weeks but it feels like a lifetime.

I went to see the horses again today before leaving on my flight to Sydney. I was so looking forward to saying goodbye and they steadfastly ignored me in a thoroughly insulting, not to say hurtful, way.

I'm having to give myself a bit of a reality check on this horse adopting situation. Horses are not children, they're not even pet dogs that sleep on the end of your bed and are privy to home life in all its intimate details. People buy horses and leave them in stables, at a livery, or agistment for weeks, months on end. Then they sell them on to the person willing to pay the price. I don't think I've ever heard that happening to a pet dog. As it happens, my parents were offered a million dollars for my brother by an American and his wife. Matthew was cute and blond and only four years old, and I'm glad to report they turned it down.

My small horses will do well without me in their green field with Jane and Doug looking after them. I know Jane and Doug are very busy but no one could be more conscientious and caring, although they have made a point of warning me that accidents do happen with horses.

It has become apparent to me that the charms of my horses are not always immediately discernible to others. Coming as they do from a world of quality Thoroughbred racehorses, Jane and Doug did not lavish me with extravagant compliments the moment they set eyes on the two pale gold brumbies, in fact there was a bit of a stunned silence. You mean these are the famous horses you are transporting three-quarters of the way around Australia? was the unspoken subtext.

But over the following weeks they quickly grew fond of Athena and Olympia and began to appreciate their unusual characters and the beauty of their flowing movement. Doug preferred Athena, while Jane preferred Olympia. That became a pattern. Athena with her flirtatious ways, her feisty independent manner covering up what I believe is really a profound need for love and protection, appeals most to the men. While the serene Olympia with her charm and her grace, and her gentle expression of affection, is the favourite amongst women.

I will miss the horses desperately over the next three months. I would like to think that they too will miss me a little.

TWENTY-ONE

Father Sanz, Arabian Horses and the Big Wet

Monday 31 January 2005

Four months had passed since I delivered Olympia and Athena to their agistment with Doug and Jane in the Swan Valley.

In early December I flew back to Perth to see the horses and put them on a truck bound for Sydney. Their condition had improved beyond all measure – they'd both filled out and matured. They looked sleek and contented and were obviously loving their life running free in a large paddock with several racehorses. I hardly recognised them. Fortunately they seemed to know me, although they were not easy to catch.

The journey to Sydney took them four or five days and nights, including a thirty-six-hour stop-over in Melbourne. They travelled in a large truck with about six other horses, probably racehorses, driving through the nights but with a break every five hours for feed and rest. After Cockatoo's experience with the loss of Olympia on the racetrack at Newman, I volunteered to go with them. In fact I was rather looking forward to the trip, 4,000 kilometres across the entire breadth of Australia sitting up in the cabin with the drivers. Unfortunately the transport company's insurance company would not hear of such a thing.

I spent Christmas in New York in the snow and freezing cold where Barry was doing a stage show on Broadway, while I muffled up every day to go down to the The Writers' Room in the Village, a wonderful urban writers' retreat.

I was longing to get back to Australia and spend time with my horses. They were now living outside Sydney on a friend's farm between Bowral and Kangaroo Valley, and they were healthy, happy and full of beans on a balanced diet including highly nutritious horse nuts. Before leaving New York, I'd taken the opportunity to work with them as often as possible to consolidate the training we had already done. I found that they were rather jumpy and eccentric after even a day without being caught, but it soon became apparent that they remembered everything they had learnt, and seemed to trust and like me, particularly Olympia who was positively affectionate. I realised I had reached the end of my horse training repertoire and, much as I was enjoying just being with them, I was also looking forward to the next stage – finding someone to help me break them in, something I hoped would happen the following year. It was hard to believe that one day I would actually sit on their backs, as I had spent so much time relating to them from the ground. This happy eventuality was still in doubt with Athena as she was barely over 13 hands. Olympia was closer to 13.2 and I was hoping she would grow to between 14 and 14.2 hands, which would make her the height of a polo pony.

The day I arrived back in Sydney, 15 January, I checked in with Susan. She was spending the Wet at the home she shares with her husband David just outside Broome, and throughout our phone conversation I could hear the rain drumming on the corrugated-iron roof of her house. 'I'm going out to the station,' Susan said. 'Celia's flying up to the Kimberley from Melbourne. We're going to meet at Athenrai, then we're going to fly on up to Kalumburu to pick up the Aboriginal children due to go back to school in Victoria. It's the beginning of the school year next week,' she continued.

'Can I come too?' was my impulsive response.

I was longing to see the horses still in the paddocks, especially the chestnut stallion Pluto, and my old friend the black gelding, Tatti. A new foal had been born in November to one of the best looking bay mares, the one that we'd named Gita. I was pretty sure this beautiful filly was Olympia's full sister. She was obviously Rex's daughter and had the same colouring as Olympia, with identical markings on her nose. Susan had emailed me pictures of all the brumbies, and I had been amazed by how well Juno had recovered from her cuts; she had filled out and transformed from a gawky yearling into a mature mare. I even had a pang of nostalgia for the Black Witch and the terrible pony Tonka, added to which, it had always been a dream to see the Kimberley transformed by the Big Wet. It had been described to me in detail – how the grasses grow high and abundant, and new saplings sprout out of nowhere, and the billabongs spread from controlled little creeks into shallow rivers and spreading marshy areas make the roads impassable.

Getting back to Kalumburu would afford me the perfect opportunity to talk to Father Sanz. The more I thought about it, the more I believed that the quality breeding I could see in these wild horses, with their magical floating gait, had to come from Arabian heritage. 'Arabs?' People around the area I'd asked had said, 'Yeah, could be. The Benedictine monks were given a couple of Arab stallions at the mission. Ask Father Sanz, he'd be able to tell you.' I was astonished that nobody seemed particularly inter-ested in the breeding of these good-looking horses. I was becoming more and more fascinated by the idea of putting together the jigsaw puzzle of their ancestry.

After speaking to Susan on the Saturday night, I spent Sunday and Monday down in Bowral with Olympia and Athena, and on the Tuesday, before dawn, flew to Broome via Perth and an unscheduled stop at Karratha.

On Thursday morning Susan and I set off early on a round-about trip to Athenrai. We were unable to drive directly to the station on the Gibb River Road (which was the route we had taken out of the Kimberley with the horses four months ago), because it would be impassable at this time of the year. Instead we drove the 1,000-kilometre distance from Broome to Kununurra on the bitumen road, and from there we planned to fly in on the mail plane.

The drive to Kununurra took us ten hours. We stopped for a toasted sandwich at the Willare Bridge Roadhouse on the Fitzroy River where I had stopped with Cockatoo all those months ago. At Kununurra we stayed overnight at the very pleasant motel, rather grandly titled 'The Country Club' but with a superior little restaurant and bar serving an interesting selection of food including an excellent steak.

The next morning we boarded the mail plane for the final stage of our journey, the flight to the station, which would take four hours, including the many stops. Fortunately, we were the only passengers so we were able to spread out a little, filling the seats behind us with water bottles, cameras, reading matter and things we might need on the flight. Our good-looking pilot Simon, was the typical smartly dressed, efficient young man building up his flying hours. The propeller plane, an Islander, was jammed with mailbags and deliveries, boxes of supplies and engine parts, and every half hour we would bump down onto another red gravelled runway carved out of the now bright green of the land. This was the lightest Wet they'd had for years; Susan told me they'd had hardly any rain at all. It was true that at the station, the rivers and the billabongs seemed almost the same as before, though the paddocks were now a startling green.

As soon as we arrived at Athenrai, I leapt onto the quad bike and went off down towards the smaller paddocks next to the cattle yards. I found it strange to be among so much intense green foliage, feeling the warm tropical damp in the air. Even the red of the earth was a darker colour. Pluto and his mares were out grazing. They were choosing to stay close to the yards, although they had the run of a 200-acre paddock.

From a distance, the horses looked well, their coats shiny and their bellies rounded with the unlimited supply of fresh feed, but close up I could see their condition was not so good. Their ribs still showed and, after spending time with the now healthy Olympia and Athena, it seemed to me that the necks of the mares, yearlings and foals were thin and angular, their energy levels distinctly low. They had not been short of sustenance, because even before the wet season had come they had been given hay that the cattle musterers had left behind. There is a theory that because the grass grows so quickly in the Wet and because of the soil type, it is low in nutrients. Unfortunately, without Ron's help they had been unable to halter the horses again to continue the worming treatment. It would have been just too dangerous and too traumatic for the horses, and even with Ron there we had never got as far as catching or working on Pluto. Pluto looked by far the best of the bunch. I remembered reading somewhere that the stallions build up some kind of resistance to parasites, and of course do not have their strength drained by the continuous gestation and feeding of foals, added to which the testosterone in their system gives their muscles that bulked-up look. Gita, as well as the Black Witch, now had pronounced ribs and jagged hips.

Within a minute Susan and I were back into our routine: coddled eggs for breakfast, Nigella Lawson pumpkin risotto for dinner, washing my clothes in the machine and hanging on the line to dry crisp and fresh in just twenty minutes.

On the second day I found Pluto and most of his herd in one of the smaller yards devouring the knee-high grass. I closed the gate and fetched a bucket of feed, and held it out between the wooden posts. Juno and one of the yearlings came up to me and thrust their noses into the bucket to investigate, and only three feet behind them Pluto was stretching his nose in my direction to see what was causing such excitement. He seemed so calm and gentle that it was tempting to climb the fence and approach him, but I was well aware that with any stallion in the presence of his mares you can never afford to take chances, let alone with a wild stallion.

Celia arrived the next day in a smart new plane. We had morning coffee and then set off for Kalumburu.

Father Sanz and I sat across from each other at a long table covered by an awning in an inner courtyard of the sprawling mission building. The Benedictine father has the appearance of a sprightly sixty-five-year-old, his face clean-shaven and fairly round, short neat grey hair, and a twinkle in his eye, as if always on the verge of a half-secret joke. I'm told that according to his passport, he is ninety-one. He was dressed in mufti – a checked cotton shirt and gabardine shorts, socks and sandals.

Father Sanz is from Paloma in Spain. He came out to Kalumburu sixty-six years ago in 1939. In those days it was called the Drysdale River Station. He'd read about the Aborigines in this part of the world and felt a calling to become a missionary but in the 1980s, the government had decided to return the land to the Aboriginal people and the church was forced to withdraw most of its presence, leaving only a small mission at Kalumburu. So Father Sanz was asked to leave and he was sent to the Benedictine monastery in New Norcia. 'I am not a monk,' he said to me in his barely audible voice, which even after all these years had a strong Spanish accent. 'I am first of all a missionary. That, I believe, is my life's work.'

And so a few months ago, Father Sanz had made his escape from New Norcia and come back to Kalumburu to die – or at least that's what he told me. 'When I leave here to go back to the monastery, it will only be by taking the road past there,' he said, smiling and pointing upwards. 'Heaven,' he added, with a satisfied sigh.

The week he had arrived back at Kalumburu, everybody in the mission had run around in a state of anxiety and anticipation preparing to nurse and look after him, until it dawned on them that with his phenomenal inner strength and determination he was going to survive a good few more years, and that he was there to stay. They settled quietly back into their daily routine.

When Father Sanz had first arrived at the Drysdale River, the settlement had been not much more than a row of tents, and there were virtually no horses, just a chestnut mare and her foal. In 1942, during the war, Father Sanz went to Perth for an operation on his back. The tiny settlement had been bombed by the Japanese; six priests had lost their lives and several had been wounded, including Father Sanz. While in hospital he had been visited by a representative of a charitable trust, whose job it was to decide where and how to distribute charitable funds. He offered to make a donation to the mission of anything they needed, up to the value of six hundred dollars. Father Sanz told them they needed horses so that they could work cattle and develop the settlement into a self-sufficient concern. The trust offered him the full six hundred dollars, and with that money Father Sanz purchased ten horses and a stallion, and took them back with him by ship all the way up the west coast to the mission.

'So what breed of horses did you buy, Father Sanz?' I asked him.

'I have no idea,' he answered. 'At that time I knew nothing about horses; some were brown, and some of them that reddy colour.'

The cattle station project was successful, and over the years other horses arrived. A cattleman employed in the early 1950s came overland with his wife, ten children, and one hundred and ten horses, presumably the usual stock horse type. Then, in the sixties, generosity came the way of Father Sanz again in the shape of a certain Mr John Morgan. A friend of Father Sanz and the mission, he was the master surveyor responsible for building the road stretching the three or four hundred kilometres up north to the mission from the Gibb River Road. Although not Catholic himself, Morgan was eager to make a contribution to the mission, and so he gave Sanz two pure-bred Arab stallions and ten pure-bred Arab mares. Of the stallions, the father said, 'One was grey, a registered stallion, he had been imported or bred by the Queensland Agricultural College, he was called Homer, and the other one was that reddy colour...'

'You mean chestnut, Father Sanz?'

'Yes, yes. The reddy one, he was also Arab, but a heavier horse, very clever, and he was a true master at cutting, the best horse we ever had for working with the cattle. Your English Prince Charles, he was coming to stay with us here and we had the horse all ready for him to ride, for him to practise cutting the cattle, but then his visit was cancelled for reasons of security and the prince never came.'

'What was the name of the chestnut horse?'

He paused for a moment. 'I can't remember. Ask Bridget. She loved the horses, she would be able to tell you.'

'Oh, who is Bridget?'

'She works for the monastery at New Norcia. I will give you her number,' he answered.

So the stories about the Arab stallions at Kalumburu were true. But what was even more exciting to me was that there had been ten pure-bred mares, and so the chance of whole generations of Arabians existing to infiltrate the area.

'So, Father Sanz, for a man who claims not to have known much about horses, you certainly seem to have acquired some phenomenally good breeding stock.'

'Yes. Very good horses . . . It's not that I'm greedy, I just like to have the best!' Father Sanz giggled to himself. It was obviously a line he'd used many times before that particularly amused him.

'What happened to the Arab horses when you left Kalumburu?'

'Well, I took with me my two stallions, Homer and the reddy brown one and ten of the pure-bred mares. But then you must remember that by now at Kalumburu we had twenty years of the pure breeding of Arabs, and so there were many very good horses that stayed. When I left, there were about two hundred and fifty here, but it seemed that no one cared any more about the cattle station or the horses and so after a time, the fences came down and the horses ran wild –'

'And what happened to the ones you took with you?'

'In New Norcia, I was just a monk, I couldn't look after horses. Ask Bridget what happened to them.'

'Do you have any photographs I could look at?'

Father Sanz went off to look. He returned a few minutes later.

'No. I can't find them, but here is where you will find Bridget.' He handed me a number scribbled on a pink Post-It. 'And now it is nearly time for lunch, they will need to lay the table,' he said, looking rather pointedly at my computer and notebooks taking up space on the table, demonstrating an elderly person's attachment to meals and routine. It was eleven-thirty but even so, a long time since we'd had breakfast.

Susan and Celia were out on the front lawn of the mission talking to parents of children who were either coming back to school this year, or intending to go the following year. They were filling in government forms. In an air-conditioned room at the side of the mission I found a couple of the fellows who worked on the mission in worn workman's shirts and RM Williams boots watching an old episode of the 'The Bill'. I joined them until it was time to leave on the plane. We were taking with us six children who were headed back to school in Victoria for the coming term. Up above us in the skies I could see thick cloud over in the direction of the property.

First we stopped at Mitchell Plateau to collect another of the children from Kandiwal, an isolated Aboriginal community. By the time we had taken off again, there was the faint rumble of thunder in the distance. At my request, I was up in the front with our pilot, looking avidly out as we bumped along in the skies, skirting along the side of a dense cloud. As the cloud was moving north-west, it was blocking our path back to the station. Worse than that, it was moving us along in the wrong direction. I was becoming rather interested in the textures of clouds, and I had recently received an email from an Argentinian friend, Maxi Gainza, who is an intrepid and enormously skilled light aircraft pilot. I happened to have his email with me, so I pulled it out of my hold-all.

When flying in the mountains and there are clouds ahead, we always keep in mind that one of them 'might have a granite core', i.e. might be hiding a mountain behind it.

With any luck we'd be safe on that count, as we were not in the Alps or the Rockies.

We also try to avoid cauliflower-shaped clouds over open ground because they denote high turbulence – you can visualise them like boiling in slow motion.

From the way the plane was jolting up and down, we were in the middle of that cloud already. I twisted around in my seat and looked back at Susan. She was smiling in a rather tense way. Was even Susan getting nervous? I turned back to the email and read the next paragraph.

We also try to give cumulonimbus clouds ('cunimbs' or 'CBs' in pilot jargon) a wide berth. These are the towering, anvil-shaped clouds you get with an approaching storm.

Now that was worrying. The pilot did not seem to be following my friend's dictum. The cloud encroaching on our left was distinctly anvil-shaped, had been getting progressively blacker and in its heart I could see intermittent streaks of lightning.

On cue, he turned in my direction. 'Maybe I'll just head right through that cloud there, the station's only just over the other side,' he said to me through the intercom. 'What do you think?'

He was asking me?

'Why don't we just keep going around the cloud?' I answered with alacrity. 'Or can't we turn around and go around the back of the cloud? It would be so much more . . . comfortable.' I tried to reassure myself that he must know what he was doing as I noted the vivid pink that had recently complemented the pale complexion of his upper cheeks. 'I mean . . . Remind me, what does actually happen if a plane is hit by lightning?'

'It's not always fatal,' he answered. Was he serious? He didn't seem the joking type. His colour did seem unnaturally high. I have always intended to take a basic pilot's course, as I believe that if you are to fly around the outback you should at least be able to land a plane. I looked at all the gleaming dials and screens around me and wondered how I would cope if my friend on the left had a sudden seizure. Could you just contact the control tower and get them to talk you through it? Like in the movies? This plane had state-of-the-art computerised navigational and piloting aids – our pilot had been grumbling about that only a few minutes earlier, saying it was all very well for the young fellows but having the plane controlled by all these computerised electronic gadgets was not his idea of flying, it was far too complicated. He much preferred the 'point the plane in the right direction, look out the window and steer' school of flying. For a moment the cloud on our left lightened from dense charcoal to dirty fog.

'Oh, I think we can make it through,' the pilot said and swung the plane into a sharp left turn. And there we were in the middle of the cloud juddering up and down with no visibility whatsoever. I held my breath, and prayed. Two or three minutes later we came out the other side, into tranquil skies and sunshine, the land below us glistening with the recent rainfall. I sighed with relief, telling myself these small-plane moments for which one needs a stoical faith and a fatalistic attitude are just part and parcel of life in the outback.

We flew low over the station runway. It was flooded, making it impossible for us to land for at least another forty minutes. By then, if we still couldn't land, we would be in danger of running out of fuel, so we turned back for the forty-minute flight to Kununurra and the Country Club Motel.

Early the next morning Celia and the children headed off for Melbourne, while Susan and I took the mail plane back to the station. From there I was able to get on the phone and follow up Father Sanz's leads.

First I called Bridget.

She was a sympathetic person, more than happy to talk to me about the history of the horses. It turned out that she was from England originally; she'd lived in a house whose garden straddled the borders of Surrey and Sussex, and had ridden and worked with Olympic horses in her younger days. Now she was no longer working at the monastery at New Norcia, but still lived nearby.

'The two stallions that Father Sanz brought from Kalumburu,' she repeated. 'I ended up buying them and keeping them to protect them.'

'Why?'

'They were being poorly treated, not fed. They didn't really know about horses there.'

'But Father Sanz loved his horses.'

'Yes, I know, but he wasn't able to look after them himself, and then he believed people back at Kalumburu had been neglecting his horses to get back at him. When Homer arrived from Kalumburu, he was in a terrible state.'

'So you bought the grey, Homer, and what about the chestnut? What was the chestnut called?'

'For the first year I called the chestnut stallion Carson, because he came from Carson River Station, you see. That was the name given to the cattle station that Father Sanz started up there next to Kalumburu.'

'But was that his name? You say that as if it wasn't.'

'No, it wasn't,' she said, laughing. 'But whenever I asked Father Sanz the horse's name, all I could hear him say was "Smmba sffa". And so I was none the wiser. It took me a year to find out that the horse's real name was Summer Safari.'

'So the chestnut, did he have any markings on his face?

'Yes. He had a blaze.'

I was getting the eerie feeling that the pieces of a puzzle were all falling into place. 'Was it crooked?' I asked.

There was a moment's silence. 'I don't remember. It was so long ago and so much has happened since those days.'

I would have to wait for the photographs that she promised to send to me in Sydney.

Along with Kimberley time, I think there is something that could be called Kimberley conversation. You talk and talk and you ask and ask, and finally your conversation enters a land of ever-diminishing circles and if you have good instincts and can guide the conversation on its concentric path, eventually you hit gold. It's almost as if you need to divine exactly the right question to get the answer, but if you knew exactly the right question, then the chances are you wouldn't need the answer.

I had heard mention of Percherons (a heavy horse breed, originally from France) in the area, then the information had gone to ground and any further questions had fallen on deaf ears. Here it was emerging again. Dusty's wife, Nina, was talking about a Percheron stallion.

'He was called Cabbage and I guess he was here about 1975.'

'Oh, that was a long time ago. Before the mining company.'

'Oh, did I say seventy-five? I meant ninety-five,' said Nina.

'So you mean there *was* a Percheron stallion here recently?'

'Yes. Part-bred.'

'Where?' I asked, almost accusingly.

'Athenrai.'

'You mean there was a Percheron stallion at Athenrai?'

'Yeah, well . . . Part Percheron. He was grey.'

Part was good enough, part was all it would take to have given Pluto his statuesque quality, his fine muscled neck, his good bone, his serenity. Arab crossed with part Percheron. It sounded like there had been a lot of general Australian stock types around and the old retired racehorse stallion which would have led to the bays and the slightly Thoroughbred look, but the Arab and Percheron genes were definitely there.

Soon after I returned to Sydney, a parcel arrived for me from New Norcia, containing a bundle of documents, a personal letter from Bridget and a small sealed envelope containing some snapshots of Father Sanz's two Arab stallions. As I opened the envelope, I felt like a detective putting together clues, a regular Sherlock Holmes. I laid out the pictures on our glass dining table. There were some snapshots of nice-looking Arab stallions and a few mares and foals, all with compact bodies, their faces only slightly dished, not the exaggerated look that has been so fashionable with the American breeders and which I have noticed has filtered through to Australia. Written on the back were the names of the horses.

I found photos of Homer, a silver-grey Arab, the first images of him looking frighteningly thin, all skin and bones, the day he arrived at New Norcia. Then photos taken a year or so later, Homer now filled out and looking magnificent, with a great big stallion neck. Was I imagining things, or could I see the shape of Rex's nose in Homer's? The pink skin, a certain square look, the way the nostrils are set, the look that is identical to little Athena's nose, and which convinces me she is Rex's daughter. And Athena has the small pointed ears of what I believe to be her Arab ancestry as well.

Then I looked through photos of Summer Safari, the chestnut. A compact horse, he looked more like a pony, and yet in real life he was probably a couple of hands higher than Pluto. I looked back at the original photograph, taken by Peter Eve, of the horse we called Sedna, the one we saw on the second day from the helicopter. It could have been the same horse. I looked at Summer

Safari from another angle – yes, a white blaze, but not particularly crooked.

I pulled out the rest of the contents of Bridget's parcel; it contained Summer Safari's pedigree, Homer's registration document – now crossed through with the word 'dead' typed after his name. There were long letters referring to plans for the horses after they reached New Norcia and the fate of some of the mares and foals, and articles and Arab horse magazines from the mid-eighties. This kind woman who loved horses had sent me her most precious things. I was touched.

For the next few hours I sat at the table and pored over the numerous papers and articles. My head was reeling with Arabian names. So many were similar and I was getting confused so I began making notes and drawing family trees. There were Summer Safari's ancestors, Naseem, Nisreen, Razina, Rathka, Rissalix and Indian Gold to mention but a few. And on Homer's side, taking the name of his sire and dam from the card and piecing them together with information from the articles: Silver Moonlight, Silver Fire, Indian Magic, Somra and then again, Naseem (who eventually ended up in Russia).

There were stories about Sir Wilfred Scawen Blunt and his wife Lady Anne, the English couple who, in the 1860s, fell in love with Arab horses during their travels to Arabia and brought some of the best horses back to England to breed from on their estate in Sussex, called Crabbet Park. I read about a Mrs A.D.D. Maclean who imported Crabbet Arabian horses to Australia from 1925 and set up a stud at her property, Fenwick, in Victoria.

What was becoming apparent to me was that Father Sanz's two Arab stallions were of the best, most classical Arabian breeding, the names on his horses' papers were the names of the most talked about and admired in the Arabian horse world, and many of them star Crabbet Arabs. In the magazines, I saw photographs of horses with marked physical resemblances to Homer and Summer Safari. And then, in a back copy of the *Australian Arabian Horse News*, I found a photograph of a mare called Sharfina, Summer Safari's great-grand-dam. She was chestnut with a creamy mane and tail, the unusual colour I had seen in the outback, the colour of Sedna's foal. It was a marked characteristic of that line of breeding. I read that these colours can be thrown back through generations. And over and over I read about that fabulous floating trot of the Arab horse.

That evening I rang my old friend Finn Guinness in England. Apart from running the family Arab horse stud in Wiltshire, for many years Finn had been president of the Arab Horse Society, and has travelled around Australia on numerous occasions judging at shows, meeting breeders, looking at studs.

'Australia? Well, you see, they imported the best Arab horses. There was Mrs A.D.D. Maclean who allegedly pawned her wedding jewels to buy one of her stallions, Indian Light, from Lady Wentworth (the daughter of Sir Wilfred and Lady Anne Blunt). You see, Lady Wentworth was happy to offer Mrs Maclean the very top horses for a good reason: if she sold her best horses to far away places like Australia and South Africa, then these horses could be guaranteed never to compete with her own horses in the show ring. You mentioned that Father Sanz's grey stallion, Homer, was bred by Queensland Agricultural College. I know they also imported Crabbet Arabs.'

I faxed through Summer Safari's pedigree and information on Homer's breeding and rang Finn back the following day. There was one particular question I was dying to ask him.

'Finn, do you recognise any of the names?'

'Yes, of course.'

'I mean, are they related to any of your horses?'

'Remember that stallion we used to have called Saladin? You

would have seen him out in the field directly in front of our house. Well, his sire, Naziri, was the full brother of Naseem, Summer Safari's great-great-grandfather.'

'What about Tamarillo – is he related to Father Sanz's two stallions?'

'As you know, Tamarillo was the son of Mellita, the mare that caught your eye when she was just a yearling. Her great-great grandfather on her mother's side was Rissalix, and she was also maternally related to Naseem.'

I couldn't believe it. Father Sanz's stallions were cousins of the horses I knew from Wiltshire, even horses I had ridden. Finn reminded me of a chestnut gelding of his called Rabadash, one of my favourite horses to ride, who, come to think of it, looked just like Summer Safari. Even Bysshe was related, the horse I had wanted to buy all those years ago, the chestnut with the creamy mane and tail that had resembled the Stubbs painting. It was so strange to think that Finn's horses, peacefully grazing in a field in Wiltshire, were the relations of the Arabs who had ended up at the Catholic mission at Kalumburu.

So were my two little duns related to these Arabs? In my view, they had to be, from their look, their tail carriage and their floating gait. Ron had told me that, among the brumbies, it was always the stallions of good blood and breeding that won out against the others – they were just more intelligent, better at fighting and prepared to engage in combat for longer to gain control of mares. Homer and Summer Safari sired pure-bred Arabs at Kalumburu from the 1960s onwards and their sons were the stallions that walked out through the broken fences around Kalumburu in the early 1980s. As heads of their own mobs, they would then have driven out the young colts and those colts would have then staked out territory of their own and stolen mares, moving gradually further and further south until they reached the areas around

Athenrai. Their connection to my horses was there, even if it meant going back quite a few generations.

I'm thankful that I followed my quest. I have two happy horses that I love, and I feel I have been reunited with myself as a child, with that rather solitary and solemn little figure I see in photographs. I've been able give that part of me the horse I have always longed for. I have regained that pure sense of love I had for horses, and for nature and the wild. I wasn't able to have children of my own to nurture, but now I have horses to bring up, teach and breed foals from.

As well as my two duns, one a horse, the other a pony, with startlingly different and original personalities, my gift has been the unique adventure of going out and finding them and making them my own, experiencing the power of the outback and the incredible characters who befriended and helped me. My part was having the courage to follow it through. I will always treasure the memories and the stories of the other horses I was lucky enough to get to know and the experience of writing this book, making another full circle with my childhood and fulfilling another life-long desire.

As for taking my horses out of the wild, I don't know if they miss their old life. I don't think horses necessarily think that way, they think about their immediate needs. If anything, I think they could miss the stimulation of life in the herd, the changing land-scape as the lead mare moved the herd around in search of grazing, the birth of foals in the family. I will do my best to give them what they need and keep them happy.

I'm not convinced that either Athena or Olympia would have been very successful in the wild. Athena, we have discovered to our surprise, is four or five years old. Three vets have confirmed this information. This makes the challenge of what we have done much greater – without knowing, we have captured and are starting to train a full-grown brumby. The question remains, if she is this old, why did she appear so scrawny and physically immature and even more strange, how come she has never had a foal?

Another suggestion was made to me by Tony Parker, one of the vets. He believes that she probably came lowest in the pecking order of the herd, and so was kept away from the good grazing by the other mares. This would result in her remaining immature because of insufficient nutrition. She was in such poor condition, if she'd had a foal, I can't imagine how they could have survived. I've been told that horses who are not strong enough to gestate the full term actually resorb their embryos. We have noticed that whenever we turn her out with other mares, she immediately becomes the lowest in the order, sometimes quite persecuted by the others, receiving bites large enough to leave a mark, and usually ending up on her own. It has been an eye-opener for me to see how unpleasant mares can be to one another, and especially to the 'lowest' in the herd. If we turn her out with a gelding, however, he affectionately nibbles her neck all day, and can't bear to be separated from her, even for a moment. Athena, true to form, seems entirely unaware of the passions she has aroused.

Olympia is far stronger as a mare, she's alpha, lead mare material, and is constantly looking for ways to dominate. But along with her charm she has a wilful, daffy side – she always makes a beeline for whatever it is she wants, usually food, and asks questions later. She doesn't have the innate, self-protective and rather suspicious nature that Athena has.

I have learnt so much from this experience, most of all I have learnt the importance of allowing horses to be horses, or else you risk destroying that which you value most in them: their magnificent free spirit living in tandem with their natural desire to please. Through my Kimberley adventure I have learnt to understand

and respect their natural state. That for me is the starting point for my relationship with them. They are not lap dogs to be coddled, nor an inferior species to be forced into obedience through subjugation and pain. You can work through their natural inclinations, remembering that in the wild there is always a stallion or a lead mare to guide them firmly but without cruelty.

But as for the call of the wild…

Sometimes I believe that humans over-romanticise the concept of the wild. It's a good sign, because it represents the realisation of our own need. For animals, it is where they live. Yes, it's glorious and beautiful, but it's also the place where they carry on their relentless daily struggle to eat and procreate while avoiding being attacked by an animal sharing the same terrain, or being eaten by a hungry neighbour. There is nothing romantic about dying of thirst, being fatally bitten by a snake, or eaten from within by parasites, or, if injured, being left behind by the herd to die a lonely death, torn apart by dingoes.

We humans live an urbanised existence, dedicated to the gods of comfort and convenience, helpless in the face of the ongoing march of progress and technology with all its many benefits but also its destructive forces. When I tell the story of my brumbies to people, they light up at the concept of horses running free in the wilderness, almost as if they want to be there with them. For a moment, they are transported. They are under that huge, night sky in the Kimberley, a canopy of dense crystal stars and the overwhelming silence of isolation. It touches some kind of primitive chord. They feel what I felt – the sense of being a soul in the presence of some indescribably powerful force. The lost sensation of how it felt to be part of nature.

Glossary and Sources

agist: to take in and feed or put to pasture horses or livestock for payment

Anglo-Arab: a Thoroughbred and Arab crossbreed

bits: metallic mouthpiece that is part of a bridle to which the reins are attached

blaze: white hair marking extending down the middle of the front of a horse's head

colt: a male horse less than four years old

double-bridle: consists of two bits (a snaffle and a bridoon, including a curb chain) controlled by two separate sets of reins, giving the rider more control

dressage: a riding discipline where a horse's obedience, deportment and responses are tested through a series of movements

filly: a female horse less than four years old

flea-bitten: small brown spots occurring on a grey coat

gelding: a castrated horse

girth: a strap which goes under the horse's stomach and holds the saddle on

gymkhana: a horseriding event featuring races and novelty events

halter or *headcollar*: a simple device, worn on a horse's head and so it can be led or tied-up

hands: measurement used for describing the height of a horse to its wither; one hand is equal to four inches; anything above 14 hands in Australia, and 14.2 hands in the UK, is a horse, anything below that is called a pony

leg-change: (change of leg) changing the leading leg while cantering *lunge*: a method of training horses where the horse moves around a person in a circle on a long rein (known as a lunge rein); can be used to improve balance and discipline

neck-reining: an American style of riding where pressure of the reins on the neck is used for turning

numnah: a saddle-shaped sheepskin or synthetic wool pad which goes on the horse's back underneath the saddle

pelham: a type of curb chain bit requiring two sets of reins

pommel: the high point at the front of the saddle

sheath: the tubular structure of skin-covered tissue that houses the horse's penis

skewbald: (also known as paint) large irregular patches of white and any other colour except black (usually brown)

snaffle: a jointed bit, widely regarding as the the simplest and most gentle type of bit; an eggbutt snaffle is a type of snaffle bit which widens out where it jointed with the side rings, to prevent the horse's mouth from being pinched

socks: solid white hair markings on a horse's leg below the knees or hocks

star: a small white hair mark on the forehead, sometimes diamond-shaped

stockings: solid white hair markings that extend above the knees or hocks

strawberry roan: chestnut or bay hairs mixed with white, giving an almost pink appearance

surcingle: a strap that goes around the horse, sometimes used in conjunction with a girth to hold the saddle in place

three-day event: a competition where riders are tested through three categories of events over three days: dressage, cross-country and show-jumping

withers: part of the horse's spine where its neck meets its back; the point from where its height is measured

Marks, Kelly *Perfect Manners*, Ebury Press, London, 2002.

Pickeral, Tamsin *The Encyclopedia of Horses and Ponies*, Parragon, Bath, 2001.

Roberts, Monty *The Man who Listens to Horses*, Arrow Books, Sydney, 1997.

Roberts, Monty *Shy Boy: The horse that came in from the wild*, HarperCollins, Sydney, 2002.

Roberts, Monty *From My Hands to Yours*, Self-published, 2002.

(For more information on Monty Roberts' books, products and schedules of his worldwide demonstrations see www.montyroberts.com)

Wright, Maurice *The Jeffery Method of Horse Handling*, Prospect, South Australia, 1973.

National Geographic Video *America's Lost Mustangs*, Questar, 2001.

Acknowledgements

My thanks first and foremost to Susan Bradley, who dispensed limitless encouragement and worked tirelessly to help me realise a lifetime dream. To Ron Kerr for catching and taming wild horses, with kindness.

To my publisher Bernadette Foley whose faith and unflagging confidence led to the publication of this book, and to Di Morrissey for kindly introducing me to Bernadette.

My thanks also to my editor Siobhan Gooley for her exhaustive attention to detail, to my agent Sandy Dijkstra for her enthusiasm, to Robin Bland and Susie Little for double-checking horse facts, and to Bridget Donovan and Finn Guinness for information about Arabian horses. To Richard Bradley, Maria Tomlins and the Hallen family for their good company and hard work.

As always, to my husband Barry Humphries for his constant support and wise counsel.

My heartfelt gratitude to Monty Roberts for his inspirational work; he has made the world a better place for horses.

Last but not least, my thanks to Maria Myers.